THE TENETEHARA INDIANS
OF BRAZIL

NUMBER 35 IN THE

COLUMBIA UNIVERSITY CONTRIBUTIONS TO ANTHROPOLOGY

Charles Wagley *and* Eduardo Galvão

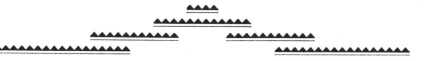

THE TENETEHARA INDIANS
OF BRAZIL

A Culture in Transition

AMS PRESS
NEW YORK

Reprinted with the permission of
Columbia University Press
From the edition of 1949, New York
First AMS EDITION published 1969
Manufactured in the United States of America

Library of Congress Catalogue Card Number: 79-82359

AMS PRESS, INC.
New York, N. Y. 10003

To

Heloisa Alberto Torres

PREFACE

THIS STUDY of the Tenetehara Indians of the state of Maranhão is the result of a training and research program cooperatively sponsored by the Department of Anthropology of Columbia University and the National Museum at Rio de Janeiro. The research program began in 1939–40, when a grant from the Council for Research in the Social Sciences of Columbia University made it possible for me to spend eighteen months in Brazil studying culture change among the Tapirapé Indians of central Brazil. This research was part of a larger program on acculturation directed by Professor Ralph Linton. The actual field work in 1939–40 was carried out under the auspices of the Museu Nacional, and during this period plans were made for continuation of research on culture change among the Brazilian Indians as well as for combining field training with research. In 1941, under the auspices of the Committee for Inter-American Artistic and Intellectual Relations, I was able to spend another year in Brazil, during which field studies among the Tenetehara were carried out.

The Tenetehara were selected as a logical succeeding step to the investigations among the Tapirapé. Although these two tribes live at a great distance from each other, both speak languages of the Tupí-Guaraní family and they share many basic culture patterns. The Tapirapé, which had been in contact with Brazilians only sporadically for less than forty years, had retained in the main their aboriginal culture. Yet the shock of the recent contact with Brazilian culture and the rapid reduction of the Tapirapé population through newly acquired diseases had so thoroughly disorganized Tapirapé culture that it was in danger of extinction. The Tenetehara, on the other hand, with more than three hundred years of contact with outside cultures, while considerably modified from its aboriginal form, had reached an adjustment both in terms of social relationships with Brazilians and in terms of resistance to foreign disease. The Tenetehara were selected therefore as a group which had made an adjustment to their new environment which at least allowed them to survive while other Brazilian tribes disappeared.

The field research among the Tenetehara was also a training program, and therefore it was a group undertaking. The materials on which this book is based were collected during two visits to the Tenetehara. During the first visit from November, 1941, to March, 1942, the field party consisted of Nelson Teixeira, Rubens Meanda, Eduardo Galvão (who were student members of the staff of the Museu Nacional) and myself. In February of 1945, Eduardo Galvão and Nelson Teixeira accompanied by Pedro Lima, a physical anthropologist, returned to the Tenetehara for four months in order to verify some of our original observations and to gather further data. During this period I was in constant communication with the field party. Nelson Teixeira and Rubens Meanda were unable to take part in the preparation of the field data for publication. They placed all their notes at our disposal and they have read long portions of this report. We wish to thank them for their close collaboration and to give them due credit for their sound field observations.

Our direct acquaintance with the Tenetehara is limited to the villages along the Pindaré River and to those along the cattle trail between the Mearim and the Pindaré Rivers (see map). We were not able to visit the Tenetehara on the Grajaú and Mearim Rivers nor the villages on the Gurupí River. We talked with many Indians, however, who lived in these regions and the descriptions of life and custom there were in complete agreement with our observations in the Pindaré region. In addition, our data is in general accordance with the descriptions of both S. Fróes Abreu (1931) and H. Snethlage (1931), who visited the Tenetehara of the Mearim-Grajaú region, as well as with the rather meager published material on the Tenetehara of the Gurupí River villages, such as that of Dodt (1939 ed.), Nimuendajú (1915), and Lopes (1932). Therefore, while the present description refers specifically to the Tenetehara of the Pindaré region, we feel certain that our observations may safely be considered as typical of Tenetehara culture in general.

During both visits to the Tenetehara each of us worked daily with a native informant whom we paid either with currency or with trade articles. Each of us collected data and made observations without limiting ourselves to any special aspect of the culture. Every evening in the field we discussed the notes we had taken during the day and the problems as they appeared to us. All of our information was collected in Portuguese and through Portuguese-speaking interpreters. A few texts were recorded in Tupí-Guaraní, and all of us were able, before we left the Tenetehara, to understand many words and phrases of the native language but no attempt was made to use it with our informants. Although we realize that much is lost of the native's point of view by using a secondary language, considerable time was gained by being able to work at once in Portuguese rather than to spend months learning a complicated language.

Our first impression of the Tenetehara whom we met at Post Gonçalves Dias was disappointing. We did not expect to meet untouched savages but, at first sight, these people at the Indian Post hardly seemed to be Indians at all. They came to meet us wearing clean shirts and European style suits—even coats—for they had been told by an Indian officer that a "Federal Commission was coming." They seemed suspicious and timid, and they would not, at first, answer the questions of the strangers. The few men who would talk with us on this first day spoke clear, well-pronounced Portuguese. During our first day at the Indian Post we had difficulty distinguishing an Indian from the *mestiço* Brazilians of the region. After a few days, however, our initial impression changed. The men soon took off their "Sunday" suits and went about their normal daily affairs. In Januaria village, which was situated then only a hundred yards or so from the headquarters of the Indian Post, they spoke only their native Tupí-Guaraní language among themselves. We had several long conversations with Manuel Viana, the village chief, who lost some of his suspicion as he grew accustomed to us. We explained our purpose for visiting the Tenetehara, and by way of example, we told something of our experiences among "his relatives" the Tapirapé. Soon Manuel was trading myths with us, and he was amused to find that other peoples told similar stories. Manuel vouched for us with others of the village, so within ten days each of our party was able to work with a native informant. Soon we were invited to witness a cure and a shamanistic exhibition in the village adjoining the Indian Post. We found that these same Indians, some of whom spoke fluent Portuguese and all of whom wore clothes, had still retained many of their aboriginal customs and attitudes.

All of the information given to us by informants was checked with others for accuracy and further verified whenever possible by actual observation. Many people—men, women, and children— therefore taught us Tenetehara culture, but a few of them spent so much time patiently answering our questions and explaining the Tenetehara way of life that they must be given special mention.

I. Miguel was one of our most intimate friends. He died in January, 1945, and we felt his loss greatly during our second trip. A quiet, middle-aged man, his information always proved trustworthy. He spoke fluent Portuguese and translated many songs and stories from his native language for us. He was not a leader in any sense, but was content to live with his wife's extended family; yet he was a good worker and provided well for his wife and their two daughters. He had never aspired to shamanism, but he did know considerable about it and was able to give us clear "on the spot" explanations of shamanistic performances. Miguel traveled with us during our first trip up the Pindaré River in 1941. Many of the myths included in this report he told to us in his quiet voice during the evenings around a camp fire.

II. João Bochecha was our most active and, without any doubt, our most valuable informant. He contributed more to our knowledge of Tenetehara culture than any other single person. João lived in Januaria village adjoining the Indian Post, but he was born in an upper Pindaré village. While he was still a young boy, he moved to a village between the Pindaré and the Grajaú Rivers, and from there to the Indian Post, where he lived in the house of the Indian Officer for a few years. He speaks Portuguese and his native language with equal fluency. In 1942, João was about thirty years of age. He was married to a widow several years his senior but soon after her death in 1944, he married a young woman. João is highly respected by the Indians and the local Brazilians alike; people of both groups speak of him as an intelligent person, an astute trader, and a capable worker. He is an excellent hunter and he always has a large garden and some surplus to sell from it. Unlike many Tenetehara who know something of local Brazilian customs and who have many dealings with Brazilians, João never expressed shame at being an Indian. On the contrary, João was a most articulate champion of the Indians' complaint in 1945 against the Indian Officer whose cattle constantly invaded Indian gardens. He is a leader in village singing. At one time he tried to organize an extended family group around him in order to become a "captain," but failed because he lacked young female relatives with which to attract young men to his group by marriage. João quickly understood our motives for visiting the Tenetehara and he became our tireless teacher, our diplomatic intermediary and interpreter in each village we visited, and our very best friend among the Tenetehara.

iii. Manuel Viana, the chief of Januaria village, spent many afternoons alone with one of our party in his house answering questions or simply talking in general about Tenetehara life. Manuel is physically a *mestiço*—the son of an Indian woman and a Brazilian father—but he is an Indian by education and by culture and he does not speak Portuguese very fluently. His point of view was always in favor of the Indian against the Brazilian. He was born near a rubber trading station, which was abandoned about 1913, on the upper Pindaré River. He grew up in an Indian village in that region but later, because of the attacks of the hostile Urubú Indians, his family moved down river to Januaria village. He was only a little over fifty years old in 1945, but he was an excellent source for information on Tenetehara life as it existed twenty to thirty years ago, and his explanations of modern Tenetehara culture were always trustworthy.

iv. Camirang, the chief of the village on the upper Pindaré River, which is known by his name, deserves special mention even though he seldom acted as an informant for us. Although his prestige declined somewhat between our visits to his village in 1942 and in 1945, he stands out among all the Tenetehara of the region as their strongest leader. In 1945 he was a man of about thirty-five to forty years of age. He speaks Portuguese with difficulty, but well enough to impress his fellow villagers, who speak the language very little or not at all, and well enough to trade with the Brazilians when he comes down river each year to sell the products of his villagers. Camirang is highly respected by the Brazilian traders as a good customer and by the Indian Service officials, who are impressed by the control he is able to maintain over his people. He is a progressive and was far more interested in learning about the outside world than in discussing his own culture, so he made us his informant to learn of big cities and of distant countries. He was eager to show us, and through us his own villagers, that he knew the ways of the outside world. When we arrived in his village, we found that he had built on to his own house an additional adobe room where we were to sleep—forgetting only to put windows in it—and he had built a table with benches in his kitchen where we were to take our meals. On the day of our arrival he wore his high shoes, a white cotton suit, and a sailor straw hat. He played sambas and waltzes (including the Merry Widow Waltz) over and over again on his portable victrola. These clothes and the victrola were purchased in the big city of São Luis, which Camirang visited twice under the guidance of the Indian Officer to sell copaíba oil. Camirang told us repeatedly of his trips to São Luis and of his impressions of the Wild West movie to which the Indian Officer took him.

Camirang told us a rather romantic, if not perhaps somewhat fictionalized, story as an explanation of his own progressive tendencies. "My grandfather was a Brazilian," [1] he said. "He was very poor" and he came to the upper Pindaré to work as a rubber gatherer. Camirang's grandmother, the daughter of an important Tenetehara village chief, saw the poor Brazilian and liked him at once. She went to her father and said she wanted to marry the stranger. "She followed him to the river when he went to take a bath" (obviously an invitation to begin an affair). The poor Brazilian told her he did not want to live in the village among the Indians, but the girl's father insisted and the Brazilian finally agreed to remain as his son-in-law. The chief gave his son-in-law new clothes, an ax, a bush knife, and food. Camirang said that his

[1] *Karaý* was the word he used. It means a white Brazilian as distinguished from a *paranã*, a Negro Brazilian.

father, the son of the couple, was "half white and half Tenetehara," and that his father spoke both Portuguese and the native language. Camirang remembers that his father took him several times to visit Brazilian settlements and that during these trips he learned to speak Portuguese.

v. Artur Vaqueiro was perhaps the most colorful of our principal informants. When we first met Vaqueiro, as he is known, he was only about twenty years old and he had always led a most haphazard existence. His father died when the boy was very young and the mother moved away from her family group to marry José Machado, by whom she had two children. She took Vaqueiro along with her, but he was badly neglected by his mother and his stepfather's family. Vaqueiro traveled for several years during his late teens visiting all the villages on the Mearim and Grajaú Rivers. For several months he accompanied a Brazilian sleight-of-hand artist who, he says, was considered a shaman (*pazé*) in the villages they visited. Vaqueiro witnessed many shamanistic cures among the Indians and Brazilians alike and he frequently compared the methods of Tenetehara and Brazilian shamans for us.

In 1942, Vaqueiro had recently returned to Januaria village from his travels. He had few relatives in the village. He seldom helped his stepfather at gardening and he was considered lazy and even dishonest. Yet, in a short time, he arranged a marriage with a young woman. Her family was not anxious at all to have Vaqueiro as a son-in-law. They fomented trouble between the two in the hope of breaking up the marriage. His married life was stormy and the subject of considerable village gossip, for neither Vaqueiro nor his wife abstained from occasional affairs with others.

By 1945, Vaqueiro's position in the village had changed. He had become a shaman, and for a young man he was already rather well known for his control over several feared and potent supernaturals. Although he now had a small garden of his own, he still worked irregularly and not very hard at agriculture. He was still married to the same wife, but now her family accepted him, since his prestige as a shaman overshadowed the fact that he was not, even in 1945, a very good provider. Vaqueiro seemed to have found the right niche for himself in Tenetehara culture.

Vaqueiro was not a very trustworthy source of information. He spun some charming tall tales for our benefit; but all his stories, details as to customs, and even the bits of gossip he fed us had to be very carefully checked with other informants, for he is blessed with a very rich imagination. Once, however, we were able to distinguish fact from fiction he became very useful to us. His wildest stories often gave us insight into Tenetehara attitudes, conflicts, and values; his lies, his dreams, and his simple exaggerations were, after all, based on his experience in his own culture.

VI. José Viana stands out among our principal informants for his meticulous and precise statements. José is a man around fifty-five years old; he is a shaman and the leader of a large extended family, thus a man of considerable prestige. He has an air of dignity and reserve about him. In 1942, José had recently moved to Januaria village from a village on the Grajaú River because, he said, the Brazilians had become so numerous on the Grajaú that there was no longer room for the Indians. He and his large family group had a hard time weathering the first year in Januaria while they waited to harvest their new gardens. Manuel Viana allowed José to harvest manioc and rice for his group. José spent considerable time with us and in return we gave him food to help tide the family over the waiting period. José, however, did not like living near Brazilians, and in 1945 he had already moved his family to a site called Jussaral Grande, near the village of Lagôa Comprida. In our many long discussions, José made it quite plain that he did not like the Brazilians. He seemed to place us in a different category, since we were obviously not a part of the local scene and since we were obviously sympathetic toward the Indian and his culture.

VII. Eleuteria, a woman of approximately forty-five years of age, was our principal female informant. She was a widow and a relative of Camirang. During our stay in Camirang's village she cooked for us and we got to know her well. She spoke fairly good Portuguese and she was very useful as an interpreter with other women, few of whom speak any Portuguese at all. Because of the linguistic barrier and because we were all men we were seldom able to have long interviews with Tenetehara women. The wives of our informants, however, often gave us information as we sat in their houses talking for hours with their husbands.

While this study owes most to our native informants, I should

like to thank several others who directly or indirectly cooperated
to make our work among the Tenetehara possible. In several long
discussions, the well-known Brazilian ethnologist, Curt Nimuendajú, gave us the benefit of his numerous contacts with the Tenetehara during his visits to Maranhão. He also made available notes
and kinship terms which he had collected years earlier among the
Tenetehara (Tembé) of the state of Pará. The Serviço de Pro-
teção aos Indios (Brazilian Indian Service) placed their facilities
and information at our disposal. The Regional Indian Inspectors
of the states of Maranhão and Pará, Sr. José Mendes and Sr. José
Maria Malcher, gave us their excellent advice drawn from practical
experience among the Tenetehara. The Indian Officer in charge
of Post Gonçalves Dias, Sr. Helio Mendes Berniz, was our host during two long visits. Francisco Mancha was not only our efficient
man-of-all-work during both trips, but also a good friend and an
excellent companion. Both visits to the Tenetehara were expeditions of the Museu Nacional of Rio de Janeiro and we wish to
thank our colleagues on the staff and especially the director, Dra.
Heloisa Alberto Torres, for their constant cooperation. The Museu
Nacional under the direction of Dra. Heloisa Alberto Torres has
become an important and stimulating center of scientific studies of
Brazil. Dr. Alfred Metraux has read the manuscript and offered
many valuable criticisms. I want to thank him not only for his
interest in this research but also for stimulating me to turn to
Brazilian ethnographic studies in 1939. To the Council for Research in the Social Sciences of Columbia University we were in-
debted for the funds which made this publication possible. Above
all, I wish personally to express my gratitude to Professor Ralph
Linton. My research among the Indians and rural populations of
Brazil since 1939 have had the benefit of his scientific orientation
and his friendly counsel.

CHARLES WAGLEY

Columbia University, New York
March, 1948

Contents

THE TENETEHARA INDIANS
OF BRAZIL

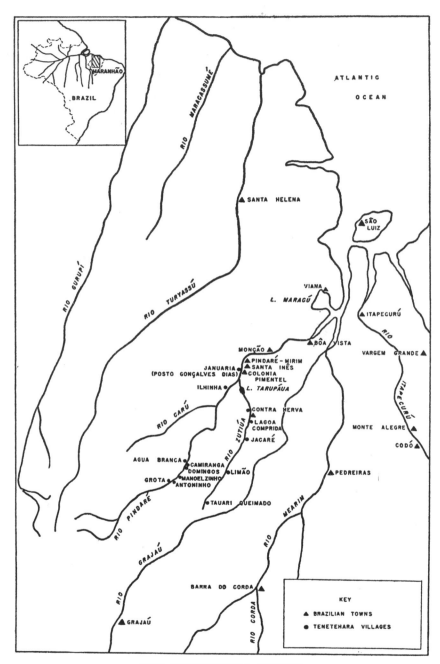

ATLANTIC

OCEAN

BRAZIL

MARANHÃO

RIO MARACASSUMÉ

RIO GURUPÍ

RIO TURYASSÚ

▲ SANTA HELENA

SÃO
LUIZ

VIANA ▲

L. MARAGÚ

▲ ITAPECURÚ

RIO

MONÇÃO ▲

▲ BÔA VISTA

VARGEM GRANDE ▲

▲PINDARÉ – MIRIM

JANUARIA ▲ ▲ SANTA INÊS

(POSTO GONÇALVES DIAS) ▲COLONIA

PIMENTEL

ILHINHA ●

● L. TARUPÁUA

RIO CARÚ

●CONTRA HERVA

ITAPECURÚ

●LAGOA

COMPRIDA

MONTE ALEGRE ▲

RIO ZUTIUA

● JACARÉ

CODÓ ▲

AGUA BRANCA ●

●CAMIRANGA

●DOMINGOS ●LIMÃO

● PEDREIRAS

GROTA ● ●MANOELZINHO

●ANTONINHO

●TAUARI QUEIMADO

RIO PINDARÉ

RIO MEARIN

RIO GRAJAÚ

RIO CORDA

BARRA DO CORDA ▲

KEY

▲ BRAZILIAN TOWNS

● TENETEHARA VILLAGES

● GRAJAÚ

THE TENETEHARA REGION

I · HISTORICAL SETTING

MODERN BRAZIL is rapidly engulfing the few Indian tribes which continue to survive in the out-of-the-way areas of the country. Tribal Indians now number no more than two or three hundred thousand people, the remnants of approximately a million American Indians who lived in the area when the Portuguese arrived in 1500. Compared to the dense aboriginal population of West Coast South America, these lowland Indians were never numerous, but they have had an influence on Brazilian national culture out of keeping with their small numbers. Their way of life was well adapted to the physical environment of tropical forest and lowland plains, and the Portuguese colonizer learned from the Indian how to live in the New World. Brazilian agricultural techniques, Brazilian foods, and Brazilian folk beliefs are to a great extent derived from the Indian. In some regions, especially in the Amazon tropics where the plantation system with large numbers of Negro slaves did not develop, the Indian formed the most important component of the population. The Portuguese colonists were few and mixed with the aboriginal women as, in the plantation regions, they did with their Negro slaves.

The process of assimilation of the Indian tribes has taken different forms at different epochs and at different places in Brazil. Some tribes were decimated long ago by new diseases acquired from Europeans and from Negroes. Others were enslaved or killed by the Portuguese during the first two hundred years of the colonial period, and still others merged slowly into the rural society, contributing both culturally and physically as they did so. Assimilation of the Indian is still taking place, somewhat differently, of course, than in earlier centuries of Brazilian history, and the phenomena may be studied at first hand. Many tribes have experienced their first contact with Brazilians during the last thirty or forty years, and some of them, such as the Tapirapé of central Brazil, are even now rapidly dying from Western diseases to which they were exposed in the twentieth century. Other tribes have resisted the impact of the foreign culture and new diseases, and, after living face to face with Brazilians for several centuries, they are slowly being assimilated into rural society. In isolated frontier regions, the rural Brazilian culture with which the Indians are in contact is not modern Western culture, for it has remained basically unchanged since colonial times. In Brazil, while Western technology is in full flower in one part of the country, aspects of earlier periods of national history may still be found in the distant frontiers.

The Tenetehara Indians are one of these tribal groups which is even now slowly merging into Brazilian rural life. They are one of the few remaining tribes of the once numerous Tupí-Guaraní speaking peoples who inhabited great portions of the country and who contributed so much to Brazilian social life. The Tenetehara have survived because the northeastern area inhabited by them was off the main roads of penetration into the hinterland and has remained, even into modern times, a frontier. After more than three hundred years of encirclement by Western civilization, they still number more than two thousand people.[1] Their villages extend over a wide territory—from near Barra da Corda on the Mearim River in the State of Maranhão north and west into the State of Pará along the Gurupí, Guamá, and Capim Rivers. Some thirteen villages are located in the region around Barra da Corda and ten more are scattered on the cattle trail between the Mearim and the Pindaré Rivers. Five villages are found along the Pindaré itself. It is estimated that there are between 350 and 400 Tenetehara (Tembé) living in several villages in the State of Pará on the Gurupí, Guamá, and Capim Rivers.[2]

[1] Census of the Brazilian Indian Service in 1940.

[2] Those living in the State of Maranhão in the Mearim, Grajaú, Pindaré drainage system have commonly been called "Guajajara" by writers and travelers, while those who migrated to the Gurupí River from the upper Pindaré during the last century are known as "Tembé." Both the so-called "Guajajara" and "Tembé" share a common language and common cultural traditions; they call themselves "Tenetehara." They regard themselves as a "people," distinct from the Tupí-Guaraní speaking Urubú tribe whose villages are found between the Gurupí and Turi-Assú Rivers in Ma-

The Tenetehara are a forest people and the territory which they inhabit is typical rain-forest country. Except for a few outcroppings of hills on the upper reaches of the Grajaú, Mearim, and Pindaré Rivers, the country is low and the streams which drain it flood into the forest during the "winter" (the rainy season, from December through June), making land transportation for this portion of the year almost impossible. During the dry season, which is locally called "summer" (July through November), small streams dry up altogether and the larger rivers are so low that navigation in small river boats is possible only along their lower courses. Neither the waterways nor the trails cut through the low tropical forest permit year-round transportation and neither the natural resources of the area nor the fertility of the soil made the region attractive to Portuguese or Brazilian colonists during the first centuries after the Portuguese discovered Brazil.

The city of São Luis do Maranhão, situated on the Island of Maranhão at the mouth of the river system which drains Tenetehara territory, was founded as early as 1611 by the French, who were at that time encroaching on the Portuguese possessions in the New World, and in 1614 the Portuguese took over the settlement. São Luis soon became an important center of colonization and expansion, but the early colonists in Maranhão clung to the coast and to the rich valley of the Itapecurú River, which offered navigation during the entire year for more than eight hundred kilometers from its mouth. The Portuguese were few in number, and until slave traffic from Africa brought large numbers of Negro slaves to Maranhão in the second half of the eighteenth century, the colonists depended entirely upon the Indians for labor. They found the Island of Maranhão inhabited by the Tupí-Guaraní Tupinambá, and the lower reaches of the rivers which empty into the ocean at São Luis by several warlike tribes such as the Gamella. In a short time, the Indians in the vicinity of the coastal settlements were either decimated by slavery or driven back into the interior. Both the French and the Portuguese early explored the Mearim and

ranhão, from the Timbira groups who inhabit the arid steppe region west of Barra de Corda, from the nomadic Guajá who appear from time to time along the upper Pindaré, and finally from the Brazilians of the region. In this study we have decided to use the name Tenetehara by which they call themselves. When quoting other authors, the name used by that author will be indicated.

the Pindaré Rivers, and many Indian slaves must have resulted from these expeditions; but, for the most part, the Indians in the dense forest country above the navigable points of the rivers were protected by the inaccessibility of their territory from early colonial expansion.

Furthermore, Jesuit missionaries came to Maranhão in 1614 with the first Portuguese colonists. The Jesuits took it upon themselves to protect the Indians, hoping to build in Maranhão a self-contained community similar to the one they created in Paraguay. There was almost constant conflict, therefore, between the Jesuits and the colonists over the Indians for almost a century and a half. The colonists, who were in need of labor, charged that the Jesuits exploited Indian labor for the benefit of the Order, isolated the Indians in their mission villages (aldeiamentos) away from contact with Europeans, and did not prepare the Indians to take part in colonial life. From time to time, colonists attacked Indian groups, both those living in Jesuit missions and those still in their own villages, under the pretext of putting down warring Indians.

The original territory of the Tenetehara seems to have centered on the upper Pindaré River; all mention of them in the seventeenth and eighteenth centuries places them on this river, above the village of Monção.[3] As early as 1615, a French expedition reported a tribe which they called the "Pinariens," undoubtedly the Tenetehara, living on the upper Pindaré River;[4] and, just one year later, the Portuguese "Capitão Mór," Jeronimo de Albuquerque, sent the famous Indian hunter Bento Maciel Parente with a force of 45 soldiers and 90 missionized Indians up the Pindaré River to search for mines. His mission was carried out "without any other fruits from their great labor but that of making war against the barbarian Tapuya Guajajara [Tenetehara] with fatal damage to that nation."[5] Other Portuguese expeditions must have been in contact with the Tenetehara during the next four decades, for the Jesuits state that in 1653, when they began their missionary activities on the Pindaré River, "the past governors had already tried to bring this

[3] Only in the 19th century are the Tenetehara mentioned as inhabiting the margins of the Mearim and the Grajaú Rivers; Gustave Dodt (1939 ed.), writing after the middle of the century, mentions the Tembé-Tenetehara along the Gurupí River.

[4] Abbéville, quoted by Metraux in La Civilization Materielle, pp. 20–21.

[5] Quoted by Fróes Abreu, p. 105. Also see "Poranduba Maranhense," p. 43.

nation down river and take them out of the labyrinth of their forest
and they were only able to bring down river one small village which
was established at the place which is today called Itaquy" on the
lower Pindaré.[6] In 1653 the Jesuit Padre Francisco Velloso traveled
up the Pindaré River to visit the Tenetehara, which he had heard
were "divided in six villages all of *lingua geral* [Tupí-Guaraní]."
He found the *aldeiamento* at Itaquy almost abandoned. Only a few
Indians were hiding near by in the forest in fear of Portuguese slave
raiders. Velloso was able to attract a few of them back into the
aldeiamento, and he sent three Indians up the Pindaré as emissaries to persuade others to come down river to the mission station.
These emissaries, however, never returned, and Velloso was forced
for lack of food to return to the Island of Maranhão with his few
missionized Tenetehara.[7]

In the next year, the Jesuit Manoel Nunes took 35 days[8] by
canoe to reach the Tenetehara village of Capiytuba on the upper
Pindaré. He was able to persuade only a few Indians to return down
river with him; most of them refused to come in fear of the Portuguese. A third Jesuit expedition under João Maria Garconi was
more successful; a "large number" was led down river to the mission
village called Cajupé. The Jesuits in 1683 moved their mission to a
new site on Lake Maracú (the present town of Viana) on the lower
Pindaré River.[9] Because so many Indians abandoned this mission,
returning up river, a mission village was also established on the
upper Pindaré, above the mouth of the Carú River[10] (see map,
p. 2). In 1730 the village at Maracú had a population of only 404
Indians, while the Aldeia de S. Francisco Xavier, the mission on the
upper Pindaré, is said to have held 779.[11] These two strategically
situated missions helped to protect the Tenetehara and their territory from the Portuguese encroachers until 1759, when the Jesuits
were expelled from Brazil.[12]

6 Moraes, I, 400.   7 *Ibid.,* pp. 399–420.
8 His trip was slow and arduous because of the "currents of the river and the
miserable plague of insects, of mosquitos and gnats (*marouins*) and another species
even smaller." Although traveling time is shorter nowadays with the commercial
launch as far as Pindaré-Mirim on the Pindaré, traveling conditions beyond this point
on the upper river remain as difficult as those described by the Jesuit. Moraes, I,
399–420.
9 Leite, p. 188.   10 Moraes, pp. 399–420.   11 Leite, pp. 189, 191.
12 *Ibid.,* pp. 192–193. Actually, the missions on the Pindaré River were not abandoned until 1760.

During the late eighteenth and the nineteenth century, control over the Indian tribes of this region passed to the civil authorities. The government attempted to attract the Indians into *Colonias* (Indian colonies) under a system of *Diretorias*. Eighteen such *Diretorias* were created in Maranhão, and Tenetehara territory on the Pindaré River was divided into three. A Director, however, was never appointed for any of the Pindaré districts, and judging from the small number of Indians attracted to the colonies established by the civil government, the system was not successful. In 1840, the *Colonia de São Pedro do Pindaré* was founded, principally to attract the Tenetehara, on more or less the same site as the modern village of Pindaré-Mirim (formerly São Pedro or Engenho Central). In 1849, only 120 Indians of "diverse tribes" were living there; by 1861, there were but 58 adults and 18 children; and by 1870, only 44 Indians remained.[13]

In 1854, the *Colonia Januaria* (not to be confused with the modern Tenetehara village at the Post Gonçalves Dias) was established on the upper Pindaré at the mouth of the Carú River, near the former Jesuit Mission of S. Francisco Xavier. There was a Tenetehara village on the site with 80 inhabitants, and in addition to these the Padre in charge was able to attract 90 adults and 38 children. About twenty years later, however, there were only 121 Indians living at this colony.[14] This small number, in contrast to the 779 Indians the Jesuits were able to assemble in 1730, shows the declining control over the Tenetehara during the nineteenth century.

In the late nineteenth century and during the first few years of the twentieth, there was an accelerated advance of Brazilians [15] into the Tenetehara country. They were living in the lower Pindaré, Grajaú, and Mearim areas, and had established two rather large settlements in the upper Pindaré region [16] at Sapucaia and at Santa Cruz, on the Carú. A group of Tenetehara established a village near the Brazilian settlement at Sapucaia,

[13] Marques, pp. 142–143.   [14] *Ibid.*, p. 143.

[15] Although the Indians themselves are, in a sense, the true "Brazilians," the term Brazilian is used throughout this study to refer to rural Brazilians who are of European, Negro, and Indian descent and who frequently are a mixture of all three of these racial groups.

[16] Marques, p. 331.

working for the traders in the extraction of copaíba oil and rubber, and considerable intermarriage seems to have taken place. At Santa Cruz, Indians became rubber gatherers and many worked as canoe men transporting rubber and trade goods. Santa Cruz was attacked repeatedly by the hostile Urubú Indians, and after the rubber crash in 1913 both the Brazilians and the Tenetehara abandoned the Carú region. Even before this time, the Brazilians had left Sapucaia on the upper Pindaré and abandoned to the Tenetehara the margins of the Pindaré River above the Brazilian town of Colonia Pimentel.

For a time, a group of Protestant missionaries resided on the upper Pindaré, but several years ago, at the insistence of the Brazilian Indian Service, they closed their mission and moved away. Each year, however, parties of Brazilians spend several months in the region cutting hardwoods and fishing. The upper reaches of the other rivers on which the Tenetehara live—the Mearim, the Grajaú, the Gurupí, and the Guamá—have been sparsely settled by Brazilians, who during the last fifty years have traveled up and down all of these rivers trading with the Indians, hunting, searching for mines, cutting hardwoods, and collecting rubber, palm nuts and other forest products.

All Tenetehara nowadays have some contact with rural Brazilians. In the middle Pindaré region, the Indians meet with their neighbors daily, since Tenetehara villages are situated within a few hours' walk from the Brazilian towns of Pindaré-Mirim, Santa Inêz, and Colonia Pimentel, and isolated Brazilian families live within a kilometer of Lagôa Comprida and Contra Herva. The people from the remote villages between the Pindaré and Grajaú Rivers and those from the upper Pindaré have relations with Brazilians only periodically, when the Indians visit their settlements to trade or when parties of Brazilians visit their territory to fish or to cut hardwood.

The Tenetehara have, in general, always lived in peace with the missionaries, traders, and settlers with whom they have been in contact. Several early writers mentioned their passivity. The Jesuit Bettendorf wrote that the Tenetehara (Guajajara) were "lazy and not very courageous; they were inconstant and deserters, for at each step, they will flee into their forests, not only the new [inhabitants of

the mission villages] but some of the older [inhabitants] as well." [17]
Later, in the nineteenth century, Cesar Marques reports that "some
aldeiamentos maintain good relations with the [Brazilian] settlements; principally those of the Guajajara [Tenetehara] Indians
who, among all [of the tribes] are the ones who have shown more
tendencies for a civilized life." [18] Antonio Pereira do Lago, writing
in 1822, says that the strongest Indians of Maranhão are the Tim-
biras and the most "perverse thieves and the laziest are the Guajajara [Tenetehara] and the Gamellas." [19] In the nineteenth century,
the two Brazilian settlements on the upper Pindaré were attacked
by Indians, but in all probability the attackers were Timbira or
Urubú. The Gamella also made war on the colonists on the lower
Pindaré over a long period. The only attack definitely attributed
to the Tenetehara was the well-known massacre of the Italian,
Capuchinhos at Alto Alegria in 1901. On this occasion, according
to S. Fróes Abreu,[20] the Tenetehara killed all the "Padres, Nuns,
students, and children of Christian families." This uprising evidently resulted from the practice of carrying off Indian infants
for training in the mission school and from resentment against the
punishments which the padres meted out to natives who practiced
polygyny.

At present, the Brazilian Indian Service of the Federal Government attempts to maintain peaceful relations between the two
groups. The Service has established stations at Colonia near the
Brazilian town of Barra da Corda on the Mearim River; at
Gonçalves Dias just above Pindaré-Mirim on the Pindaré River;
and at two points on the Gurupí River.[21] Each Indian post has an
Indian Officer, an assistant, a schoolteacher and several day laborers
—all of whom are generally Brazilians. These posts were established
to serve as centers of attraction for the Indian population, where

[17] Bettendorf, p. 271.   [18] Marques, p. 143.
[19] Pereira do Lago, *Itinerario*, p. 88.   [20] Fróes Abreu, pp. 215–227.
[21] Post Felipe Camarão and Post Pedro Dantas on the Gurupí River as well as Post
Gonçalves Dias on the Pindaré River are also points of contact with the Tupí-Guaraní
speaking Urubú tribe. During each dry season, groups of Urubú Indians appear
periodically at Gonçalves Dias, several days' walk from their villages near the Turi-
Assú River, in order to receive gifts of metal tools and cloth, which the Service provides them. A small number of Urubú are said to have settled near the posts on the
Gurupí River, and each year groups of Urubú visit these posts from the villages between the Turi-Assú and the Gurupí Rivers.

they might be given the necessary instruction, medical assistance, and material aids which could enable them eventually to take their place as citizens of the nation. They also serve as points of control protecting the Indians from attacks, exploitation, and loss of land to the encroaching Brazilian population. There has been some effort on the part of the Service to demarcate "Indian lands." Thus the area east of the Pindaré River above Pindaré-Mirim and on both sides of the river above Colonia Pimentel is "Indian land," and the Indian Service prohibits Brazilians from settling on them and even from traveling above Colonia Pimentel without previous permission of the Indian Officer. Similarly, lands have been set aside for the Tenetehara in the Mearim River region. Nevertheless, in spite of the efforts of the Indian Service, Brazilians are steadily invading traditional Tenetehara lands all along the Grajaú River and on the middle Pindaré River, and it is only a question of time until they begin to push into the upper Pindaré region. Even at the present time they make their way each year up the Pindaré River above Colonia Pimentel in defiance of the rules of the Indian Service. The police power of the Indian Officer is theoretical only; he is merely able to make formal protest to local authorities against such transgressions.

The Indian post tries to protect the Tenetehara from economic exploitation by regulating trade between the Brazilians and the Indians. It is forbidden to sell alcohol in any form to the Indians. Brazilians are not permitted to go to the Indian villages to buy and sell. When a Tenetehara wishes to sell his products to a Brazilian trader and to buy manufactured articles from him, the post rules that he must be accompanied by a member of the Indian Service staff who sees to it that a fair price is paid for the products and that the Indian is charged the normal price for his purchases. Several times each year the Tenetehara from the upper Pindaré villages come down river to trade and the Indian Officer or his assistant accompany them to Pindaré-Mirim to buy and sell.

Real control over trade, however, is impossible. The Indians themselves complain that the Service hinders their commerce with the Brazilians. They say that the Indian Officers tell them what they must buy, and they complain that they often have to wait at the post for several days until the Officer or his assistant finds the time to go with them to the Brazilian settlement to trade. The Indians like to buy *aguardente* and they like to buy on credit, neither of which the Indian Service allows them to do. Considerable trading therefore takes place without the Indian Officer's knowledge. In the Pindaré region, the Indians by-pass the post on their way to Pindaré-Mirim or stop to trade at Colonia Pimentel before they arrive at Post Gonçalves Dias. Brazilian traders visit Indian villages frequently, against regulations, carrying goods with which they purchase *babassú* nuts, rice, pelts, and manioc flour. While we were living in the villages of Lagôa Comprida and Jacaré, two Brazilian traders arrived with pack animals loaded with trade goods to exchange for *babassú* nuts and rice. Although we warned the Indians that the prices paid to them were low, they explained that they preferred to sell to these traders rather than be forced to transport heavy loads of *babassú* nuts and rice on their own shoulders to the Brazilian settlements.

The efforts of the Indian Service to "protect" the Indians have met with hidden, even open, hostility from the Brazilians, who believe, and try to convince the Indians, that the employees of the Service are exploiting the Indians for their own benefit. In 1934, a group of Brazilians from Pindaré-Mirim attacked and machine-gunned Post Gonçalves Dias; the Indian Officer was arrested under the pretense that he was a communist. The simple Brazilians of the region, whose standard of living is little, if at all, superior to that of the Tenetehara, find it hard to understand why the Federal Government takes such pains to protect the Indian when they themselves are exploited almost as much as the Indian. They fail to understand why the Federal Government doles out tools, clothes, and farming equipment to the Indian and not to them, when they are almost as poor. Local Brazilian authorities level the same criticism against the Federal Indian Service which the Portuguese colonists made against the Jesuit missionaries in the seventeenth and eighteenth centuries. In short, they complain that the Indian Service wishes to isolate the Indians and to preserve them in a vacuum, and that the Service does not have a realistic program for educating the Indian to take an active part in national life.

The inefficiency of the Indian Officers and their staff and their lack of knowledge of the Indian culture does not make the situation any better. The Post Gonçalves Dias, for example, does maintain a school, but the effect of this school is to fortify the general belief among the local Brazilians and the authorities that the Tenetehara will never be able to learn and that the Indians are "lazy and no good." Each day the schoolteacher at the post, who takes her duties very seriously, must go through the near-by village to collect enough children, and adults, to make up a class. None of these Indians have learned to read or write. In fact, some of them moved away in order to avoid having to send their children to school. On the Mearim River at Post Colonia, however, it is reported that several Tenetehara have learned to read and write and that the school-teacher is an Indian.[22]

Although the *civilizado* [23] of the region is hardly more civilized than the Indian, in the sense of sharing modern industrial culture, he considers himself socially superior and refers to the Indian as "a savage." Even many Indians accept this view and some of them are ashamed of being Indian. Our Tenetehara informants at first tried to convince us that they followed Brazilian customs, and a few of them claimed to have Brazilian ancestors, thinking that they would thereby gain prestige in our eyes. While many Tenetehara are completely bilingual, using their native Tupí-Guaraní and Portuguese with almost equal facility, we did not meet one local Brazilian who had found it necessary or worthwhile to learn the aboriginal language. Intermarriage between the Tenetehara and Brazilians is relatively infrequent. Only about thirty acknowledged halfbreeds were noted in the villages we visited in the Pindaré region. All of them were children of Brazilian men who had spent some time in an Indian village and of Indian mothers. We heard of only two permanent unions between Brazilians and Indians in the Pindaré region, but we heard of many temporary sexual unions, even between Indian men and Brazilian women. The relationship

[22] Their slowness in learning is due to the system by which they are taught rather than to a lack of native intelligence. Young Indian boys, whose knowledge of the world comprises a short stretch of the Pindaré River and whose ideas of astronomical bodies comes from Indian myths, are asked to copy again and again such sentences as: "*O mundo faz parte do sistema universal* (The world is part of the universal system)."

[23] In the Pindaré region, the Brazilians are called the "Civilized" or the "Christians" and the Indians are usually referred to as *caboclos*—a term generally used in north Brazil to refer to the rural Brazilian population of mixed Indian, Negro, and Portuguese ancestry.

between the Brazilians and Indians who are neighbors is one neither of caste nor of class; it is a relationship between people of two different cultures, one of which is considered superior.

The core of Tenetehara culture is still essentially aboriginal. In spite of their long contacts with Brazilians, they have retained many aboriginal patterns in more or less the same form as in ancient times. The basis of their social organization is still the extended family, and they distinguish relatives by the native kinship system. They still celebrate, although in a slightly attenuated form, their native puberty ceremonies and their seasonal festivals. They believe in native supernaturals, and shamanism is still a strong force in modern Tenetehara life. Even borrowed customs have been molded into the framework of their native culture pattern. Tenetehara culture is still distinctly an American Indian culture, yet it has undergone numerous modifications. The Tenetehara have acquired new material desires and necessities; there have been changes in their customs, institutions, values, and behavior patterns since aboriginal times. Furthermore, such changes are currently taking place with increasing velocity with the rapid expansion of modern.Brazil. Day by day, acculturation of the Tenetehara is taking place, not as the Indian Service might plan it, but in essentially the same haphazard way that numerous other tribal groups have been assimilated into Brazilian life. Tenetehara culture as we find it today offers a rich field for the student of culture change and for the student of the social history of Brazil. It gives us a picture of a cross-section, in a sense, in the process of the formation of rural society in north Brazil.

II · SOCIAL ORGANIZATION

THE TENETEHARA are a "people" rather than a politically organized tribe or a nation. There is no tribal organization of any
kind; each village is an independent political unit. The Tenetehara
are united only by a common language and by a common body of
cultural tradition. Even though men of several villages are said to
have taken part in the attack on the missionaries of Alto Alegria in
1901, this was quite casual and obviously a momentary union of a
group with common grievances rather than a confederation of
villages for war. The Tenetehara are not even aware of the extent
of their own territory and the extent of the population among
themselves. Although visiting between villages is frequent, the
travel of most people is limited to those villages in the general
neighborhood of their own. The villagers in the Pindaré region
knew the names and approximate size of each village on the Pindaré and those on the trail between the Grajaú and the Pindaré
Rivers, but most people had only the vaguest idea of the location,
the size, and the number of Tenetehara villages on the Grajaú,
Mearim, and Gurupí Rivers. A few men had traveled to these villages and there were a few immigrants from the Grajaú villages to
the Pindaré region. Everyone was surprised when we told them a
few Tenetehara lived beyond the Gurupí on the Guamá River.
People from distant villages are strangers, but if they appear they
are recognized as Tenetehara—that is to say, as "people"—and hospitality is extended to them.

The direct knowledge of most people is limited to a zone of easy
communication, such as the Pindaré River drainage. Within this
zone, people visit other villages frequently. They take part in each
others' festivals and ceremonials, and young men, especially, wan-

der from village to village, living for a short time in each until they finally marry and settle down. One young man, for example, resided for short periods in four villages situated between the Grajaú and the Pindaré River before he finally married a girl at Januaria and settled there. There is frequent intervillage marriage within a limited zone; thus most people have relatives in several villages. One of our informants, Miguel, who lived in Januaria village, had a brother's son, a sister, a sister's son, and several more distant relatives in the village of Camirang on the upper Pindaré. He also had kin in Lagôa Comprida and in Ilhinha. People visit their relatives in other near-by villages, and, should they wish to change residence from one village to another, they move to join relatives.

Even the sense of belonging to a particular village is not strong among the Tenetehara. Although people generally live for many years in their native village, sometimes even pass their entire lives there, the size and constituents of a particular village change considerably over a long period. In fact, entire family groups frequently move from one village to another. When we visited the upper Pindaré in 1942, for example, a large group of relatives had just left one village and moved to another after a quarrel between two important leaders. Several months before our arrival in Lagôa Comprida (in 1942) a small extended family from the village of Limão had moved to Lagôa Comprida because Limão was "too isolated." Such moves require a previous understanding with the chief of the village which the family wishes to join, since the newcomers frequently must depend for food upon the gardens of others, at least for one season, until their own gardens are producing. Furthermore, according to Manuel Viana, each village owns the surrounding land, and outsiders should ask permission to plant on another village's terrain. Manuel was unable to describe the limits of the lands of his village any more specifically than to say that the neighboring village of Ilhinha should not plant on "our side of the river" without asking permission, but he remembered at least one occasion when a group was refused hospitality when they moved without previous arrangement. Years ago, when he was a boy, a group arrived unannounced from the Gurupí River to join his grandfather's village on the Carú River. They began to build houses and clear forest for gardens. His grandfather, the village chief, did not want them to remain and he asked them to leave. There was a quarrel and a fight with clubs—not with bows and arrows—and the group left, returning to the Gurupí.

THE VILLAGE

Tenetehara villages are usually situated on high ground about a half kilometer from the river or *igarapé* (small stream) which furnishes them with household water. They live at this distance from their water supply because the rivers and smaller streams generally overflow their banks during the rainy season. The houses in a village are usually laid out in two lines facing an open plaza from which all grass and brush have been cleared. Informants spoke of "streets of houses like the villages of the civilized." The village of Camirang [1] had three rows of houses or "three streets." At the village of Antonhinho, on the upper Pindaré, however, the houses are scattered about without any apparent order, due perhaps to the broken terrain of the site; Snethlage mentions that the village of Colonia was oriented in a quadrangular form.[2] One old Tenetehara told us that many years ago on the Carú River he had seen a village with houses arranged in a circle around a plaza. He drew a plan of it on the ground showing houses in a large circle and paths cleared from a central ceremonial house to each house. This is the general plan of the village of the Eastern Timbira who during the last century lived on the Carú, and he may well have been confusing a Timbira village with one of the numerous Tenetehara villages in which he had lived. Other informants do not remember having seen any other form of village than one laid out in "streets."

Formerly, a large ceremonial house (*tupuizuhú*) was constructed

---

[1] We have decided to use the Portuguese names for the Tenetehara villages, although each village has a native name. The Tenetehara use the Portuguese name almost as often as the native name—even when speaking the native language. The two names for the villages in the Pindaré area are:

PORTUGUESE	TENETEHARA	PORTUGUESE	TENETEHARA
Januaria	Kriwirí	Ilhinha	Neirí
Lagôa Comprida	Ipururupokú	Contra Herva	Purupaháwo
Limão	Limaináwo	Cigana	Mahuriáwo
Tawari Queimado	Tawarí pehumira	Camirang	Camirang
Manuelzinho	Kapitari kwaháwo	Antonhinho	Tunirí kwaháwo

[2] Snethlage, "Unter Nordostbrasilianischen Indianer," p. 121.

in the central plaza and used by both men and women for ceremonial singing and dancing. It was a large shelter without walls built for the occasion of a ceremonial (usually the Honey Feast, see p. 122) and destroyed after the ceremony ended. Nowadays, the Tenetehara on the Pindaré hold their festivals under roof extensions of private dwellings or in the center of the plaza. None of the Pindaré villages we visited had built a ceremonial house, nor have they held the Honey Feast, for several years. In the village of Colonia on the Mearim, Snethlage saw a ceremonial house which was situated toward the end of a village "street" [3] and not in the center of the open plaza, where our informants said it should be.

While the Tenetehara in general prefer the sociability of village life, a few family groups live isolated from the others near their gardens outside the village proper. At Lagôa Comprida, for example, two family groups lived about fifteen minutes' walk from the village. A few years ago, Lagôa Comprida contained only a few houses. The majority of residences were scattered about in the vicinity. The Indian Service persuaded the villagers to concentrate their dwellings so that the Indian Officer could have better control, but in 1939 a fire destroyed one side of the village. Rather than rebuild on the site, the two family groups elected to live as before near their source of food on their garden sites. In 1942 the village of Contra Herva consisted of only four houses, and six more houses were located in the general vicinity near the gardens.

Tenetehara villages vary considerably in size. The largest on the upper Pindaré, the village of Camirang, had twenty houses and 130 people in 1942, while the near-by village of Manuelzinho had only six houses and 19 people. In 1942 Januaria at the Post Gonçalves Dias had a population of 85 Indians living in twelve houses, and Tawari Queimado near the Grajaú River on the cattle trail, one of the largest Tenetehara settlements, had more than 250 people. According to a recent census of the Indian Service, the villages around Barra da Corda on the Mearim vary from 160 (village of Uchôa) to 15 (village of Genipapo) Indians.

At a short distance from each Tenetehara village there is always

3 *Ibid.*, p. 122.

a "center," that is to say, a group of temporary shelters situated near the plantations where sometimes an oven for toasting manioc flour is installed.[4] From time to time, when garden work becomes pressing during the period of clearing, planting, or harvest, entire families move to the "center" for a few days. At other times, families go at intervals to prepare manioc flour; they leave there the necessary equipment for preparation of the flour such as *tipitis*,[5] graters, baskets. In a few villages, the Indians preferred to carry the heavy manioc tubers from their gardens to the village for preparation of flour, but in such villages as Januaria, Contra Herva, Lagôa Comprida, and others the plantations are distant, and a few families are always absent from the village "making flour at the center." There is a well-beaten path between the village and the center.

Whenever possible, Tenetehara villages move their location each five to seven years within a limited territory. As the surrounding country is cut and burned for garden plots, they must go out farther and farther each year to find high virgin forest desirable for agriculture, and it is soon preferable to move the village rather than to travel so far to reach choice agricultural land. The village of Camirang on the upper Pindaré, for example, had been situated on its then present site for five years (in 1942); villagers had to go two or three kilometers to find first growth forest suitable for new gardens. They told us, therefore, that they planned to move the next year to a site some thirty kilometers down river. The men, they said, would clear and plant gardens near the new village site, and

4 While most "centers" are only temporary sites near the gardens where people go to work for a few days, now and again they are sometimes so distant from the village that the people construct more permanent houses and spend most of their time in the "center." Although the residents of such a "center" continue to consider themselves as belonging to the main village, they lead a life almost entirely independent of it. In 1942, for example, Januaria had more than 120 inhabitants, but by 1945 suitable sites for gardens could be found only at such a great distance that only sixteen people continued to reside permanently in the village. One family group numbering more than thirty people lived almost ten kilometers away and another extended family had established themselves about five kilometers away. Yet both of these groups considered themselves as inhabitants of Januaria village. In the village of Camirang, not only the distance to the gardens but also dissension between family leaders caused one extended family group to move to their "center," and finally to form a separate village.

5 A long palm fiber tube used to squeeze the poisonous juice from manioc.

only after the gardens were producing would their people build houses and move their families there.[6] While the Tenetehara agricultural system ideally calls for such moves each five to seven years, many settlements have actually remained on the same spot for as long as twenty years. Villages such as Contra Herva, Lagôa Comprida, and Ilhinha, which are hemmed in by Brazilian settlers, have exhausted most of the possible village sites in the vicinity, and the Indians do not want to move too far away for commerce with the Brazilians.

VILLAGE CHIEFS

Each Tenetehara village has a "Capitão," who is appointed by and recognized as chief by the Indian Service. He is theoretically responsible to the Indian Service for the government of the people of the village. Each "Capitão" is given a document by the Indian Officer stating that he has been appointed "Captain" of the village. S. Fróes Abreu published two documents shown to him by village Captains in the Mearim region which indicate that the appointment of chiefs by outsiders did not originate with the Indian Service. One of these documents, dated 1912, appointed an Indian "Major of the Indians"; and the second, issued in 1919 by the Governor's Palace of the State of Maranhão, appointed an Indian "Lt. Colonel" with authority over the Indians of a specific village.[7] Fróes Abreu makes the following observations regarding the appointed village Captains: "From what we observed, we concluded that among the semi-civilized Guajajara (Tenetehara) the chief of the village is not an individual with the authority which is generally attributed to him. We had occasion to observe that the captain, in order to show his prestige, always tried to take steps which would not be disagreeable to his followers; some of them attained the perfection of not taking any initiative at all in fear that their orders might not be carried out."[8] Our observations in the villages of the Pindaré region agree in general with those of Fróes Abreu.

[6] The entire village did not move, but in 1945 when we visited the village of Camirang again, we found one of the largest extended family groups had indeed moved to this new site.

[7] Fróes Abreu, p. 122.

[8] *Ibid.*, p. 113. Citations from this source are translated by the authors from Portuguese.

The fact that a man has been appointed "Capitão" by the Indian Service does not assure authority in his own village. It simply means that he will act more or less as an intermediary between the Indians and the Service and that he gains a certain prestige thereby. Some village chiefs, however, do wield authority. These are men with strong individual qualities, who are leaders of one of the large extended family groups, and who are at the same time the appointed Captains of their village. The fact that they are respected by outsiders emphasizes their prestige in the eyes of the villagers. The best example of this type is Camirang. He actually governs his village. He gives orders daily and they are carried out. Yet, even Camirang diplomatically confers constantly with the leaders of family groups of his village. We first met Camirang at Post Gonçalves Dias during one of his trading trips down river and made arrangements with him to visit his village. He said that he would "give an order to delay" a forthcoming puberty ceremony until after we arrived. During our stay he ordered that all men of the village hunt to provide for the feast at the puberty ceremony. Camirang gave orders for the clearing of forest for gardens, for the cooperative planting of manioc, and for many other activities, but before giving such orders he always discussed them with Ambrosio and Domingo, important family heads of the village.

Now and again Camirang uses his relationship with the Indian Service to accomplish his ends by threats. Once when several Indians were poking around in our baggage, we heard Camirang threaten that if they stole anything he would "send them down river with the karaý (white Brazilians)" and have them "put in jail in São Pedro (Pindaré-Mirim)." Several Indians told us that Camirang had threatened to report them to the Indian Officer at Post Gonçalves Dias if they did not work in the collection of copaíba oil, which the village sells each year through the Indian post.

In other villages the chief is somewhat of a figurehead with little authority. Capitão Picó of the village of Lagôa Comprida seldom gives an order to anyone outside of his own family. Capitão José Verissimo of Jacaré makes a pretense of authority in front of visitors; yet the people of his village pay little attention to him. He insisted that the two of us who visited Jacaré stay in his house. He publicly demanded presents of us and pay for the people of the village. Yet, when he ordered the young men of his village to forage for palm hearts for our horses, they ignored him. We soon learned to go directly to an individual, avoiding the Captain as an intermediary, if we wanted a favor of anyone in Jacaré. When José Verissimo visits Post Gonçalves Dias, however, he is the spokesman for his village. Most village chiefs speak Portuguese fluently.

FAMILY AND KINSHIP GROUPS

Tenetehara family dwellings are constructed in the same general style as those of the simple Brazilians of the region. Their houses have a rectangular floor plan with hip roofs; the sides and the roof are covered with *babassú* palm fronds. Unlike those of local Brazilians, however, Tenetehara houses have no windows. In general, there is only one room, but frequently an extension of the roof is left open to form a porch where people gather for gossip and where shamans perform their cures. The Tenetehara do not remember any other kind of house. In 1924, Snethlage found Tenetehara houses on the middle Mearim built in the same manner as those of the Brazilians of the region, and even in the last century, Gustave Dodt described Tenetehara (Tembé) houses on the Gurupí River as straw-roofed with clay adobe walls, definitely a copy of the Brazilian house type of that region.[9] Snethlage mentions seeing roofs covered with bark, but he considered this a temporary expedient in the absence of appropriate palm leaves in certain districts.[10]

As a rule, the interior of a typical Tenetehara house forms one large room, but, sometimes, when the house is shared with relatives beyond the immediate family, partitions are built dividing the house into two or more rooms. Cooking is done on sunny days just outside the door under the porch-like extension of the house roof. On rainy days, one corner of the house serves as a kitchen and, since there is no opening for ventilation, the smoke from the fire curls through the door and seeps through the cracks in the palm-leaf walls and roof. Cooking is done over a fireplace constructed of several large stones. The family hammocks are suspended from the upright house poles and from the rafters to within a comfortable

[9] Dodt (1939 ed.), p. 194.
[10] Snethlage, "Unter Nordostbrasilianischen Indianer," p. 122.

sitting distance from the floor. The portion of the house allotted to the father and mother of the family is generally a particularly desirable part of the house, some distance from the fireplace and with access to the door. Possessions, such as weapons, steel tools, scissors, and baskets are usually stored on the rafters or hung on pegs driven into the upright house posts. Many Tenetehara keep small belongings either in little tin trunks, which they buy from Brazilian traders, or in woven baskets which they make themselves. Trunks and storage baskets are placed alongside the wall nearest the owner's hammock. Occasionally a Tenetehara house contains a wooden bench or a canvas chair, but usually people sit either in their hammocks or on palm mats thrown on the clay floor. Because there are no windows, the interior is dark, and the crisscross of hammocks and the personal possessions on the walls and on the rafters give the household a cluttered appearance.

In each dwelling resides, ideally, one simple family (a man, his wife or wives, and their children), yet the majority of Tenetehara houses hold other close relatives. In Lagôa Comprida, nine of the twenty houses in the village were occupied by simple families; eleven were shared with relatives. One house, for example, held not only a man, his wife, and their young daughter, but also three young unmarried men—a brother's son and two adopted sons. Since residence is matrilocal for a year or two after marriage, during which the groom works for his father-in-law, many young couples live with the bride's parents. As a rule, after a year or two they build a house for themselves, generally near the dwelling of the wife's parents. No one among the Tenetehara remembered having seen a large multifamily dwelling, such as those used by the coastal Tupinambá and by other Tupí-Guaraní tribes of Brazil. As long as people can remember they have lived in single family houses similar to those of the local Brazilians.

Most Tenetehara men are monogamous; in 1942, we noted only nine men with two wives and one man with three wives. Polygynous families occupy one house. Coresidence of the wives of one man does not generally result in disharmony and quarrels because the wives in such cases are usually close relatives. In five cases, men were married to a woman and her daughter by a former marriage. One man had a woman and her sister's daughter (whom she called

"daughter" according to the kinship system) as wives; and a woman
and her classificatory "granddaughter" were co-wives of still
another man. The marriage between a man and two women who are
close relatives generally takes place in the following manner: he
first marries the older woman and then helps raise her younger
relative. Instead of exercising a stepfather's control over his young
charge and thereby gaining a worker for the extended family group
by marrying her to a young man, he decides to keep her as a
second wife. Informants told us that an older wife sometimes sug-
gests this to her husband in order to keep an active husband and a
good provider for herself and for her young relative and in order
to keep her "daughter" to whom she is attached in the same house.
Quarrels and jealousy between two co-wives under such circum-
stances are rare. The genealogies of Tenetehara men and women
which we gathered did not show a single case of sororal polygyny
with two sisters as co-wives of a man, nor could our informants remember such a case. Genealogies did show, however, that polygyny
was more prevalent a generation ago. For example, the father of one
of our informants, who died more than twenty years ago, had as
many as five wives at one time. Manuel Viana told us of several
men of great prestige, whom he knew as a young man and who had
four or five wives. Nowadays, the Indian Service prohibits polygyny.
During our residence at the Post the Indian Officer threatened to
arrest two men because he had heard that they had more than one
wife. Yet, right under his nose in the village of Januaria itself, one
man had two wives. He simply explained to the administrator that
the older woman was his wife and that the younger woman was his
wife's daughter who lived with them. All the Indians, however,
knew that both were his wives.[11]

The Tenetehara system of classifying kin is a bilateral system;
that is, there is no emphasis on either the father's or the mother's
side. According to this system, all relatives of one's own generation—
brothers, sisters, parallel or cross-cousins—are called "brother" or
"sister." There are terms for "older brother" and for "younger
brother" when a man is speaking, and there are terms for "older
sister" and "younger sister" when a woman is speaking. The father's

[11] Snethlage (op. cit., p. 129), writes that polygyny was not frequent, but that the
chief of the village of Aratoria had three wives.

brothers are classified with "father," although the term for this
relative is slightly different; and the mother's sisters are classed
with "mother," although again the term differs somewhat. Uncles
and aunts of a different sex from one's own parent (that is, the
mother's brothers and the father's sisters) and their children are
distinguished by completely different terms. This system is internally consistent, for a man calls the children of a brother by the
same term he calls his own children, and a woman calls here sister's
children as she does her own children, but the children of a man's
sister and of a woman's brother are given special terms. There are
kinship terms for grandparents which distinguish them only according to sex and which extend even to the brothers and sisters
of one's real grandparents on either side. There is one term only
for grandchildren, which differs according to the sex of the person
speaking.[12]

This Tenetehara system of classifying kin is characterized by a
wide extension of the terms to include distant relatives; a man's
father's brother's son is his "brother," this "brother's" children are
"sons" and "daughters" to him and "brothers" and "sisters" to his
own children. Theoretically, such extensions may continue almost
ad infinitum. Actually, however, kinship terms are only used for a
limited number of people and the system is never followed out to
extreme lengths.

Beyond the immediate biological family, the most important unit
of relatives is the extended family, made up of several biological
families bound together by kinship. This larger group is perhaps
even more important in Tenetehara social structure than the more
restricted biological family. It is the basic unit of economic production and it survives when the single family unit breaks up, thus pro-
viding greater security for the individual. Ideally, an extended
family is based on the control of an older man over his "daughters"
(his own daughters and those of his "brothers"). Thus, the core of
the Tenetehara extended family is made up of a group of related
females, yet it is led by a male. A leader of an extended family is
always willing to adopt a "daughter," on the death of one of the
men whom he calls "brother." Through the marriage of these
young women, he draws younger men into his group by matrilocal

12 See Appendix for complete list of kinship terms.

residence. A young man is obligated to work for his father-in-law for a year or so after marriage, and, depending on the prestige of the family leader, the young couple may remain permanently with the group. A few young husbands, however, become dissatisfied with the wife's family group and adhere to the group of a strong leader to whom they are related by kinship.

The composition of such extended families and the relationship of the people who compose them is best explained by describing the composition of several specific groups. In 1942, José Viana had just moved to the village of Januaria, bringing more than twenty people of his extended family with him; he explained that a few of the family remained behind but planned to join him later. José is a man of great prestige; he is a strong family leader, a shaman, and a very careful diplomat. The female "core" of his group was made up of his three real daughters; five "daughters" (daughters of two deceased brothers); a younger "sister" (father's sister's daughter); and an adult granddaughter (see Chart I). Through the marriage of these ten women and by the rule of matrilocal residence, José has garnered ten "sons-in-law," who plant their gardens cooperatively. José sells the pelts, *babassú* palm nuts, or surplus crops for the group, rewarding each son-in-law according to his contribution. He makes a special effort to satisfy the best workers among them. Because José is known as a wealthy man at the head of a strong extended family group, young men are attracted to him. As members of his group, they have greater security than with a leader of less renown.

The extended family group of Camirang, the chief of the largest village on the upper Pindaré, illustrates how an ambitious and skillful man can use kinship in Tenetehara society to bring people under his control. Camirang himself has no children. His group consists of his two younger sisters, their husbands and young children; his wife's two sisters and their husbands; three "sisters" (father's sister's daughters) and their husbands; a younger brother and his wife; as well as several unmarried young men whom he adopted when they were very young (see Chart II). Camirang gained leadership of the group at the death of his father and he has steadily added people to the group. Thus, his younger brother brought his wife and son from her father's group to join Camirang

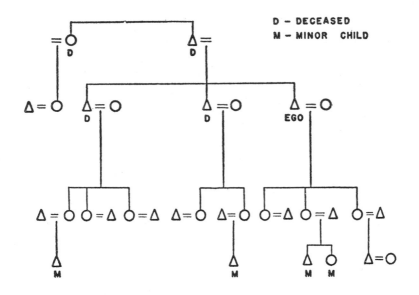

CHART I

EXTENDED FAMILY OF JOSÉ VIANA

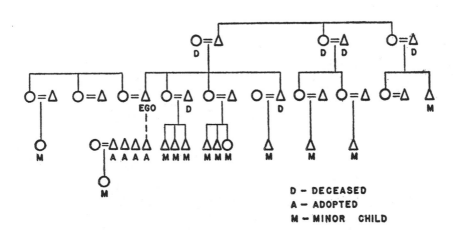

CHART II

EXTENDED FAMILY OF CAMIRANG

and one of his adopted sons also returned after a short period of residence with his father-in-law.

Enterprising family leaders make every effort to hold the women in their group and to retain the male workers who join the group by marriage. Most quarrels between family groups involve women. Pedro, a young shaman who was forced to flee from the village of Januaria, for example, took his young wife with him. People were glad to see Pedro go, because he was suspected of evil sorcery, but Manuel Viana, his "father-in-law" (the young wife was Manuel's brother's daughter, thus his "daughter"), was angry because the woman left. Manuel arranged with the Indian Officer to have Pedro arrested and the girl returned to the village.[13] On another occasion, a young widow left the village of Ilhinha soon after her husband's death, and moved to Januaria, the village at the Indian Service Post. She complained that her own extended family group was not treating her justly. Soon, Joãozinho, the leader of her family group, came to the Post, complaining to the administrator that she had been stolen by Raimundinho, a family leader in Januaria. Both men claimed her as a "sister." After much litigation, the Indian Officer allowed the woman to remain with Raimundinho following her own desires, and the Ilhinha group retired in anger. Our Tenetehara informants told us of several similar quarrels between family groups when a woman left one group to join another.

Each Tenetehara village is made up of several extended families. In the village of Camirang in 1942, for example, there were four such groups. Camirang's extended family has already been described; the other three groups were led by Domingo, by Pedro, and by Ambrosio. The first consisting of Domingo, his wife, his two married daughters and their husbands, and one unmarried son, lived about a kilometer away from the village proper. Seven houses belonging to Pedro's group occupied the northeastern part of the village. In terms of kinship, Pedro's extended family was rather exceptional in its composition; Pedro's three married sons lived with their father's group. People told us that Pedro had re-

---

[13] The Indian Service has made a special effort to unite a large village at Januaria and has prohibited Indians living there from moving away without permission. This rule was used by Manuel Viana as reason to have Pedro arrested. The gist of the charge was that Pedro not only left the Post but took one of the women away with him.

fused to allow the sons to leave to get married and had arranged
wives for them with great difficulty. Several unmarried children and
one married daughter and her husband also belonged to Pedro's
extended family. The largest extended family of the village in 1942,
however, was that of Ambrósio. His group was larger than that led
by Captain Camirang himself. Although Ambrósio was only
about forty years of age, comparatively young for a leader of a large
extended family, he had several younger sisters, many "daughters"
and "granddaughters," and they brought young men into his group.
Moreover, he had adopted several boys, who were still unmarried
youths and who worked with his group.

Camirang, because of his facility with Portuguese and his ability
to deal with outsiders, had been appointed Capitão of the village
by the Indian Service. Fortified by this relationship with the Indian
Service, he wielded considerable authority, but it was based primarily on his rare diplomacy and his intimate relationship with
the leaders of the other three extended families. Pedro was Camirang's father's brother; they called each other (in terms of the
Tenetehara kinship system) "father" and "son," and Camirang
made the most of this kinship tie. He also worked hand in hand
with Ambrósio, and consulted with him before giving any order
for village activity. Neither Domingo nor Ambrósio spoke Portuguese fluently and thus it was to their advantage to let Camirang
take all their products down river to market. Both seemed to feel
somewhat dependent upon him as their intermediary with the Indian Service and with traders. A certain amount of wealth stuck
to Camirang's hands in passing, and he was able to maintain a
higher standard of living than the other three leaders, thus increasing his prestige among the men of the village. His authority
within the village, however, rested primarily on the goodwill of
these family leaders.

Now and again an extended family, dissatisfied with the village
chief, decides to move en masse to another village. When a Captain
of an upper Pindaré village died a few years ago, the Indian Service
appointed his son as his successor. The young man at the time
was living at the Post Gonçalves Dias but went up river to govern
"his village." Within two years, he had quarreled with two family
leaders of the village and both moved with their people to other

villages. One of them, Domingo, joined Camirang's village and the other moved to a village where his father's brother was captain. The family leaders complained that the newly appointed young captain exploited their men, asking them to work each day on his own gardens; they said that he never consulted them in regard to cooperative endeavor and that he did not bring them enough in return for the skins and surplus products they sent down river with him to sell. The young captain was left with a village of eighteeen people—his own extended family—and these were drifting away slowly. By 1945, he had moved down river to the village at the Indian Post with a handful of survivors who remained with him.

The size of an extended family depends upon the leader—his capacity to maintain authority and his astuteness in protecting his group. Now that the Tenetehara are dependent upon trade with Brazilians, a man who understands trade and commerce has a great advantage. A successful family leader stimulates his people to produce surplus garden products, collect *babassú*, or copaíba oil, and markets these products for them in order to buy clothes, salt, arms, hardware, and other manufactured objects. Many leaders are fluent in Portuguese and are therefore better middlemen in trade. A young and ambitious leader such as Benedito, for example, will prosper and gradually gather about him an increasingly large number of people. In 1942 Benedito had only his brother and four unmarried youths living with him in the village of Lagôa Comprida. By 1945, however, he had adopted two young girls who would soon be marriageable. The six men worked cooperatively, Benedito selling their surplus products and palm nuts to Brazilian traders. Together they bought a horse, since theirs is an inland village, which they used not only to haul their own products but also to transport the goods of other villagers to market. This provides them with an extra source of revenue; and Benedito is an active and acute trader, who speaks fluent Portuguese. He persuaded the Indian Service to present his group with a large griddle for toasting manioc flour, and he maintains excellent relations with the Indian Officer. Benedito may lose the four unmarried youths who were working with him through marriage, but he will add two sons-in-law and others will undoubtedly join his group.

On the other hand, the extended family of Captain Picó in the same village is slowly dwindling. At one time Picó was an important man, the head of a large group. Now he is old and poor; he has practically no control over the ten or twelve relatives who remain, and there is no energetic young man among them. Each man of Picó's group makes his garden individually and each sells any surplus to passing traders. His relatives are moving off to join other extended families whose leaders offer greater advantages. The extended family, however, does not always break up when the leader gets old and loses his capacity for leadership. The largest extended family in the Pindaré region in 1942 and 1945 was led by Manuelzinho. There were eleven individual families totaling forty-one people. Manuelzinho was an old man—probably sixty years of age —but his son had returned to live with his father and was the active leader in trading and in group work. Manuelzinho was also a well-known shaman (pazé). The Tenetehara depend upon the shaman to defend them from sorcery and from malevolent supernaturals, and the shaman is the central figure in most ceremonials. The leader of an extended family who is also a shaman has an added control over his people. We were told that formerly almost all family leaders were shamans.[14] Among most Tupí-Guaraní peoples, the shaman holds both religious and secular powers over the people, and a Tenetehara shaman-family leader—with religion, kinship bonds, and economic controls validating his authority—has the maximum control over his group.

[14] Snethlage (op. cit., p. 129) mentions a "cacique" who was a shaman (pazé) at the same time.

III · ECONOMIC LIFE

THE TERRITORY inhabited by the Tenetehara is ecologically speaking part of the Amazon Valley, although all of the main rivers drain directly north into the Atlantic Ocean. The dense tropical rain forest is rich in various hard woods and palms common to the Amazon, and the climate is tropical, with a mean temperature of 85 degrees Fahrenheit and with abundant rainfall. The region is sparsely populated: the average is less than one person to two square kilometers. Only slightly more than 10,000 people, including Indians and Brazilians, live in the Pindaré River valley above (and including) the Brazilian town of Pindaré-Mirim. Most of them are concentrated in or near three Brazilian settlements, Colonia Pimentel, Santa Inês, and Pindaré-Mirim—all in the municipality of Pindaré-Mirim.[1] Although several important Tenetehara villages are situated near these settlments, most of the Indian population lives in the upper reaches of the Pindaré or along the cattle trail which follows the Zutiua River between the Pindaré and the Grajaú Rivers. There are no Indian villages below Pindaré-Mirim on the Pindaré River; above Colonia Pimentel the land is officially reserved for Indians, and there are no permanent Brazilian settlers. Only along the middle region of the river, in the munici-

[1] Until recently the town of Pindaré-Mirim was called São Pedro; it is also well known throughout the region as Engenho Central. The administrative center of the municipality, which in Brazil corresponds to the county in the United States, its population is about 2,000. The two other centers, Colonia Pimentel and Santa Inês, have approximately 1,000 and 2,000 people, respectively. There are 10,475 people in the municipality. There was a sugar mill at Pindaré-Mirim until 1938, when it was sold and dismounted. The town immediately declined, and many people moved away. The agricultural center, Santa Inês, two leagues away, began to be more important, though Pindaré-Mirim remained the administrative center of the municipality and the river port for the region.

pality of Pindaré-Mirim, do the Tenetehara of the Pindaré have any serious conflict with the Brazilians regarding land.

Compared to other rural areas throughout the world, the middle Pindaré would seem to have more than enough land for its present population. Yet the Brazilians feel considerable antagonism toward the Indian Service for prohibiting them from expanding into the upper Pindaré, while the Indians constantly complain that the Brazilians have encroached upon their land. The basis of this conflict lies in the agricultural techniques used by both Indians and Brazilians, namely, the *roça* system of cultivation. By this system virgin forest is cut and burned each year to provide new clearings for planting. A clearing is thought to be productive for only two or three years. The land covered with the secondary growth (*capoeira*) that soon springs up over abandoned sites, is considered inferior for agriculture. Since almost the entire area of the middle Pindaré is now secondary growth, both Indians and Brazilians are forced to plant what they consider "used land."

Even on the upper Pindaré, where there are no permanent Brazilian settlers, suitable areas for *roça* agriculture are rare. Except in the uppermost reaches of the river, where there are a few hills, the region is low and badly drained. During the rainy season, from January through April, rivers and streams overflow their banks each year, flooding extensive areas, and such land is not used for agriculture. Garden sites are restricted to high virgin forest.[2] After a few years of planting near a site, suitable sites for new gardens can be found only at a considerable distance, and in the neighborhood of such Tenetehara villages as Januaria, Ilhinha, Lagôa Comprida, and Contra Herva, which are near Brazilian settlements, there is competition for garden land. This conflict is absent only if the villagers have access to vast uninhabited areas in which it is possible to move about periodically in search of new forests for gardens. The agricultural system of the Pindaré region, as in much of the rest of Brazil, requires tremendous areas to support a small population. The resulting "land problem," which causes antago-

---

[2] In the Delta region of the lower Amazon, however, local Brazilians prefer to plant land which is flooded each year. This low land, which they call *vargem*, is used for quick-growing crops, such as corn, squash, and beans, which are planted and harvested during the dry season while the river is low. Manioc is planted only on high land, which is considered inferior.

nism between local Indians and Brazilians, must be understood in terms of their inefficient system of *roça* agriculture.

Both the Indians and the Brazilians of the region supplement agriculture by collecting such native products of the tropical forests as *babassú* palm nuts, copaíba oil, jatobá rosin, hard woods, and wild animal pelts. The region along the lower and middle stretches of the Pindaré is especially rich in *babassú* palms, from the nut of which is extracted a palm oil. From 1942 to 1945 this oil was considered an essential war material and the nuts were eagerly sought by buyers from coastal ports. Even in normal times many Indians and Brazilians collect and husk *babassú* nuts during part of each year, but in 1944 and 1945 the high price of *babassú* nuts led many to neglect or entirely abandon their gardens. As a result, in 1945 there was a critical shortage of food in the region, and basic foodstuffs imported from outside were sold at excessive prices. Manioc flour, the basic staple in the diet of both Indians and Brazilians, was imported from the city of São Luiz and sold in Colonia Pimentel and Pindaré-Mirim for approximately 10 cents or two *cruzeiros* [3] per kilo. In 1942 the price of manioc flour was from one to one and one-half cents per kilo. In contrast with enormously inflated prices for basic foodstuffs and other necessary articles, the highest price for *babassú* in 1945 was about ten cents per kilo as against six cents in 1942. Still the 1945 price enticed a large number of Indians and Brazilians to neglect subsistence entirely, which in turn forced them to buy foods at exorbitant prices.[4] The Pindaré region has been tied into the international commercial system, and both the Tenetehara and the simple rural Brazilians of the region felt the impact of the war crisis.[5]

[3] At this time the local unit of currency, the *cruzeiro*, was worth about five cents in U.S. money.

[4] The price paid for *babassú* nuts varied between 1942 and 1945 from five to ten cents. When we left the Pindaré region at the end of May, 1945, the price was six cents. At this price, a man could earn about 30 cents per day, since the average man is able to break open a sufficient quantity of *babassú* fruit to yield five kilos of nuts. At the time, the Brazilians were paying only 25 cents per day for work in the field, and in general a whole family could work at collecting and breaking *babassú*. When a man, his wife, and their children all worked, they sometimes earned from one to two dollars per day.

[5] Even the Indians of the more isolated villages were affected, although they did not suffer for lack of food as did both the Indians and the Brazilians down river. Since *babassú* is not so abundant on the upper Pindaré, it did not take so many people away from agricultural production. There was a relative abundance of food

AGRICULTURE

The Tenetehara plant a large variety of crops in their gardens.
They raise maize, beans, squash, peppers, yams (Dioscorea sp.),
watermelon, tobacco, peanuts, cotton, and manioc, which are aboriginal plants, and from the Brazilians they have borrowed rice,
okra, cucumbers, onions, sugar cane, bananas, papaya, castor beans,
and hashish. Their "staff of life" and staple crop, however, is
manioc, or cassava as it is sometimes called. In one form or another
manioc forms the basis of every Tenetehara meal. It is reflected in
the native mythology. One story relates how in legendary times
the Tenetehara lived on wild fruit called *kamamô* (*Solanacea*),
which the women collected in the forest. Then a great culture hero,
Maíra, brought them manioc, which miraculously planted itself,
matured in one day, and was harvested without any labor. This was
a golden age of leisure and plenty. But Maíra's wife finally grew old
and sick and he took a new young wife. When he told her to fetch in
the manioc which he had ordered to plant itself just the day before,
she doubted her husband's word, and refused. Maíra was infuriated
and said, "Now you (people) henceforth will wait through the entire winter (rainy season) for manioc to grow." From that day to
this, manioc has grown slowly, and mankind has had to plant, harvest, and make it into flour for food. Despite these mundane difficulties, however, manioc still provides the Tenetehara with an almost certain food supply. It is an amazingly hearty plant. It seldom, if ever, fails. Whether rainfall is scant or excessive, it grows
well in almost any soil—clay, sandy or loom—and it resists the
numerous insect enemies which beset plants in the tropics. Once
planted, manioc requires little or no attention until time to dig up
the giant tubers at harvest. The Tenetehara plant both the poisonous (*Manihot utilissima*) and the sweet variety of manioc (*Manihot
palmats aypi*); the latter may be eaten in the form of a soup or
baked or boiled like a yam.

---

in the up-river villages in 1945; the people sold food down river, yet they toc had to
pay prices which were double and triple those current in 1942 for new tools and other
necessities.

GARDEN MAKING

Most Tenetehara believe that the steel instruments which they use nowadays for gardening came to them, along with their aboriginal agricultural plants, as gifts from their legendary culture heroes. In a myth which explains the origin of agriculture, steel tools are presumably already a part of the culture; in one version of the story, axes and bush knives do the work themselves for mankind, and in another version men sharpened their steel axes and cleared the forest so that the manioc shoots could plant themselves with ease. One informant, Manuel Viana, remembered that his grandfather had described how the Tenetehara cleared the forest in the old days. His grandfather told him that in those days gardens were very small and that all men had to work many days to prepare a small site for planting. A large extended family had only one small garden as a result of their cooperative efforts. Low underbrush was pulled up by hand. Small trees were doubled over the blade of a stone ax which was held upright with the feet. The trunk was beaten against the blade with a hardwood club. Large trees were brought down by a fire kindled at the base of the trunk. Manuel himself hardly believed that the Tenetehara had ever been forced to such primitive practices, and reflected that the "Tenetehara were very stupid" in those days.

Nowadays steel axes and large bush knives, which are purchased from local Brazilian traders or received as gifts from the Indian Service, are used to clear garden plots. At the height of the dry season, in late July or August, the work of clearing begins. The first job (called *roçagem* in Portuguese) is to cut away the underbrush and low vegetation with a bush knife. Next, the large trees are felled with the ax (this task is called *derrubada* in Portuguese), and the vegetation is left to dry at least two or three weeks before it is burned.

The ideal time for burning the dry brush and felled trees is mid-September. The longer the brush is allowed to dry, however, the better it will burn and the cleaner the garden site will be. Therefore the Tenetehara frequently gamble. They delay burning until the last possible day before the first rains wet down the forest. Often they lose. The rains catch them by surprise, and they are forced to try to burn the partially wet brush. In such cases, it is often necessary to pile up and set fire to the half-burned logs and brush several times before the site is clean enough for planting.[6] In 1942, and again in 1945, the first rains came unexpectedly and many Indians were able to make use of only part of their garden sites. They piled up the semi-burned brush, hoping to be able to burn it again if there were a few days of sun to dry it out. In three villages (Camirang, Lagôa Comprida, and Januaria) they were still cleaning up and reburning logs and brush in order to give more area for planting manioc as late as February of 1942, when maize was almost ready for harvest. In fact, Tenetehara gardens are never really clean. They are always crisscrossed and tangled with trunks of great trees, branches, and stumps which never burn completely and which rob them of much valuable space for planting. It is not easy to walk through a Tenetehara garden, so great is the disorder and litter of unburned brush blocking the way.[7]

There is no systematic daily routine. The Tenetehara work in their gardens for the most part irregular, whenever the spirit moves them. Sometimes they will put in several full days in succession; at other times only a few hours a day. The work of clearing a site of approximately 3,000 square meters, which should not take more than four full work days- -two days to clear away the underbrush and two days to cut down the larger trees—often extends over a month or more. It is therefore very difficult for them to estimate the number of days necessary to clear a garden site. The estimates given us on the work days involved in clearing specific sites, which we measured, varied greatly because of this, as well as because of the differences in terrain. One man told us that he had taken only two days working alone to clear away the underbrush and another two days to fell the larger trees on a site which measured less than 5,000 square meters. Another estimated that it had taken six men two days to cut away the low vegetation and five days to bring down the trees and *palmeiras* on their garden site, which was only about 7,500 square meters. Still another remembered that a group of four men

[6] The first burning is called *queimada* and the reburning *coivara* in Portuguese. These Portuguese terms are given here because they are used throughout rural Brazil for these same gardening tasks.

[7] The same is true of the gardens of the local Brazilians who share these same processes of agriculture with the Indians.

spent three full work days to clear away the underbrush and three days to cut down the larger trees on a site of approximately 8,750 square meters. Other estimates varied between these extremes.[8] The Tenetehara have no compulsion to complete any specific amount of work in one day. They never pay others to work for them in units of money or kind, and thus they seldom calculate work in terms of time. A lazy man is one who does not have food and necessities for himself and family, and not the man who does not work steadily day by day.

The agricultural cycle of the year is determined by the two seasons. Clearing is a dry season or "summer" task, and planting begins soon after the first light rains of November. The best time for planting is in December or even as late as early January, after the "winter" rains have softened the earth. Maize, watermelons, squash, and castor beans are planted as early as mid-November, and bananas, beans, yams, and peanuts soon afterwards. Rice is planted in late January or February. Manioc may be planted at any time during the "winter" months. Since the Tenetehara do not store large quantities of manioc flour, they plant at intervals throughout the rainy season, so that not all of the crops will mature at once. Since the tubers do not rot in the ground after they are mature, manioc may be, in a sense, stored in the ground and harvested as it is needed.

Most of any Tenetehara garden is planted in manioc. Even the space given to short-term crops, such as maize, squash, and beans, is replanted in manioc as soon as these have been harvested. It is replanted for two or three years in the same garden. Cultivation is started with shoots or cuts, taken from the lower main branches of the bush. Two or three cuts, twenty to thirty centimeters in length, are stuck into the earth at about a 45-degree angle and loose earth is heaped around them in a small mound. The cuts take root without any special care.

Rice is frequently planted in the same field with manioc. In February, manioc bushes which were set out in December are trimmed to the level of the ground in order to assure better de-

8 That is, the estimates varied between 600 and 2,500 sq. m., as the area from which one man might clear underbrush in one day, and between 250 and 2,000 sq. m. as the area from which one man might cut away the large trees.

velopment of the tuber roots, and dry rice is planted in the open space. The rapid growth of the rice (three months) allows it to be harvested before the manioc bushes have grown again sufficiently to cover the rice. Rice cultivation is nowadays quite common in the villages along the Pindaré River and its tributaries, not as a food crop, since the Tenetehara seldom eat rice, but as a product to be sold to local Brazilians.

Maize is planted in a shallow hole made in the earth with a pointed hoe, and four or five grains are covered with earth. The Tenetehara have planted less maize in recent years than they did formerly and in some gardens it was not planted at all. Formerly, we were told, maize was almost as important as manioc as a garden product. It is the only crop for which supernatural sanctions are necessary; throughout the whole period of its growth the Maize Festival was observed. This is now seldom celebrated. The modern Tenetehara do not have time for the long ceremonial, without which large-scale planting is a risky undertaking.

Harvesting takes place whenever the various plants mature, except for manioc, which is harvested throughout the year. Tenetehara diet depends upon the garden produce of the moment, for except for maize, manioc, and rice, garden products spoil within a few days after they ripen, and the Tenetehara have no way of conserving such foods. Thus, in January they eat watermelon and squash in great quantities. In February of 1945 there was a great shortage of manioc flour and many families were living almost entirely on a diet of baked squash. Since Tenetehara maize has a three to four months' period of growth, in March and April there is generally new maize to be eaten, boiled or roasted on the cob, or ground into a soft meal called *pamonha*.[9] By May such plants as rice, peanuts, beans, yams, *maxixe,* and cucumbers are ready for harvest, so that May and June is usually the epoch of plenty for the Tenetehara.

Manioc has a period of growth of nine to ten months and the mature tubers may be left in the ground for as long as three or four

[9] Maize which is not eaten at once is left to dry in the sun on the stalk. The stalks are bent double, leaving the ears of maize hanging upside down; in this position the husk protects the grains from the rain. The dry ears are broken from the stalks during the next few months and carried home as they are needed for food. The largest and most uniform ears are saved for seed.

years before rotting. Formerly, it was a man's work to dig up the tubers and woman's work to carry them in a basket to a stream or to the village. Nowadays, both a man and his wife may be seen carrying heavily loaded baskets of manioc roots from the garden to the stream or pool where they must be soaked before they can be worked into the so-called *farinha d'agua* or "water" type of flour. A palm leaf barrier is constructed across a small stream to prevent the tubers from being carried away by the current, or, sometimes, a submerged canoe is used both as a barrier in the stream and as a receptacle in which to soak the manioc. The tubers must be soaked for a minimum of four to five days, and often they are left as many as seven or eight days until decomposition and fermentation begin. A strong, sour odor of decomposition from these cakes of manioc is characteristic of all Tenetehara villages and garden centers.

As soon as the tubers are *puba*,[10] that is to say, of a soft, pulpy consistency, they are taken from the water and carried to a trough made of a hollowed log, where they are peeled and mashed into a thick dough. Then the liquid, which contains poisonous prussic acid, must be squeezed from the pulp. Traditionally, the Tenetehara use for this purpose a tubular basket called the *tipiti*, which throughout rural Brazil is associated with the manioc complex. The pulp is stuffed into this long, flexible tube and as the *tipiti* is stretched, the liquid is squeezed out. Usually one end of the *tipiti* is attached to a house beam and a person places all his weight on the other end to stretch the basket. Nowadays, the Tenetehara also often use several types of presses which they have borrowed from the neighboring Brazilians. The most common of these is a series of levers which crush the pulp, held in a palm leaf basket, between two platforms.

After the liquid has been removed, the pulp is passed through a sieve to take out the lumps and the large stringy fibers. Then, after it has been allowed to dry, it is broken into particles and toasted over a large copper griddle (one and one-half to two meters in diameter). Formerly, the Tenetehara constructed these oven-grills of clay and rocks and covered them with a large ceramic plate. We were told that the Tupí-Guaraní Urubú tribe, neighbors of the

[10] This process of allowing the manioc to decompose in the water is called, in local Portuguese, *pubar*.

Tenetehara, still use similar ceramic griddles. A hot fire is made in the fireplace under the griddle, and the pulverized dough is toasted slowly. As it toasts, it is stirred constantly with a long wooden rake-like instrument, so that it will not form into large grains and balls. When the flour turns from white to a light brown or yellow color, it is ready to take off the griddle.

A second type of manioc flour, known as *farinha sêca,* or dry flour, is made by a different process. This dry flour, which is more common in south Brazil than in the north, is used now and again by both Indians and Brazilians of the Pindaré region. Instead of being soaked in water, the manioc tubers are peeled dry and then grated. Sheets of zinc or tin are used nowadays for graters, but in the past a grater was made of a block of wood into which bone or hard wood pegs were inserted. After the manioc is grated, the liquid is crushed out with the hands, and the dough is placed on a banana leaf and left in the sun to dry thoroughly before it is toasted over the griddle. Sometimes the Tenetehara and the rural Brazilians of the region mix dough made by soaking tubers in water with the dough of grated manioc to make a flour which is thought to be definitely superior to the flour made by either single process.

Manioc flour is stored in large plaited baskets made of *pindova* [11] and lined with banana leaves. These baskets, called *paneiros* by the local Brazilians, hold about thirty or forty kilos of flour. In its final form, ready for consumption, the flour represents only about 20 percent of the weight of the original harvest; thus, a day's harvest of, say, 150 kilos of manioc tubers would produce only about thirty kilos of flour (one *paneiro*).

The liquid squeezed from the grated manioc—not that which has been decomposed by soaking in water—produces *tapioca,* a by-product of manioc. This liquid is caught in a trough and allowed to stand one day, then poured out. A fine white powder is deposited in the bottom of the trough. The powder is mixed again with water and left to settle a second time and the water is poured off. Then the powder is allowed to dry; it is passed through a fine sieve and is slowly roasted over a hot griddle. *Tapioca* is rich in the natural sugar starch of the manioc; it is prepared and eaten as a small cake (*beijú*).

[11] New fronds of the *babassú* palm.

The Tenetehara also cultivate tobacco and hashish (*Cannabis indica*). Tobacco is a necessity for curing and for all other shaministic activities, and is smoked constantly by individuals of both sexes; it is therefore an important crop. In March, tobacco is planted in baskets filled with earth and placed on platforms above the ground, out of reach of domestic animals. Sprouts are transplanted in May, either in the gardens, or in small plots near the village. In one village, tobacco sprouts were transplanted in a plot situated in the central plaza. In harvesting, the larger nervures are extracted from the leaves and hung on strings to dry. As soon as they are dry, the leaves are stacked one on top of the other and rolled into tubelike bundles, wrapped with leaves of the *sororoca* plant (*Ravenala guianensis Beuth*) and tied with a vine. Tobacco is cut from the roll and shredded as needed. Men and women make cigarettes by wrapping tobacco in the *tawari* bark (*Couratari tauary Berg*) and women often smoke small clay pipes. Shamans generally prefer to use whole dry leaves of the tobacco for their large cigars (sometimes forty to fifty centimeters long), instead of the roll tobacco. In past times, the cultivation was entirely native and tobacco was traded between villages. On the upper Pindaré, it is still grown in quantity for local use and is still exchanged between villages, but the Tenetehara who live near Brazilian settlements prefer nowadays to buy it from local traders.

The African Negroes, who were brought to Brazil by the first European colonizers as plantation laborers, were undoubtedly responsible for introducing hashish into this region.[12] It is in wide use by both the Tenetehara and the Brazilians of this region. Cultivation follows closely the same procedures as those described for tobacco. Hashish is sown in baskets in fertilized earth and then transplanted to gardens near the village. The flower and the leaf are dried in the sun to be smoked in cigarettes similar to those made of tobacco. Since hashish is said to be "strong," four or five men smoke the same cigarette. Brazilians smoke the leaves in cigarettes or in water pipes made of gourds. Although the Indians speak of cases of hallucination caused by hashish, the Tenetehara generally use hashish moderately. As a stimulant, its effects are very much

[12] It is known locally as *diamba* and in southern Brazil by the name of *herva do sono* (sleep herb) and *maconha*.

appreciated; "hashish makes one feel like working," they explain.
The Indians smoke hashish frequently before working on their
gardens and during hard trips on the river. In shamanistic activities its use to induce trance is frowned upon. There were ugly
rumors in Januaria village that the young *pazé* called Vaqueiro had
to smoke hashish to get his spectacular trances. Tobacco is the only
traditional stimulant for shamans.

The rural Brazilian of this region most commonly measures the
area of his plantations in terms of "lines" (in Portuguese, *linhas*), [13]
which are, on the average, units of 2,500 square meters; the Indians
have adopted this unit in calculating the size of their gardens. Most
Tenetehara men, and any local Brazilian, can estimate the size of a
garden plot with rather amazing exactness. On several occasions
we checked their estimates by actual measurements and found
them some 10 to 20 percent low, corresponding more closely to the
area planted than to the area cleared. For example, José Machado
and Manuel Luis—both Indians—estimated their gardens to be
four "lines" (10,000 square meters), but by actual measurement
they were found to be 12,300 and 11,400 square meters, respectively.
The local Brazilians, with a general idea of the yields to expect
per "line," [14] plan the size of their gardens in terms of their own
necessities and of their specific plans to sell on the local market. The
Indians, on the other hand, have no such definite ideas as to yield;
and when we attempted to find out just how large a garden an in-

[13] A "line" is defined locally as "twenty-five *braças*" on each side. A *braça* is the
distance from the ground to the finger tips of a man holding his arms vertically above
his head (approximately two meters). This measurement is marked on a pole used to
measure the sides of the gardens. There is also a larger unit of area, the "square"
(*quadra*), which is 16 "lines," but most gardens are too small to be measured by this
unit.

[14] Local Brazilians gave us the following rough estimate of the yield of a "line" of
land planted in manioc, maize, and rice:

PLANT	AMOUNT OF SEED	YIELD
Maize	2.5 kgm.	250 kgm.
Manioc	2 bundles	150 kgm.
Rice	5 kgm.	750 kgm.

They also estimate that one "line" of relatively good land when planted in one
crop should produce 30 *alqueires* (900 kilograms) of rice; or 240 kilograms (6 *alqueires*
of 40 kilograms each) of maize; or 1,000 kilograms of manioc flour; or 1,000–1,200
kilograms of sugar; or 10 *arrobas* (10 kilograms per *arroba* or 100 kilograms) of tobacco;
or 10 *arrobas* (100 kilograms) of cotton.

dividual must plant to support a simple family (man, wife, and two or three children), we were assured that he should plant "at lease one and a half lines" (approximately 4,250 square meters). This assumption seems to be based on experience rather than on any sort of planning.

From our own calculations, however, it seems apparent that if a man made a new garden of this size each year and also replanted his old site, he would at least be assured of sufficient food for his family and might have some surplus to sell or exchange for necessities. A "line" of moderately good land planted entirely in manioc should produce about twenty-five *alqueires* or 1,000 kilograms of manioc flour, according to the estimates of local Brazilians. A Tenetehara family, of a man, his wife, and two children, consume on the average about 40 to 50 kilograms each month, or 480 to 600 kilograms per year. Since manioc is planted for the most part on old garden sites, and on new sites only after quick maturing crops have been harvested, there would be, at least theoretically, considerable space in the new garden site for other crops such as bananas, rice, beans, maize, to supplement the diet and to sell.

The individual gardens which we measured in 1942 in Lagôa Comprida, a village near the Brazilian towns, varied from two "lines" (5,000 square meters) to slightly more than ten "lines" (25,730 square meters).[15] All of these gardens supplied more than enough manioc for use of the owners, who sold or exchanged some flour, rice, beans, tobacco, or sugar cane for manufactured products. One of these men of Lagôa Comprida, who planted a garden of approximately two "lines" in 1941, not only provided his family

[15] The following measurements of new gardens were made in 1942 in Lagôa Comprida. Without exception these were cleared from secondary growth.

OWNER	SQUARE METERS	LINES
Vicente	19,500	8
Pedrinho	25,730	10
Nicolau	5,000	2
Leandro	5,000	2
Antonio	12,800	5
Picó	6,000	2½
Antoninho	13,600	5½
João	6,200	2½
Manuel Raimundo	5,000	2
Antonio José	10,000	4
Manuel	6,300	2½
Sabino	15,000	6

with sufficient manioc flour, sweet manioc, some maize, squash, beans, and yams, but had been able to sell eighteen *alqueires* (540 kilograms) of rice and ten rolls of tobacco. For the rice he told us that he received enough cloth to make pants and a shirt for himself and a skirt for his wife, and for the tobacco, only a comb. He was obviously cheated by a Brazilian trader, but his garden was small and his surplus products were few, so he was forced to work at collecting *babassú* nuts to purchase the other trade articles which he and his family needed during the year. In contrast, another man, Sabino, who had planted one of the largest gardens in Lagôa Comprida in 1942 (six "lines," or 15,000 square meters) sold considerable produce in Colonia Pimentel and Pindaré-Mirim. He had planted sweet and poisonous manioc, beans, watermelon, sweet potatoes, squash, and two hundred banana plants for his own use, and almost four "lines" of land were planted in rice, which would be sold. Sabino also had considerable manioc in his old garden, which he planted the year before, and from time to time he sold manioc flour, which he and his wife prepared.

The twelve gardens measured in 1945 near the village of Januaria were much smaller than those described above and, according to our informants, smaller than those the same people cleared in that year to be harvested in 1946. They varied from less than one "line" up to something more than five "lines" (2,500 to 11,400 square meters).[16] The larger gardens of this group belonged to large families in which there were adult sons-in-law, or adult unmarried males. The largest garden belonging to a simple family (man, wife and small children) was less than one and one-half "lines" (3,654 square meters). These gardens were scarcely big enough to supply the minimum food requirements for the families concerned, and certainly not large enough to supply surplus

[16] Individual gardens measured in 1945 at Januaria village:

Owner	Square Meters	Owner	Square Meters
Zézinho	1,500	Vicente	5,000
Avelino	3,022	Manuel Viana	5,850
Marinheiro	2,176	Teodomiro	9,600
João Bochecha	3,255	Inácio	10,000
Vaqueiro	3,654	Antonio	10,800
José Lins	2,500	Manuel Lins	11,400

The six largest were gardens belonging to large families with more than one adult male, yet they were not the large communal gardens of extended family groups.

products for sale to traders. The size of these gardens in 1945 was indicative of the general neglect of agriculture by the Indians in favor of collecting *babassú* nuts.

There was a general shortage of foodstuffs in the Pindaré region in 1945. Both the Tenetehara and the Brazilians depended upon imported foods, and in many instances people were actually hungry. The Tenetehara system of distribution of garden products is normally based upon an abundance of basic foods. In 1942 it was common for people to have rather free access to the gardens of their relatives of the same extended family. Pedro, at Lagôa Comprida, had lived for more than a year on produce from his father-in-law's gardens, until he could clear and plant his own; both Nicolau and Leandro of the same village, who had planted only two "lines" in 1942, told us that they frequently asked a relative, who had a larger garden, for permission to dig manioc when they were short. In 1942 we did not hear anyone express a fear of going hungry for lack of, at least, manioc flour, nor was there any suspicion of theft; but in 1945 when food was scarce several people were accused of stealing from gardens, and the shortage of food was a general topic of conversation.[17] In normal times, in an extended family property rights in gardens are not jealously guarded, and relatives frequently help themselves, even when the gardens are considered as individual property.

Frequently, in fact, they have helped to clear and plant the garden. Young men traditionally work with fathers-in-law in their gardens for a few years after marriage. Later, even when they have their own gardens, young men sometimes continue to help their fathers-in-law with their larger gardens. Various combinations of relatives cooperate in helping each other. For example, José Antonio, the owner of a large garden in Lagôa Comprida, in 1942 was aided by his three brothers-in-law—his wife's sisters' husbands—and he, in turn, worked with them in their gardens. Since his was the largest garden, these brothers-in-law had access to José Antonio's manioc plantations for food. To give other examples,

---

[17] In 1945 Manuel Viana accused Miguelzinho, a young married man who did not have a garden and who lived entirely from collecting babassú nuts and from his brother-in-law's garden, of stealing manioc, maize and squash from his garden. Manuel never accused the young man face to face, but only threatened vaguely that he would shoot the thief if he caught him. Everyone in the village seemed to accept the fact that it was Miguelzinho who was stealing, but nothing was done about it.

Nicolau exchanged work with each of his five brothers, and
Leandro worked with his brother, Benedito, who had a much
larger garden; in return Benedito gave him gifts of food and allowed him to harvest manioc freely from the gardens. People never
expected an exact exchange for work in each other's fields; instead
there is a rather free and easy use of each other's gardens for basic
food supplies.[18]

Besides these individual gardens, many large extended family
groups, such as those of Manuelzinho in the village of the same
name, of Camirang and of Raimundo in the village of Camirang,
and of Antoninho on the upper Pindaré, cultivate large plots
cooperatively. These gardens are spoken of as the property of the
family leader (as, "the garden of Camirang"), but they are actually
group property. Many of the men of such an extended family have
individual gardens of their own and, at the same time, share in the
cooperative garden. The family leader lives on the produce from
the communal garden, selling the surplus to purchase manufactured articles which, theoretically, are to be distributed among
the entire group. Members of the group often harvest maize and
manioc out of the communal gardens for their own use, but they
always ask permission first from the family leader.

The size of such cooperative plantations depends upon the family
leader, and on the unity as well as the size of the extended family
group. The extended family of Picó, at the village of Lagôa Comprida, did not have communal gardens in 1942. Picó was old and had
been recognized as a man of considerable prestige. Thus, the
younger men of his family group helped him clear and plant a small
garden (two and one-half "lines," or approximately 5,000 square
meters) for his own use, but it was not in any way considered a communal garden. The largest communal plantations in 1942 and in
1945 were those belonging to Camirang, who was the outstanding
family leader of the upper Pindaré. In 1945, his gardens totaled
more than 70,000 square meters in area, approximately half of
which were new gardens and half second-year sites replanted in
manioc. Besides these large cooperative plantations, many of Cami-

18 This free access and use of another's garden seems to be limited to foodstuff for
one's own use. We never heard of anyone giving another access to manioc flour which
had already been prepared or of rice which is generally produced for sale and not for
consumption.

rang's men cleared and planted individual plots. The extended family of Raimundo this same year had planted 27,900 square meters, and Manuelzinho's group, which had moved from the upper Pindaré to the vicinity of Januaria, had almost 26,000 square meters of cooperative gardens. These relatively extensive plantations not only guarantee a basic food supply to the extended family group, but also provide surplus crops whose sale the family leader negotiates with the Brazilian traders in Colonia Pimentel and Pindaré-Mirim on the middle Pindaré. The large extended family group offers an individual the maximum in economic security and the members of such groups are bound together not only by kinship but by strong economic ties. With the tendency toward the breakdown of the extended family into smaller units, the individual loses economic security.

DIVISION OF LABOR

Formerly, the Tenetehara followed rather rigid rules governing sexual division of labor. The men did the heavy work of clearing the garden site and planting and harvesting the manioc. Women planted and harvested all other plants—maize, cotton, yams, sweet potatoes, peanuts, bananas, watermelon, and the rest—and carried all these products, even the heavy manioc tubers, from the garden to the village on their shoulders in the carrying basket. A man seen doing such women's work would have been ashamed. The preparation of manioc flour was, some years ago, entirely a feminine activity. Besides the domestic activities of cooking, carrying water for the household, and clearing the house, the women made pottery and the cotton-string hammocks for the family. Men hunted and fished; they plaited baskets, made bows and arrows and traps for hunting, shaped utensils and benches out of wood, manufactured canoes, and built the family houses. The woman, however, was the provider of the basic foods and was responsible for the necessary activities of everyday life.

At present, in most Tenetehara villages, this sexual division of labor has become less rigid. In only a few villages on the upper Pindaré do women still manufacture manioc flour. In the other villages, both men and women carry the heavy tubers from the garden to the stream, and men, more frequently than women,

nowadays assume the responsibility for preparing manioc flour. Men
for the most part do the work of planting and harvesting all garden
crops and can even be seen carrying water from the river or spring
to the house, a task which in former times would have made them
the laughing stock of the village. Most men are fully aware that
these are traditionally female activities, but they are little concerned about the problem. They justify the change in attitude by
saying, "We are stronger than women," and thus, "We can make
more flour than a woman can." And it is a fact that, while formerly
manioc flour was manufactured only for the consumption of the
family group, nowadays it is often produced on a larger scale for
commercial sale. Finally, all Tenetehara men have seen Brazilian
men of the region work at these same activities and they have
imitated the "superior" Brazilians. Perhaps, because it coincides
with the local Brazilian sexual division of labor, there has been no
change in regard to manual techniques, such as the making of hammocks by women, and canoes, bows and arrows, traps, and baskets
by men who also build the dwelling houses. Today both men and
women collect *babassú* nuts and break open the shells, but the men
do the heavy work of carrying them from the forest to the village
and transporting them to the Brazilian centers to be sold. Due to
the necessity of trade for manufactured articles [19] and the breakdown of the old rules of sexual division of labor, the man has taken
on greater importance in Tenetehara economic life.

There is no leisure class among the Tenetehara. Even the shamans, although they are given presents for their cures, have gardens
to provide their basic subsistence, just as all other men do. A
village captain and family leader, such as Camirang, works with
his men in their cooperative gardens. A young girl begins at a very
early age to participate in household duties and, since very frequently her betrothed comes to live with her family, she may at
eleven or twelve years of age have the duties of an adult woman (see
p. 78). In contrast, young men, at least until they have passed
through the puberty rites and often until they are married, are not
expected to work with any regularity. In fact, it is not considered ad-
visable to try to teach young men manual techniques, such as bas-
ketry and manufacture of arrows, until they have gone through the
puberty rites. Only when a young man is ready for marriage is he

[19] Ceramics are no longer made but metal pots are purchased from Brazilian traders.

forced to prove that he is at least potentially a good worker, so that an older man will select him as a son-in-law.

All adults must work. Lazy women are held in disapproval by other women of their family group and they soon lose their husbands. Men who do not have gardens are considered lazy even though they may work hard at collecting and breaking *babassú* nuts, for the money or credit earned thereby is often not enough to purchase sufficient food (principally manioc flour) for the family. Miguelzinho, for example, was not taken seriously at all by the other men of Januaria village. They said that he was very lazy. Although he was married, he had no garden of his own nor did he make one with his father-in-law. He worked and supported his family only by selling *babassú* nuts and for this the men laughed at him. "Miguelzinho's garden is all *babassú* palms," they said, making fun of him. A lazy man is not generally welcome as a member of a large extended family, and thus he does not have the security of group cooperative activity. Vaqueiro, for instance, was considered lazy when we first knew him in 1942. His father-in-law tried several times to break up the marriage and thus rid the family group of a nonproductive member. In 1945, however, Vaqueiro had his own gardens and was a shaman of some renown. He now brought prestige to his wife's family and was a productive member of the group. Their attitude toward him had changed accordingly.

Unless an aged man has built up around him a strong extended family which he is able to direct with some astuteness so that he makes his living without great effort on his part, he must work as hard as any young man to earn his living. The Tenetehara make no provision for old people as such. We did not see any very old people among them during either of our visits; the oldest were Picó and his wife in Lagôa Comprida, Pedro in the village of Camirang, and José Viana at Januaria. They were only in their late fifties and all of them worked in the fields and at collecting and husking *babassú* nuts, but since they were family leaders they profited from their family gardens and from the cooperative exchange labor of their group. When we asked Manuel Viana what a person would do if he were too old to work at all, he answered, "The only way would be to steal or die of hunger." He did not seem to have any idea that younger relatives might take the responsibility for the support of the old. Yet Miguel, the half-witted youth at

Lagôa Comprida, was protected by his mother. People told us that Miguel was not able to plant his own garden, but "he is strong" and "works hard" at bringing in firewood, carrying water for household use and transporting heavy carrying baskets from the garden to the house. When we asked what would happen to Miguel if his mother died, they told us they "supposed that someone would give him food." Even his mother did not think it necessary to clothe him, and he wore only a breechcloth.

PROPERTY

The territory around a village is thought to belong to that village. Manuel Viana told us that people from one village did not move to the neighborhood of another without first asking permission of the chief. João Bochecha told us that the land belonging to Januaria village extended west of the Pindaré River from a near-by stream "until the sun set." He added, however, that the villagers never went further than "one day's trip" (afoot) back from the Pindaré River on hunting expeditions and thus did not know the country beyond. In such a sparsely populated region as the Pindaré drainage system, great areas are completely uninhabited and the concept of exactly what land belongs to each village is a vague one.

Garden lands, that is to say, lands on which people have expanded labor, are either individual or group property. During the time a man still has crops on the site, it belongs to him. But as soon as he has harvested all his crops and abandoned the land to the secondary growth which begins to cover it, it may be used by anyone. Yet old sites are often identified as "Miguel's old garden" or "Manuel's old garden" (*capoeira*) for many years after one has abandoned the plot. Although communal gardens, the result of cooperative efforts of an extended family, are spoken of as the individual property of the family leader, the entire group benefits from them to some degree. As we have noted, with the family leader's permission they may take foodstuffs from the gardens, and the leader sells the produce to secure trade goods for the group.

Hunting-blinds and barriers built across streams are the personal property of the man who builds them. They may not be used by anyone else without his permission until they have been completely abandoned. While houses are constructed by men and are referred to as "Miguel's house" or "Manuel's house," they are in reality considered to be the property of the wife. When more than one couple share a house, then it is the property of the wife of the oldest male in the household. Since most Tenetehara couples live in a house adjoining that of the wife's relatives, in case of divorce the wife remains in her house and the husband moves away.

Gardens belong to men, but garden products, after they have been brought into her house, belong to the wife. The same is true for game and fish brought by the husband to his wife. In the house, hammocks, cooking utensils, and all household equipment are the property of the woman. Clothes are the personal property of the individual who wears them. Men own knives, bows and arrows, guns, garden implements, and various odds and ends of personal use. Dogs are a man's property, since he hunts with them.

Some idea of the objects owned by an average Tenetehara man and his wife may be had from the lists which we noted down in 1942 in two Tenetehara houses. House I belonged to Miguel (see p. x), who owned about the average number of odds and ends, and House II to Manuel Viana (see p. xi), a man of more prestige, who had several young men working with him and who with his wife owned somewhat more property than the average Tenetehara.

HOUSE I

PROPERTY OF THE HUSBAND	PROPERTY OF THE WIFE
1 ax	5 hammocks
1 bush knife	2 new enameled plates
1 bow and 2 arrows	4 spoons
2 large hoes	4 gourd water containers
2 knives	10 decorated half-gourd bowls
1 pair of wooden-soled slippers	15 half-gourd containers
1 broken paddle	2 plaited sieves
2 fish poles and lines	15 kilograms of manioc flour
1 muzzle-loading rifle	10 empty bottles
1 shoulder-strap case	1 old bedspread
2 dogs	1 iron pot
3 pairs of pants	1 enameled pot
2 shirts	½ kilogram of coffee
1 pajama shirt	1 small knife
2 spoons of lead shot	1 small kerosene lamp
2 spoons of gun powder	1 comb
	1 mirror
	2 dresses
	2 fish caught that day

HOUSE II

PROPERTY OF THE HUSBAND	PROPERTY OF THE WIFE
1 large hoe	1 wooden bench
1 smooth stone used to sharpen knives	1 muzzle-loading rifle [b]
1 saw	2 large hoes
1 new ax and 2 old axes	1 large iron pot
1 steel file	3 palm sieves
2 bows and 2 arrows [a]	2 plaited palm-fiber containers
3 sickles	1 basket container
2 fishing poles	1 large iron stew pot
1 wooden packing case	3 medium enameled pots
1 copper griddle used to toast manioc flour	1 canvas deck chair
2 new bush knives	1 commercially manufactured clay pipe
1 straight razor	4 aluminum soup bowls
1 pair of shoes	2 cotton dresses
1 fishline and hooks	1 small kerosene lamp
1 palm-leaf container	2 pair of scissors
1 roll of cord made of vines	1 clay pot of local Brazilian manufacture
1 harmonica	15 half-gourds used as eating utensils
1 mirror	1 tin can used as drinking cup
1 gourd rattle	1 enameled plate
1 pair of blue linen pants and a shirt	1 enameled wash basin
2 old pairs of pants	2 baskets
1 old shirt	2 *tipitís* for squeezing manioc pulp
1 pair of wooden sandals	1 vessel for working manioc pulp
1 shoulder-strap case	3 hammocks
1 woolen Brazilian-style business suit	3 ripe squashes
1 document issued by the Indian Service appointing him "village chief"	15 kilograms of manioc flour
1 canoe paddle	1 grater for preparing manioc flour
1 pig	
1 small knife	

[a] Purchased from visiting Urubú Indians for one shirt.

[b] Inherited from her father. Manuel and his mother-in-law, who lives in adjacent house, are considered joint owners.

Besides these objects, Manuel's house contained a land tortoise, twelve chicks, one pig, two chickens, a young tapir, and a small dress

—all of which he described as the property of his small daughter, Auta. The household property possessed by other couples was more or less the same as that of Miguel and Manuel and their wives; a few owned more, a few less—but all owned the essential objects for preparing manioc flour, for hunting, for cooking and eating, and for gardening.

From the lists given above, it may be readily noted that most of these are manufactured articles which must be purchased. Only a few are made by the people themselves. Metal tools, and especially clothes, are the possessions which bring prestige. Almost all Tenetehara men try to own at least one cotton suit (coat and pants) besides their work clothes. They use this "Sunday suit" only on special occasions, when, for example, they attend a Brazilian-style dance (see p. 175), or make a trip to a near-by Brazilian settlement, or honor officials visiting their village. A poor man often owns only a shirt and pants, and, in order to save his good clothes for dress-up occasions, he may be forced to work in his garden clad only in a breechcloth, despite the great prudery of the Tenetehara on the subject of nudity. Most Tenetehara, however, make a point of owning dress-up clothes for themselves, and men are proud of the number of cotton dresses their wives possess. A great family leader, such as Camirang, for example, owns four suits of clothes and several suit coats and extra pants for everyday. Next to clothes, metal tools are the most prized possessions. Men need an ax, a bush knife, and a large hoe for work in their gardens, but beyond their actual needs, they like to store up unused tools. Miguel (House I) had the tools he needed, but Manuel Viana (House II), a wealthier man of greater prestige, owned a new ax and two new bush knives, which he was not using but was keeping for the future. Camirang kept in a trunk several new bush knives, new axes, several hoes, and many steel knives, and he showed us with pride several rolls of uncut cloth, enough for several shirts and pants, which were stored in a wooden box.

In the case of strong leaders of united extended families, there is a certain confusion between what is owned individually by the leader and what is group property. Since the leader often makes purchases for the whole group, he distributes the materials purchased—a piece of cloth, some salt, a bush knife, and an ax, for example, for each man. He often holds back materials to be distributed to the group later from time to time, and while they are in his hands, they are said to be his property. Generally he keeps a large share for himself. Camirang's bush knives, hoes, axes, and cloth were acquired in this manner. Now and again he gives such articles to people of his group who have worked for him. He also "owned" seven or eight rifles which had been purchased with the proceeds of the sale of products of his family group. Members of the group who wished to hunt would ask for the loan of a rifle and several loadings of lead shot and gunpowder. In return Camirang expected a share in the results of the hunt. Camirang also owned three copper-plate griddles used for toasting manioc flour. He used one himself and the others were used by his family group. He levied a high tax on his family for use of the griddles (as much as one half of the manioc flour), but most group leaders expect only a small return. Such property, although it is the result of group effort, is "owned" and controlled by the family leader. The family leader holds such property as leverage to maintain his position, and the display of surplus tools, clothes, and articles brings him prestige.

Since Tenetehara villages are relatively small and since people have relatively few belongings, almost everyone knows what the others own. Furthermore, almost everyone knows when anyone acquires a new belonging and where it came from. It is therefore very easy to identify stolen property, and theft is not only infrequent but disgraceful. Now and again, a man "who does not have gardens" and "who lives from *babassú*" will be seen with an object which is recognizably not his and he will be suspected of having stolen it. People are very careful to ask permission before using the personal property of others, and let it be known publicly that permission to do so has been obtained. The young orphan boys at the village at the Indian post sometimes steal, but then they are expected to be untrustworthy since they do not have relatives to help them. But theft is rare and the Tenetehara would never accuse a suspected thief face to face. "One is ashamed to speak about it to him," they say, and in several instances of theft of small objects, such as glass beads or a mirror, which occurred while we were in Tenetehara villages, the owners merely gossiped and never quarreled with the thief or sought to punish him. Our closest friends among the Tenetehara found it quite natural that we did not face down an Indian who had stolen a small amount of money from our house.

Personal property is theoretically supposed to pass to the widow or to a son on the death of the owner. Several people explained that the widow should retain her husband's property only until his children were old enough to take it over. What actually seems to take place, however, is that the leader of the extended family takes over the property, or at least in some way manages to keep it within the family group. João Bochecha explained that the five rifles owned by the family leader, Manuelzinho, came into his possession in this manner: he had taken them from the widows of his deceased brothers. João felt that there was some injustice in Manuelzinho's action, since one of the widows happened to be João's sister and the rifle might well have come to him instead. When the family leader, Apuá, died several years ago, his widow and his one-year-old son were left in a precarious position. His two rifles and all his garden implements were dispersed among several male relatives; his own brother and his wife's brother each took a rifle. The widow went to live with her brother, who, according to our informants, gave her food "only when he had more than he needed." The only dress she owned when we visited Januaria village was given her by a female relative, and the small objects, such as glass beads and combs, and some extra food she received from the young men of the village in return for her sexual favors. Finally she married one of the shamans of the village who was a widower.

In the litigation already mentioned (see p. 27) between two groups involving a widow and her property, the widow left her extended family in the village of Ilhinha because her relatives had not only seized all her dead husband's property, including the garden which he had planted that year, but had treated her badly as well. After she had to move to Januaria village, where she joined a "brother" and took another husband, the group from Ilhinha complained that she had been stolen. Her new husband made a countercharge, asking that he be allowed to harvest from "her" garden in Ilhinha, but he really had no thought of gaining this right.

The mother of our informant Vaqueiro was another widow who had not received anything from her husband. He had left a rifle and many other objects which her family soon took for themselves, and even her cooking utensils were borrowed and used by her own female relatives. Now and again, however, a widow does hold on to her husband's property. Manuel Viana's wife inherited a rifle from her father. Manuel uses the rifle "on loan," but she says that it will be the property of her daughter when she marries. It is interesting that a man's property among the Tenetehara is used by others after his death and practically nothing is buried with the body. This is contrary to the practice among other Tupí-Guaraní tribes, who bury or destroy the property of a man when he dies.

HUNTING AND FISHING

Domestic animals were introduced into the Tenetehara region by Brazilians, but there are relatively few of them even in the villages near the Brazilian settlements. Each village will have a few chickens and, sometimes, a few ducks, pigs, sheep or even goats, but these animals are not numerous and are treated more as pets than as a source of food supply. In the Pindaré River region, the Tenetehara still resort to hunting and fishing to supplement their diet. The region is rich in fauna, especially the little-inhabited upper Pindaré; and even in the middle Pindaré region, which is more densely inhabited, the Indians depend for meat primarily on hunting and fishing rather than on domestic animals. Such animals as the tapir (*Tapirus Americanus*), wild pork (*Tayassú albirostris*), peccary (*Tayassú tajassú*), deer, capivara (*Hydrocherus capivara*), paca (*Cuniculus paca Acs.*), various types of monkeys, armadillo, and such birds as *mutum* (*Crax*), *jacú* (*Penelope*), red macaws (*Ara chloroptera*), and blue macaws (*Ara arauna*) are common in the more isolated parts of the tropical forest. Deer, wild pork, and peccary are hunted not only for food but also for their hides, which can be sold to Brazilian traders. Birds, such as the red and blue macaw as well as the small parrot, are used as food but are hunted principally for their feathers, which are used to make decorations. Paca, peccary, wild pork, deer, and tapir are the animals whose meat is most appreciated, but they are hard to hunt in the dense forest and only rarely do the Tenetehara men bring them back from the hunt. Most often a man returns with land tortoises (*Testudo tabulata*), an agouti (*Dasyprocta aguti*), a *jacú,* or a monkey.

Most of the Tenetehara nowadays hunt with muzzle-loading rifles, which are manufactured in southern Brazil. Since they are flimsy affairs made from inferior metal, a hunter must be careful just how much gunpowder and shot he uses or he may burst the barrel. Before each shot, he must measure out gunpowder, shot, and wadding, and must replace the fuse under the trigger hammer. When the rifle is fired, the report can be heard miles away. These rifles sold for approximately nine or ten dollars in 1942, and in 1945 for twelve and a half to fifteen dollars. Any man who possibly can purchase one (with trade objects or on credit) owns a rifle. Most men also have bows and arrows, but only young men and those whose economic situation is so precarious that they cannot afford a rifle use the bow and arrow for hunting.

The rainy season, when animals are driven to high forest regions by the excessive flooding of the lowlands, is the best time for hunting. These so-called "islands" of highland are well known to the Tenetehara, who make for them by foot or by canoe, knowing that the chances of game are good. When a man sees tracks of a band of wild pork or peccary on such an "island," he frequently returns to his village, spreads the word and the villagers turn out *en masse*. Since the animals cannot escape from the island, mass hunts are frequently very successful, and as many as twenty to thirty wild pigs may be killed in one day. One leader of an extended family, José Verissimo of the village of Jacaré, is well known as an organizer of collective hunts to the "islands" during the rainy season. He hunts not only for meat, but for pelts, which he sells to the local traders.

Throughout the entire year, however, the Tenetehara hunt from time to time. They carry their rifles when they go to and from their gardens, leaving the path now and again to search for something to shoot at in the forest. Many men habitually spend at least one day each week in hunting. At the village of Januaria near the Indian Service post and at Lagôa Comprida Village, where the Tenetehara are in constant contact with Brazilians, the Indians customarily hunt on Saturday or Sunday in imitation of the local Brazilians, who look upon hunting as "resting."

The Tenetehara know the best places to hunt each type of animal' —on "islands" in the rainy season, near a water hole in the dry season, or under a tree the fruit of which attracts game. At these spots they often construct a blind, called by both the Tenetehara and the Brazilians a *tocaia*. Some blinds are small conical shelters made of palm leaves, others are platforms built in the trees and covered with palm leaves. The Indians often wait for as long as 24 hours in a blind for a shot at a paca or a band of wild pork. When a family moves to the "center" to make manioc flour, men take the opportunity to hunt, since the "centers" are generally located in a region of virgin forest some distance from the village.

In the vicinity of those villages which have occupied the same site for many years, game becomes scarce. In Lagôa Comprida, for example, which has been situated on the spot for twenty years, hunters killed only agoutis, tortoises, and occasionally a paca. At the village of Camirang, which has not moved for almost eight years, hunters had to go miles to hunt larger animals, such as deer and wild pork. In such cases, they make an excursion of several days' length. The animals they kill are roasted slowly over a low fire in order to preserve the meat for a few days. The scarcity of game as well as the necessity of high virgin forest for gardens is a motive in the moving of the village.

Hunting can be a dangerous occupation for a man. Many animals of the forest are thought to have "spirits" called *piwára* (see p. 104), and some spirits are very dangerous, especially to a man whose wife is pregnant or who is himself the father of a young infant. Many animals such as wild pigs are thought to be owned and protected by the supernatural Marana ýwa, the Owner of the Forest (see p. 102). Needless slaughter of his charges may anger this supernatural and he may punish the offender by sickness or even death. Sometimes a hunter who has angered a supernatural becomes *panema*— "unlucky" at hunting. José Verissimo, for example, told us that for many months he did not have any success at all in hunting or fishing. He explained, "I was *panema*," and he attributed this state to the fact that he had washed blood from his hands into a stream and had thus offended Ywan, the supernatural Owner of the Water (see p. 102). Very frequently, however, it is not the hunter who becomes "unlucky" but an object such as his pouch, his gun, his fish traps, or even his fishhooks. Our informants found it hard to explain why such objects are "unlucky," except that now and again they become so when a menstruating woman steps over them or even when they are used by a woman. The object is only "unlucky" for its owner and it may, therefore, be passed on to a companion who will try to see if it is "unlucky for him." If it is found to be "unlucky" for several men, the article must then be destroyed. Tenetehara hunters frequently carry the umbilical cord of a newborn child in their hunting pouch as a preventive against *panema*.

The Tenetehara seldom give as much time to fishing as they do to hunting, yet from time to time throughout the year those who live along the Pindaré River fish during leisure hours with hook and line. The dry season, when the river is low and the fish are driven to deep pools, is the most propitious time on the main river for this method of fishing. The Zutiua River and the smaller tributaries on which such villages as Lagôa Comprida and Jacaré are situated are dry during the late part of the summer months, and people in these "inland" villages are able to fish only during the rainy season. Soon after the rainy season begins, when the river and small streams begin to rise, fish seek the headwaters to lay their eggs, and the Indians living along small streams are able to kill many fish [20] with clubs, bow and arrows, and bush knives. During the early rainy season, Tenetehara often stretch a trotline, bearing fifteen or twenty hooks across a narrow part of the river to catch *surubim*. This is a comparatively large fish with few bones, and is considered a delicacy.

Three different types of fish traps, all called *pari*, are also used by the Tenetehara, mostly for fishing in small streams. One is a cone-shaped trap provided with a funnel entrance; a second is constructed of strips of the stalk of the *tucum* palm stuck upright in the stream in the form of a labyrinth into which the fish wanders and from which it is then unable to escape. The third, a cone-shaped trap made of *tucum* fibers, used more as a net than a trap is thrown over the fish that can be seen moving about in shallow water during the late dry season. The Tenetehara sometimes use *timbó* vine (*Paullina pinnata*) to poison fish in the pools left when the small streams dry up. Pieces of the vine are mashed

[20] Among others, the following fish are found in the Pindaré River and its tributaries and are often caught: *piranha* (Serrasal minae), *surubim* (Platystoma sp.), *curimatá* (Prochilodus sp.), *mandubé* (Hypophtalmos edendatus), *cascudo* (fam. Loricaridae), *pirapema* (Tarpon atlanticus), *sarapó* (fam. Gymnotidae), and *jejú* (fam. Characidae).

and soaked in the water and in a short time the stupified fish rise to the surface.

The Tenetehara collect various wild fruits from the forest for food. Such fruits generally ripen during the rainy season and provide a substitute for fresh garden products during the first days of the dry season in April and May. Among these fruits, *kamamô* (see p. 34) deserves special emphasis for its traditional role in Tenetehara culture. This is a seed which grows on a bush and is sometimes even planted near gardens and abandoned garden sites; it is well known where natural groves of it may be found. The Tenetehara find the *kamamô* seed extremely tasty. *Jussara (Euterpe)* or *assaí*, as it is also known, and *bacaba (Oenocarpus)* are picked mainly between January and March. Both of these are palm nuts and the Tenetehara drink the juice squeezed from the nut. During the early rainy season such fruits as *piquí (Caryocar)*, wild *cajéw (Anacardium)* and *cupú açú (Theobroma grandiflorum Spreng)* may be found in the forest. In general, however, people do not count on wild fruits for food, and collect them only now and again as occasion arises.

Babassú nuts and copaíba oil are collected, not as food, but as an object of trade with the Brazilians. The most important of the two, *babassú*, grows extensively in the middle Pindaré and is infrequently found on the upper reaches of the river. It grows natively in the low forests where the high trees have been cleared away. The leaves of the *babassú* palm are considered the best material for house building both by the Brazilians and the Indians, and the heart of the palm is used as food for pack animals. The main product of the palm, however, is the nut which produces an oil of considerable industrial importance. The fruit grows in large bunches high on the trunk. It falls to the ground as it ripens; men and women then gather it into piles near a small shelter erected to protect them from rain or sun while the husking is carried on. To remove the husk, the fruit is held against the blade of an ax and is struck with a hardwood club. It is first split in half and then into fourths, so as to release the four small nuts inside. In general, Indian and Brazilian women, more often than men, do the work of opening *babassú* fruit, but frequently an entire family—man, wife, and children—work at it together.[21]

The copaíba tree, of which there are several species,[22] is found along the upper Pindaré, the Maracassumé, and the Gurupí Rivers. Early writers mention it as the source of an oil used by the local Indians,[23] and according to S. Fróes Abreu the oil has been used as an article of trade since early in the nineteenth century.[24] It is gathered by tapping, much like rubber and turpentine. An incision is made in the trunk and a gourd is tied below it to catch the oil. A tree can be tapped only once, during the dry season, and the yield is about ten liters.

The people of Camirang's village are the most intensive collectors. The Indian Service helped them acquire several large iron drums in which the oil is stored and shipped down river. Each year a large number of men from Camirang's extended family and from the other families of his village go into the forest to collect the oil. They make a long expedition of it, spreading out through the forest to spot and tap the trees. While waiting in camp for the gourds to fill, they hunt for meat and animal pelts. Almost every year the drums of oil, the surplus manioc flour, and the animal pelts collected by the group are taken down river to be sold or traded for manufactured products. Frequently Camirang sells as much as $125 worth of oil in one transaction; in 1944 his total sale of oil, manioc flour, and pelts, through the Indian Service post amounted to more than $350.[25]

The traditional methods of agriculture are hardly adaptable to

21 Brazilians sometimes organize cooperative work parties, called locally *puxirões*, to open the *babassú*. Neighbors congregate at one house and crack open all the fruit gathered by that family and on following days go on to the houses of the rest of the group.

22 Fróes Abreu (p. 69) states that the principal producers of the oil are *Copaifera reticulata,* Ducke; *Copaifera multijuga,* Mayne, and *Copaifera Lagsdorffi*—all of them found in Maranhao.

23 Fernão Cardim, p. 61, and notes on p. 124.

24 *Ibid.,* p. 69: "At present Maranhão exports a relatively large amount of copaíba [oil]. The historians say that it was in 1806 that they began to export this product. In 1854, President Eduardo Olympio Machado informed us that the forest of the Upper Pindaré and of the Maracassumé and Gurupí contained an abundance of copaíba; in the last five years the production has grown and is now as much as 50 barrels. . . . The industry was a primitive one of the Indians; they exchanged the oil for metal tools and cloth with the traders who visited the more accessible villages."

25 In the registry of the Indian Service, Camirang sold approximately $117.50 worth of oil, flour and pelts in 1942; in 1943, approximately $51 worth, and about $360 worth

large-scale commercial production and the salable surplus is generally small, but from the sale of *babassú* nuts and copaíba oil, it
is possible to purchase iron tools, clothes, salt, gunpowder and shot,
fishhooks and lines, kerosene, and other items that the Tenetehara
consider necessary.

---

in 1944. These figures do not represent the sum total of his trade, however, since
Camirang, like the other Indians, trades in Colonia Pimentel and in Pindaré-Mirim,
and also with Brazilians who come to his village, without the knowledge of the Indian
Service.

IV · PERSONAL LIFE

THE ONSET of pregnancy marks the beginning of a rigid set of restrictions for both a Tenetehara woman and her husband which last until the infant which is born is able to walk. The development of the child during the prenatal period and early infancy is considered to be dependent upon the careful observance of these rules by both parents. The behavior of the father is as important as that of the mother in safeguarding the child—guarding the foetus against evil influences, insuring a smooth delivery, and making certain the normal early growth and development of the infant. This physical bond between father and child begins at conception; it is thought that conception does not result from a single sexual union but from continued sexual relations between a specific man and a woman. The Tenetehara believe that a woman becomes pregnant only when she has intercourse several times during a period of ten or fifteen days with the same man. It is hard for them, therefore, to credit pregnancy to the casual affairs of unsettled young women or of widows who are sexually free. A bond between the father and his child is recognized even in rare cases when the man leaves his wife when she is pregnant.[1] Even though he moves to a distant village, he must still respect the restrictions imposed during the prenatal period, during the birth, and during the early infancy of the child. A young woman who has had a series of husbands will be called on to name the procreator of the child; in general, she indicates her current husband as the "father," sometimes without much respect for the cold fact that they were not living

[1] In one case, for example, the man left the woman before she knew that she was pregnant. Her family sent word to him that she was expecting his child and warning him to observe the necessary taboos.

together as man and wife when conception took place, for pregnancy of the wife generally solidifies the marriage.

Tenetehara men told us that they were "sad" when their wives told them that their menses had stopped. They were "sad," it seems, mainly because of the long sexual continence imposed by the pregnancy and birth. Sexual contact should be suspended for a few days immediately after the wife announces her pregnancy and then may be resumed for a few months. As soon as the woman is visibly large, however, sexual relations between the man and wife should end entirely, to be resumed only when the child is "hard" (when it is six or seven months old and has some control over its muscles), or even when it begins to walk. Sexual intercourse during the last months of pregnancy is thought to cause physical abnormalities in the foetus and always to cause a difficult delivery. The same results would follow if the father had sexual contact with another woman.

According to the Tenetehara, if a mother and father begin sexual relations too soon after the birth of the child, the infant will be sickly and may die. One infant in the village of Januaria was notably thin and weak in spite of the great efforts of the parents to feed it. A shaman was called in several times, but everyone told us that nothing could be done and that the child would undoubtedly die because the parents had already begun sexual relations. Some Tenetehara reasoned that sexual contact should be avoided during this period because the woman should not be pregnant again while she is carrying a young baby. "She cannot carry her child on her stomach [astride her hip, to be more specific] while her stomach is big with another baby."

The most complex rules are those against killing and eating certain animals. Transgressions bring supernatural punishment upon the unborn child and even upon the parents themselves. A large series of animals and birds are said to be *tapiwára*, that is, carriers of spirits. If the father kills one of these animals or birds, or if either the mother or father eat of its meat, the spirit "will enter" the foetus, causing some undesirable feature or even physical abnormality in the child; it may even bring about a miscarriage. Such abnormal or ugly features are generally characteristic of the animal in question. Below are listed the animals in the prohibited group, together with the effect upon the child if the animal is killed or eaten by the parents.[2]

ANIMAL	EFFECT ON THE CHILD
Red macaw	Born halfwitted or with a beak instead of a nose
Blue macaw	Born halfwitted
Anteater: *Tamandúa bandeira* in Portuguese (*Myrmecophaga jubata*).	Born with a white mark on shoulders similar to the marking of the pelt
Anteater: *Tamanduá jaleco* in Portuguese (*M. tetradactyla*)	Born almost without a nose
Toucan: *Rhamphastos toco,* having an enormous beak	Born with large nose
jacú	Born with white hair; perhaps an albino
japú-urú (a small bird)	Born with an ugly finger
jacâmim: a large forest fowl (*Psophia obscura. Pelz.*)	Born halfwitted
mutûm: a forest fowl (*Crax alector*)	Born with a red beaklike nose
Boa constrictor	Born with a flat head
Black jaguar	Born halfwitted and "with the flat face and ugly features of a jaguar"
Brown jaguar	Born halfwitted or with a tail
Wild cat	Born with weak hands—"will not be able to hold anything in its hands"
Sloth	Born halfwitted and slow of movement
Otter: (*Lontra* in Portuguese; *Pteronura brazileinsis*)	Born with hands "backward"—palms outside
Hawk	Born with a hooked nose and claws

Our informants explained that, even otherwise apparently normal, infants born with such abnormalities, should be buried at birth for they are certain to lack normal mental capacities. Obviously, a few cases of infanticide do take place each year among the Tenetehara because of these beliefs, yet many such children are permitted to live, since they do no harm and trouble no one but the parents. Several cases of the kind were reported to us, and two youths were pointed out as examples. One of them, Miguel, was a halfwit.

---

[2] These same animals can be dangerous to a hunter even though he is not a "father" and some of them are forbidden to young people as food until after the puberty rites (see p. 79).

He was about eighteen years old and lived with his mother and her relatives in the village of Lagôa Comprida. Miguel wandered harmlessly about the village and vicinity carrying a staff, for which he had a terrific attachment. He would not sleep without his staff by his side and cried until it was returned to him. He was unable to talk intelligibly but he seemed to understand most of what was said to him. He did only light work and was treated with reasonable kindness. Everyone explained that Miguel was born "crazy" (*hehó*) because, during his mother's pregnancy, his father killed two jaguars (a spotted jaguar and a brown one). A spirit of one of these two animals followed the father home and entered into the foetus, causing Miguel's plight. His mother wished to bury the child, but his father insisted that the son looked normal, and they allowed it to live. The second young man, who lived in the village of Januaria, had an atrophied arm and leg. It was said that his father killed an otter while his mother was pregnant. People pointed out the resemblance of his atrophied arm to the finlike member of the otter.

The restrictions against killing or eating animals and birds which are *tapiwára* continue after the child is born and until it is strong, or until it begins to walk. At the village of Jacaré one man refused to shoot a red macaw while hunting with one of our party because, as he explained, he had a new baby at home (eight to ten months old). After the child is approximately a year old, however, the restrictions are relaxed and the parents return to their normal diets.

Women are said to want children and to be happy when they know they are pregnant. One woman in the village of Januaria left her husband because he did not give her children,[3] and such cases are evidently not infrequent. A story of an obviously frustrated woman who was living at the time in the village of Lagôa Comprida was told to us to show how desperately some women want children. She had been married to two different men and had not had children by either of them. Several times she pretended pregnancy and childbirth, going through all the motions for the benefit of the neighbors (and it seems for her husband, too) telling them that the child was born dead. We were told that she stuffed cloth under her

[3] It is interesting to note in this case, as in the others related to us, that the woman considers it the man's fault that their union is childless.

dress for several months and told people she was pregnant. One evening when her husband arrived from hunting she told him that she was in labor pains but refused to let him call other women to help her. She moaned most of the night. During the night she spread the blood of a land tortoise on the floor and buried the tortoise and the cloth in the corner of the house. The next morning she told her neighbors that the child was born dead. She rested in her hammock but when she left the house several days later to bathe, women neighbors dug up the tortoise and the cloth. People said that she was strange and a liar; they did not face her down on the matter. "She does this," said one man, "to fool the others, but they know that it is a lie."

Women know several ways to "secure the child" by preventing an early abortion or a miscarriage. One should drink a soup made of corn husks and water, of *koroeira* of manioc, or of the flower of the banana arm to insure that the pregnancy will hold.

In spite of a woman's desire for children, however, the Tenetehara know and sometimes use several methods of contraception and for inducing abortion. One woman told us that to prevent conception she and her married daughters used a tea made from the bark of the *zawa ýwa* tree each month at the time of menstruation or during the new moon. These women already had children and did not want more. Another woman explained that abortion could be brought about during the first months of pregnancy by rubbing over the stomach the grated cinchona bark (*kaá-yw* or *Ywiratazyw*) soaked in water. Another recommended the similar use of white onion soaked in *aguardente* or olive oil. Snethlage relates that in order to induce abortion Tenetehara women take baths in still water in which *tinguy* vine (*Tephrosia toxicaria,* which produces a poison used to stupify fish) has been soaked.[4] It is quite probable that the Tenetehara have learned some of these methods from the Brazilians of the region.

DELIVERY

A Tenetehara woman continues her normal household pursuits during the early months of pregnancy, but "when she gets big" she should confine herself to light household tasks and she should not

4 "Unter Nordostbrasilianschon Indianer," p. 130.

go far from her house. The husband should also take precautions during the last months of her pregnancy. He should not travel far and should avoid such heavy work as housebuilding or clearing forest for garden space. Heavy work, on the part of either the woman or her husband, was given as the reason for several stillbirths.

Snethlage states that birth takes place in the forest.[5] Although we did not witness a birth, our informants told us that it always takes place inside the house.[6] A woven palm mat is spread on the floor; the woman either squats over this mat or rests on a low wooden stool. She is supported under the arms from the back by one of her female relatives and is attended by her mother or an older sister. Her husband should not be present at the delivery but should remain near by in the village. The woman herself massages her abdomen in an effort to speed the delivery; sometimes she rubs chili pepper over her abdomen for added help.

In case of a difficult delivery, a shaman is called. A difficult birth is thought to be caused either by the spirit of an animal or by a shaman who may have worked sorcery against the couple. It is said that shamans, even from a distant village, are able to tie the foetus by the neck with a vine inside the mother. Then "when the time comes for it to be born, the child cannot come down and the woman dies." Another shaman, however, may be able to fumigate the woman with tobacco smoke, to massage her and, if he is a strong shaman and has many spirit helpers, to aid in removing the vine from the neck of the foetus. The mother's life is saved and the child will be born. A few days before we arrived in the village of Januaria, a woman had been delivered in what seems to have been a breech birth. A shaman from a distant village was thought to have tied the child by the neck, causing it to turn and come out feet first. One of the shamans of the village, however, was able to overcome this evil influence and save mother and child.

As soon as the child is born, it is placed across the mother's knees and water is brought to her with which to bathe it. The umbilical cord is cut with a pair of scissors or with a piece of bamboo. The placenta is buried near the wall inside the house; we were told that

5 *Ibid.* His information comes from Plagge.
6 In 1945, Manuel Viana's wife gave birth at night "without anyone's help." Manuel had promised to call us but he was away from the house and she did not even call him.

if the placenta were found and eaten by a dog or some other animal, the child would certainly die. The mother is moved to her hammock where she should remain for several days. She is given a scratching stick to be used until the end of the lying-in period, for if she scratches her body or head with her hands, the child will certainly break out with severe skin eruptions; if she rubs her eyes with her hands, the child may become blind.

Both parents are subject to rather rigid lying-in rules which end, for the husband, when the navel cord drops off and, for the mother, several days later.[7] The mother should remain prone in her hammock as much as possible, and the husband should also rest. Both should eat only manioc flour, small fish (usually the *piabanha*), and roasted maize; and they should drink only warm water. Cold water is said to make one cold inside, upsetting the internal organs. Neither the mother nor her husband are considered as yet normal internally. One informant told us that on the day that the navel cord drops, the woman's mother, or an older relative, paints both parents with black genipa dye over legs and arms, and that on this day the couple drink a beverage made of the bark of the *ywira ró* tree to end the lying-in period. The mother, however, should, for safety, continue a restricted life for a few days more.

We were told of several instances of transgression of the lying-in rule. One man went hunting, killing a deer the day after the birth of his son; two days later the infant's stomach became bloated and the child soon died. It was explained that a man in Januaria is blind because he did not follow the rules when one of his daughters was born.

During the lying-in period, it is believed that the bodies of the new parents are weak from the delivery and cannot stand strong foods. The physical bond between the parents and the child is especially close at this time, and the parents must continue to respect the restriction on sexual relations and to avoid specific dangerous meats. The story was told of a woman who kept complaining that she was hungry. Only two days after her delivery she insisted that her husband kill a chicken for her. She ate the chicken, and three

---

[7] Even a stepfather, the husband of a woman, is subject to these lying-in rules. Manuel Viana married a young widow who was pregnant. When the child was born he was subject to all the regulations for the child's protection.

days later she died. Her child died a month later, ostensibly from a cold, but most people believed from its mother's actions.

The navel cord of a male child is frequently carried by the father as a luck piece in hunting. It is wrapped in a piece of cloth and hidden from the eyes of the infant, for should the child see it, the navel cord immediately loses value as a luck piece. After a few months, a son's navel cord loses its efficacy for the father, but may be passed on to a male relative for whom it will still bring luck for a time. Finally, however, it loses all power and should be buried in the house floor. We were told that a man should not touch the navel cord of a daughter; it will bring him bad luck in hunting.

Twins are not wanted by the Tenetehara. People were not anxious to discuss the subject of twins with us, intimating that it was an unpleasant subject. After a time, however, it was made clear that twins are not usually allowed to live but are buried immediately. For fear that we would report them to the Indian Service for infanticide, our informants were guarded about discussing this matter. But aside from this fear, the very idea of the birth of twins is decidedly unpleasant to them. A woman who gives birth to twins is thought to have copulated with the evil forest demon, Marana ẏwa. In two examples which were related to us, both mothers died after giving birth to twins. "She was ashamed," our informant explained, referring to one of the women. In both cases, the husbands moved away to distant villages. Their wives had disgraced them and they were afraid that they would be reported to Brazilian Indian Service authorities for infanticide.

CHILDHOOD

Children are named, generally by the mother, a few days after birth. Frequently a boy is given his maternal grandfather's name and a girl her maternal grandmother's name. Since the parents normally live with the wife's family group, mothers usually name the first children after her parents to please them. Formerly, we were told, the maternal grandparents themselves named the newborn. Almost all children are given native names such as *wariwa* (guariba monkey), *zawarehú* (jaguar), *tonaí* (*inhambú*), *chiakwá* (up-turned nose), *tapiíre* (tapir), and *marakazá* (wild cat). A few, however, are given only Christian names and a few are even baptized by Brazilians, who act as godfathers. If a Tenetehara has no Christian name, he usually adopts one for use at the Indian Post and in Brazilian settlements. Often this Christian name is used even by the Indians rather than the native Tupí-Guaraní name. There is a tendency nowadays to be somewhat ashamed of native names; we never suspected, for example, that João Bochecha had a native name until we heard him called *wariwa* (guariba monkey) in the villages on the upper Pindaré; in the village of Januaria and at the Indian Post he was called by Indians and Brazilians alike by his Christian name. The use of Christian rather than native names is, of course, more common near the Indian Post and in those villages near Brazilian settlements.

Tenetehara mothers worry little about the feeding of a newborn infant. It is given the breast several times during the first twenty-four hours to insure that the mother will have milk. There are no regular hours for feeding, but at the slightest whimper from the child the mother offers her breast. During the first two or three months, the mother holds the nursing baby in her arms, but after the child is fairly strong, it is carried in a band swung from the mother's shoulder in a position somewhat astride her hip so it can easily reach the breast. The mother rubs a paste of sweet manioc over her breast believing it will increase the production and flow of milk. When the child does not nurse well, or when a woman temporarily lacks milk, the infant is fed a tea made from sweet herbs or a fine meal prepared especially from manioc.[8] The tuber is soaked several days in water until it is soft, and is then passed through a fine sieve. The stringy, rough material and the juice are thrown away and the thin dough which results is set out to dry thoroughly in the sun. A thin soup made of the dough is usually the first food, other than mother's milk, given to Tenetehara children. If the mother lacks milk entirely or cannot nurse the child for one reason or another, the infant is given this manioc soup as a basic diet.

Until a child is eight or nine months of age, it is seldom out of its mother's sight. Although a few families fabricate small hammocks for infants of five or six months, most children sleep with their mothers, or with the mother and father when they share a hammock,

[8] There is an identical commercial production of doubtful nutritive value used widely throughout northern Brazil.

until they are two or three years of age. Nights in this region are apt to be uncomfortably cool, especially during the early morning hours, and the child undoubtedly welcomes the body warmth of the parents. It is thought best to keep a fire going during the night in a room where a small infant sleeps, not for warmth, but to drive away ghosts (*azang*, see p. 104) which might come to harm the child. During the day, the mother carries the child in her arms or astride her hip as she moves about the village. As she works in the house, she may leave the child sleeping in the hammock, but she never leaves it alone in the house.[9]

During the first few days, the baby is bathed once a day with warm water by the mother's female kin; later, the mother bathes the infant herself, with unheated water, on the average of twice each day, usually during the sunny portions of the morning and afternoon. The young infant receives considerable attention during its first months from the mother and from her female relatives of the extended family group.

In general, Tenetehara children are weaned gradually. After six or seven months, a mother begins to give her baby other foods, first manioc soup and then small bites of baked sweet manioc, yam, or squash. The child continues to take the breast at irregular intervals even after it has learned to eat other foods; it is not unusual to see a child of eighteen months or two years, already walking, but still nursing now and again at its mother's breast. We were told that a mother should nurse her child "until it eats other foods" and "until it is tired of the breast." If the mother should become pregnant, however, then it is considered imperative to wean the baby immediately. A nursing child is thought to suck the milk which should nourish the unborn baby and the Tenetehara women do not believe it possible to nourish two children at once. Accordingly, the woman is forced to wean her child quickly; she rubs pepper or ginger powder on the nipples of her breast in full view of the baby and after a few unpleasant trials the child will refuse to nurse. However, few infants are weaned so violently because the sexual con-

---

[9] We saw several children with scars resulting from falls from the hammock into the house fire. Sometimes children fall from the hammock during the night while the mother is asleep, especially after they become active and hard to control.

tinence imposed on the parents of an infant ordinarily assures a spacing of children.

As soon as a child is able to crawl, the mother and her female relatives perform an informal ceremony called *wira o háwo-i*,[10] to protect against illness from the meat which is now added to the child's diet. The father or a mother's brother provides a forest fowl such as an *inhambú*. The meat is roasted, torn from the carcass, and ground with manioc flour into a meal. The mother and her companions eat of this preparation and then offer some to the child. We were told that it was a simple family occasion; dancing and singing does not occur.

During the first year, parents pay little attention to sphincter and bladder control of the child. Several times each day the mother places the infant on the ground to urinate or to defecate. She then simply calls an older child to sweep up the feces on a banana leaf and to throw it into the near-by underbrush. At night the mother, without even leaving her hammock, holds a child out over the floor to urinate or even to defecate. After the child is able to walk, however, she sometimes shames it when it soils the hammock or the house floor. Older siblings or cousins usually take a two or three-year-old child just outside the house for such necessities. These older children laugh at the child who does not ask to be taken outside, and both adults and older children shame the child who urinates or defecates in the house in front of the family. Although several people told us that it was customary to "spank the child lightly" (on the buttocks) when it continued to lack sphincter and bladder control after it was walking, we did not observe one instance of such punishment for these reasons. Instead we often saw children three or four years old defecate on the floor of a Tenetehara house without being punished at all.[11]

Children are soon, however, made to feel ashamed of these body functions and by the time they are adult, they are not only ashamed to urinate or defecate in view of a person of the opposite sex but also in the company of people of the same sex. Men on hunting trips

[10] *Wira o háwo* is the name given to the puberty ceremony, after which boys and girls may eat any type of meat; *i* is diminutive.

[11] One informant told us that some parents rubbed herbs on the navel of a child to keep it from wetting or soiling the hammock.

move a distance away from their companions to urinate and go to
infinite trouble for privacy for excretory functions. The same is true
for women with other women. The attitudes of personal shame in
regard to sphincter and bladder functions are passed on to children
during the first three or four years of their life—not by corporal
punishment but by ridicule and shame.

A conscious effort is made to teach children to walk and talk. Parents and older brothers and sisters hold a baby while it toddles and
much comment is passed as to how well it learns. We sometimes
heard fathers, mothers, or older children repeating a phrase over
and over again for a young child. Manuel Viana, for example, was
heard repeating slowly for his small daughter, "This is your mother's
brother," and he laughed as she repeated it back to him. He named
objects in the house and was delighted when she could distinguish
them when asked again. Manuel told us that there was no special
"baby talk" but that children pronounced badly at first.

As soon as a child learns to toddle about, it must be taught where
and with whom it may play. Adults believe that "a small child is
not welcome in other people's houses." Thus, a toddler is shown his
mother's brother's house, his mother's sister's house, and the houses
of other close kin where he may go and come at will. The toddler is
scolded for entering houses outside this family group. When there
is an older sister, she is given the job of watching the child and told
not to let it "bother other people." In general, the size of Tenetehara extended family groups provides for the younger child several accessible houses and a large number of people with whom it
soon feels at home. But, except in its own father's house, a child is
taught never to ask for food. Children almost always refused our
offers of food while we were in residence in Tenetehara villages.
Parents are "ashamed" when children ask for or accept food in another's house. We were told that people will say, "Ah, in your
father's house is there not enough for all to eat?" The Tenetehara
complain that children give considerable trouble from the time they
learn to walk until they are five or six years old. "They do not know.
They enter others' houses (the homes of distant relatives or non-
relatives) and they ask for things. One has to watch everything they
do," said Manuel Viana.

Only on rare occasions did we observe a parent spank a child.

Even the parents of an unusually bad-tempered little girl limited themselves "to talking to her" when she cried because they would not let her enter a neighbor's house. Manuel Viana said that "to talk to the child" was better than "spanking." "To talk to the child" seem to be an effort both to convince the child through affection to do what is wanted and to threaten or frighten it into obeying. Auta, Manuel Viana's daughter, would respond when he "talked to her" because she knew that her father would be sad if she refused. A child is told that "his fingernails will show a black streak" if he lies; [12] that if he steals, he will have twisted hands; and that ghosts (azang) will come and carry him off if he does not stop crying, or if he disobeys his parents.

In general, Tenetehara parents treat their children with great affection in spite of their statements that they do not want children because of the dietary and sexual restrictions which their coming entails and the nuisance of rearing and training them. Small children spend most of their time with the mother, yet it is common to see a Tenetehara father carrying one about the village or playing with it in front of the house during late evening. On the days when he did not work Manuel Viana always took his small daughter wherever he went within the village. Sebastião brought his eighteen-month-old son with him each time he visited our camp in Lagôa Comprida. Fathers also try to please their children in other ways. Manuel Viana explained, for example, that his daughter, Auta, liked fish heads, tortoise eggs, and special pieces of certain game, and that he was especially anxious to bring these things for her to eat. In fact, Manuel knew Auta's eating preferences in detail. She wanted meat above all and would only eat squash and sweet potato when she was very hungry. He was obviously deeply attached to his small daughter. Once when he returned from a trip he told us that he had been very worried about Auta while he was away. During the trip he dreamed twice that some harm had come to her. He dreamed one night that she had been bitten by a dog, and another night that he killed a jaguar and exposed Auta to the harm of the dangerous jaguar spirit.

Until they are four or five years old, there is no great difference

[12] Rural Brazilians say that the nail "shows a white mark from lying." This trait was evidently modified by the Tenetehara in borrowing.

between the education of Tenetehara boys and girls. It is, however, obvious that parents have a preference for girls and this affection for a small daughter was always explained by such statements as "girls grow faster," "girls walk earlier than boys" and "learn easier." It was notable that almost all small girls wore decorative necklaces made of agouti or jaguar teeth and of glass beads and that small boys never did. Many more small girls had individual hammocks than did boys. We saw a few boys of eight to ten years old sleeping on the floor, while all girls of this age had their own hammocks. Young girls who are left orphans are without exception adopted immediately by near or distant relatives and treated with some care and attention. On the other hand, in every Tenetehara village we visited, there were several ill-kept orphan boys between five and twelve years old who had no clothes at all or only a few rags. Many of them slept on the floor, and ate irregularly at a relative's house. In 1945 several boys were living at Post Gonçalves Dias ostensibly under the care of the Indian Officer to whom they had been charged by distant relatives on the death of their parents. Just as many girls were left without parents by the epidemics of smallpox and whooping cough which killed so many Tenetehara in 1943 and 1944, but none of them were "given" to the Indian Post. Although this preference for girls is obviously based on their economic and social value to the family group, we never heard anyone explain it in such terms. Young males do not have a productive place in Tenetehara society until they are past adolescence; soon after they begin to be economically valuable as workers, they are likely to marry and move away from the family group. Young females, on the other hand, begin household work very early, soon after puberty or even before it, and at marriage they attract a male worker to the group.

At five or six years of age, striking differences begin to appear in the education of boys and girls. Boys acquire more liberty and freedom to roam about the village. They perform odd jobs such as carrying firewood and running errands for older people, but in general they do not have any specific obligations or work to do. One father laughed and said, "Boys only return home to eat" (a boy would be punished if he embarrassed his parents by eating elsewhere). Youngsters of seven and eight join the young men of the village when they return in the late afternoon from the garden or from the hunt. They

smoke small cigarettes made from *tawari* bark and tobacco given
them by the young men, and they take part in the conversations no
matter what the subject matter may be. In the afternoon the youngsters play with tops made out of small palm nuts or play at hunting
with small bows and arrows made from bamboo, shooting at lizards
or even only at leaves. They build small shelters near the village
in the underbrush in imitation of the hunting blinds built by men
in the forest. Sometimes they play "deer," a popular game similar
to our "fox and the hounds." One boy is selected as the "deer" and
the others become "dogs." The "dogs" chase the "deer" through the
underbrush, imitating the barking of the hunting dogs until they
run the "deer" to bay. Then one of the boys who is "the owner of
the dogs" carries the "deer" to an open space and imitates the
process of skinning it. Then the game begins again.

At nine or ten years of age, a Tenetehara boy sometimes accom-
panies his father on short hunting or fishing trips and sometimes his
father takes him to the garden to teach him various agricultural
techniques. For example, Severino, who lived in the village of
Jacaré often took his son with him when he went to the garden; the
boy did not spend all his time at work, but often played near by
at hunting while his father was busy. Severino said that the boy
would grow up to be a good hunter because several times while he
was playing he found land tortoises. Severino assured us that it was
the boy's own idea to accompany him to the garden; he evidently
did not consider that the son had any obligation to do so. Other
men explained that it was better for boys to learn to hunt only after
they had passed through their puberty rites and that generally until
that time boys did not help out in the garden work. They said that
if a father tried to force a small boy to help, the boy would disappear
from the house early in the morning before it was time to leave for
the garden. Most adult males remembered that they had not learned
such techniques as the manufacturing of bows and arrows, the plaiting of baskets, and the decorating of gourd vessels until they were
fourteen or fifteen years old, after they "had sung alone" in the
puberty rites—and sometimes even later. Even if a youngster asks
to be taught manual techniques, he may be told that "it is too early
for you to learn." People told us that a boy who learned such adult
skills as plaiting baskets or forming a bow "too early" would die

young. Until they are at least twelve or thirteen years old, boys have
no serious part at all in economic life and usually not until they are
about fifteen years of age are they considered old enough to begin
productive work.

The feminine role during these same years, from five through
adolescence, contrasts markedly with that of the male. The young
girl begins exceedingly early to help her mother in household tasks,
first in play, imitating the mother as she works; then by the time she
is eight or nine years old, definite tasks are expected of her. It is
commonplace to see a Tenetehara girl of ten sweeping out the
house, carrying drinking water from the spring or stream, tending
the cooking pots and the fireplace, spinning cotton thread, and taking care of younger brothers or sisters. A few seven or eight-year-old
girls are sometimes seen playing in front of the houses, and now and
again the boys, whose major preoccupation is to invent new means
of amusements for themselves, are able to entice girls into the
near-by brush to play house in imitation of adult life. In general,
however, girls stay close to their mothers and female relatives, helping them in the household tasks. Often a young girl is "married"
by the time she is ten years old—that is, a young man many years
her senior has entered her father's household as a son-in-law in order
"to raise her as his wife." In the course of these years her duties
are almost those of an adult woman; although her mother and aunts
help her with all the heavy tasks until she is strong enough to under-
take them by herself.

Tenetehara children of both sexes have at a rather early age a
fairly complete knowledge of the facts about sex and of adult sexual
affairs. Girls learn from the conversation of the women in the household and boys from playmates and from the conversations of young
men. No effort is made by adults to hide such facts from children
and adult conversation is not changed to suit the children present.
One day, for example, Auta, who was then seven years old, explained
to her father that her mother's brother was having secret sexual relations with a young married woman of the village. Manuel laughed
and asked his companions if it was true. Small boys invariably know
of all extramarital affairs in the village. Both boys and girls are said
to wake up frequently during the night while their parents are having intercourse, and parents do not place any importance on the

matter. One informant, explaining that children were well aware
of sexual matters, pointing to a group of boys ranging from five to
nine years of age, said, "All of them know everything."

Boys are said to masturbate now and again. When they are discovered by adults, they are warned—"the head (glans) of your penis
will stick out and the foreskin will stretch as far as your feet if you
do not stop. This is shameful." One of the men with whom we had
many intimate discussions confessed that as a small boy (eight or
nine years old) he had masturbated for a short time and he said
all boys probably do so now and then. He assured us, however, that
masturbation was preadolescent experimentation, and that as soon
as boys were older, even before their puberty rites, they procure
women. There is also some sex play with girls. Groups of boys tempt
a young girl to leave her household duties and play house with them
in the small houses the boys build near the village. Many girls take
part in such sex play at one time or another, but in general they soon
tire of it and refuse to cooperate further. While we were visiting in
Januaria village a group of boys (eight to twelve years old) were discovered one day in sex play with two small girls in such a shelter near
the village.[13] There was some comment among the adults in the
village regarding their behavior but neither the boys nor the girls
concerned were punished. The parents were not angry with the
children, nor were any particular children singled out as the leaders
of the culprits. Instead, one of the parents explained, "They do not
as yet know everything. They do not know even who their relatives
are." Adults were not upset even though one of the boys and one
of the girls involved were real cousins (the boy's mother's sister's
daughter). Somewhat later in the same village several small boys
were seen in sex play using a smaller boy of about five years of age
"as the girl." This was considered ridiculous and funny but not abnormal.

During the years which precede adolescence, children of both
sexes are restricted as to the meats they may eat. Wild goose,
mutûm, jacú, and the red and blue macaw as well as several other
forest fowls are prohibited to them. These birds and animals are

---

[13] A young man told us that usually a group of girls invites the boys to go with
them to the brush for sex play. His statement was obviously inexact. He was repeating
the male attitude that sex aggression always comes from the female.

among those with dangerous spirits (*piwára*, see p. 104), and in general they are the ones that are prohibited in the diet of the parents during the pregnancy of the woman and the early infancy of the child. A girl or boy who breaks these diet taboos and eats of these meats will suffer insanity. As soon as the youth has "sung alone" and the girl has tasted of the ceremonial meal at the puberty rites they are allowed to eat of the prohibited meats; but as soon as they are to become parents the restrictions of childhood are imposed again.

The Tenetehara told us that, in the old days, when the boy was about five or six years old, his lower lip was pierced with the pointed tip of a deer horn. This custom must have been abandoned more than fifty years ago since we did not see a single individual among the Tenetehara, even among the older people, with such a perforation or with a scar from such an operation.

Nowadays many Tenetehara of both sexes have pointed incisor teeth.[14] The operation of pointing the teeth is performed by an older man and takes place soon after the second dentition. The teeth are not filed to a point; in fact when we asked people whether it was done by filing, they seemed somewhat horrified with the idea. One man held his hands to his head imitating great pain in reply to this question. The teeth are chipped with the blade of a small knife. A block of wood is placed between the patient's teeth to prop the mouth open. The knife blade is placed against the incisor and it is tapped with a small hardwood club. In this way, bit by bit, the incisor is worked to a sharp point. As soon as the operation is finished, the patient should bite into a warm potato or yam "to harden the teeth." The operation is described as painful and the patient always suffers the first night afterwards from an intense headache. Within a few days, however, there is little discomfort except that the teeth are sensitive to heat and cold. Young people are said to cut their tongues on the sharp teeth until they become accustomed to them.

[14] The custom of sharpening the incisors is probably of African origin. The Brazilians of this region and even the Eastern Timbira share the custom. The custom may well have been introduced into the region by escaped Negro slaves in the 18th and 19th centuries. See Baldus (1945), p. 45.

PUBERTY

The Tenetehara mark the passage of childhood and the beginning of adulthood with a single ceremony in which adolescents of both sexes participate. Formerly, both boys and girls were required to go through a period of isolation before celebrating these rites. About forty or fifty meters from the village proper, a small hut of *jussára* palm was set up for each adolescent, and here the boy or girl remained in solitude for a period of ten days or more. Girls were painted black with genipa dye over their entire bodies; boys were similarly painted, except that the upper half of the face was left free. The adolescent was not allowed to leave the hut at all during the period of isolation and spent his time lying prone in his hammock. The mother or a female relative brought food at intervals and emptied the gourd vessel which the adolescent had used for urinating or defecating. No meat was eaten during this period, only maize, manioc flour, a soup made from the sweet manioc, and sometimes a few small fish, and there was only warmed water to drink. The adolescents were allowed to talk only to their mothers or the other relatives who came to tend to their necessities, and normally no one else approached the huts. They were warned that they must always look straight ahead, for if for any reason they turned to look at something, they might become insane.

On the last day of isolation, the entrails of the agouti were stretched across the door of the hut. The next morning the parents of the youth approached the hut and called to him to leave. He would leave by breaking the entrails across the door. A girl was not called by her parents but by a young man of the village. At dawn he came near her hut, calling to her. She would break through the agouti intestines and run for a near-by stream, chased by the young men of the village. At the stream they gave her a bath and she returned to her parents' house. It was not explained what would take place should the young men catch her before she reached the stream; in fact, it did not seem to occur to our informants that they might.

We were told that in former times a father or a grandfather would inspect a boy's penis after his isolation period for signs of masturbation. If there were any signs of irritation that might indicate masturbation, the boy was whipped with a piece of vine. Also, formerly, before Tenetehara men wore trousers, the boys were given a piece of palm fiber at this time to bind the prepuce over the glans penis (see p. 93), and, we were told, he was sometimes scratched over legs, arms, and chest with the sharpened teeth of the agouti. Following the isolation period both boys and girls were scarified with the tribal insignia. According to two of our informants, this tribal mark or insignia was made by cutting a thin line from the elbow to the wrist on the inside of each arm, and by etching four circles with radiating lines like the rays of the sun—one figure over and one under each breast. A straight line was formed from each corner of the mouth almost to the ears. Snethlage mentions this last marking as a tribal symbol and says that it passed horizontally from the nose to the ear lobe. He observed only a few people with the marking.[15] The operations seem to have been performed with the incisor of the agouti and genipa dye was rubbed into the wounds to give them permanent coloring.

Nowadays the puberty rites are carried out in a simplified form. Only two people in the villages we visited had ever seen the act of scarification. We found no one wearing the old tribal markings. In describing these old customs of isolation and preparation of adolescents for the ceremony, our informants were somewhat vague. They agreed on details but, for example, one man told us that scarification took place in the old days before the isolation period and that isolation ended for the adolescent when the wounds healed. Others corrected him and stated that scarification took place following the isolation period and that the puberty ceremony, properly speaking, was postponed until the wounds healed. Many Tenetehara had never heard of the inspection of genitals for masturbation, nor could they describe the scarified tribal markings.

Nowadays boys are seldom isolated before the puberty ceremony. The five who celebrated the ceremony in 1941 in the village of Jacaré, instead of being isolated, were told not to wander into the forest nor to take a bath in the stream. They were instructed to walk about only in the village plaza and to retire early. Water was brought from the stream for them to drink and to bathe in. Such precautions were taken because the youths are considered vulnerable during this time to the evil supernaturals, especially Ywan, the water

[15] Snethlage, "Unter nordostbrazilianischen Indianer," p. 120.

spirit, and the *azang*, the wandering ghosts. No restrictions at all were placed on the adolescent boys in the village of Camirang, who passed through the puberty ceremony of 1942.

Girls, however, are still isolated just after menstruation appears for the first time. Instead of being sent to a special hut inside the village, as in the old days, a palm-leaf screen is stretched across a corner of the family dwelling and the girl lies in her hammock hidden from the view of the family and visitors. The rules are much the same as in former times. There are the same restrictions on her diet; she may drink warmed water only; she must look straight ahead, and she must not leave her isolation even for necessary physiological functions. The isolation period lasts approximately the same length of time—ten days or more—as before. At the end of it, the agouti entrails are stretched across the door of the family dwelling and the girl is called and chased to the stream, as formerly, by the young men of the village. Likewise, girls are still painted black with genipa dye before their isolation period, and the puberty ceremony should not take place until all signs of the paint have worn off. In modern Tenetehara society, the rules and restrictions at puberty have relaxed to a greater extent for males than for females. Because women have less contact with Brazilian culture than men, they are more conservative and native customs concerning them seem to have changed less than have those which refer to males.

The puberty ceremony is still celebrated in all Tenetehara villages. In 1941, the rites were observed in Jacaré for five boys and—in Januaria for one girl; in February of 1942 they were held in Camirang for four youths and two girls. Although informants described the other ceremonies to us, we were actually present at only the one held in Camirang. This was under the patronage of Ambrósio, one of the strong family leaders of the village, whose group consisted of his own son, a sister's daughter, two classificatory "brother's sons" (whom he addresses as "son"), and a classificatory "younger sister." With the exception of one youth who was a relative of the village chief, all the initiates were members of this extended family. Two days before the day set for the ceremony, Ambrósio spoke with Camirang, the village chief, who gave orders for a cooperative hunt of all men of the village to collect meat for the ceremonial feast. The men of Ambrósio's extended family, most of those of Camirang's group, and a few from Pedro's extended family complied. Camirang distributed gunpowder and shot to each man who had a gun. The result of the first day's hunt was poor. Only a few tortoises and three howler monkeys were killed, so it was decided that a second day's communal hunt was necessary. This time the men returned with many land tortoises and two deer. There was enough meat for the feast, and the ceremony was announced for the next day.

As we have said, the same ceremony serves to celebrate the passage of puberty for boys and girls. It takes place during the rainy season; in fact, it is a phase of the annual rainy season ceremony for maize (see p. 125). The dancing, the singing, and the shamanistic activity which provide the background during the puberty rites are the same as those for the Maize Festival. The ceremony begins early the morning of one day and ends at dawn of the next. Formerly it was always held in the "big house" a central feature which was in all Tenetehara villages, but in 1942, as the village of Camirang did not have a "big house," the palm-thatched walls were removed from one large room of Ambrósio's house to provide an open shelter against the hot sun.

Early in the morning, the youths were decorated by their immediate families. Cotton-string bands dyed red with *urucú* were tied just above the elbow and a little above the knee. The whole body was dyed black with genipa, leaving the face untouched above a line that ran from the nose to the ear lobe.[16] Each boy wore a headband of cotton string from which dangled flowers made of yellow toucan feathers. White bird-down was glued to the shoulders in a line down the arms to the elbow, and a V-shaped line of bird-down was fixed to the chest. White down and feathers were stuck into the hair with rosin glue. Relatives loaned necklaces of glass beads, and each celebrant carried a decorated arrow shaft. Ambrósio's own son carried a wand made of at least thirty long tail feathers of the red macaw, stuck into a wooden handle.

At the same time, the mothers and other women of the extended family group prepared the young girls for the ceremony, painting their bodies black with genipa and fastening white bird-down in their hair. Actually the girls were less elaborately decorated than

---

[16] Formerly the scarified facial marking ran from the nose to the ear lobe.

casual participants. Most adults of the village decorated themselves in some way. Many painted red lines with *urucú* on their faces and many women wore narrow string headbands. Ambrósio, who was the patron of the ceremony, decorated his arms and chest with bird-down in the same design used by the boys.

The ceremony consisted mainly of group singing and dancing. The songs began about midmorning. Ambrósio sat down on a bench with two of the young male initiates at his side and began to sing, keeping time with a gourd rattle and stamping out the rhythm of the song with his right foot. The other two young male initiates joined the group seated on the bench. The initiates did not sing, but kept time to the rhythm with one foot. After a time, the women brought the two girl initiates to the other side of the house, where they stood quietly, hanging their heads as if with shame. Some of the women slowly grouped themselves behind the girls while some of the men gathered near Ambrósio and the boys. All joined in the chorus of the song. The women, with the two girl initiates in front, moved a few paces toward the men, then returned, using a hopping step. The men then advanced and retreated in a line, stamping out the beat of the music heavily with one foot. The two lines, each led by the initiates of its sex, simultaneously approached and retreated. Ambrósio led the singing; the chorus was again picked up by the men and women participants. As usual in Tenetehara singing, the women sang in a high, almost falsetto, tone, in counterpoint to the men. The singing is unusually melodious even to Western ears.

About midday, after a few minutes' rest, Ambrósio changed the form of dancing. With boy initiates on each side of him he began to dance in a circle around the center pole of the house. Joining hands, they formed a line which revolved around the house pole like the spoke of a wheel. The two girls joined hands and fell in behind them. Like additional spokes in the revolving wheel, lines of men with their arms over each other's shoulders and lines of women clasping each other's hands danced until sundown around the circle to the rhythm of the song.

In the midst of the dancing and singing, the shamans began to call their familiar spirits. They puffed on long strong cigars, dragging great drafts of tobacco smoke into their lungs until they were intoxicated thoroughly. They staggered about, singing the songs of their spirits, without regard to the songs being sung by the group. Two shamans and several shaman novices performed all that afternoon, while the group singing and dancing continued. The shamans were possessed by several supernaturals. One of them, Inácio, fell to the ground in a trance under the influence of the deer spirit, and the other, André, was possessed by the dangerous hawk spirit. Such shamanistic exhibitions are characteristic of the Maize Festival, and this afternoon portion of the puberty ceremonial seems to be but a more elaborate session of this seasonal festival.

At sundown, the group singing and dancing and the shamanistic activity came to an end. Exactly at sunset, Ambrósio fired twice into the air with his rifle "to show that his son was now a man." All the dancers then ran to the central plaza of the village and formed a large irregular circle. Each male initiate now had a young woman dancing at his side. The large circle of dancers sang and moved in toward the center and then withdrew. At this time the youths are supposed to "sing alone," leading the group by introducing each verse of the song. Ambrósio danced beside them, giving support by singing softly with them. All four of the youths were timid, and each sang so low that he could hardly be heard. After about an hour, the singing and dancing in the plaza broke up and the people returned to Ambrósio's house for general night singing. Although the boys must participate in this group singing through the night, to all purposes they have now taken their place as adults.

The nocturnal portion of the puberty rites was a "group sing" or *zingar-eté* (to sing much)—the name given to any song fest which is not a specific festival. During the night villagers came and went informally, sitting about on benches or on the floor, joining in the singing for a time, and then retiring to their hammocks to rest awhile. Ambrósio also stopped to rest, passing the rattle to a companion who beat out the time of the song and led the singing in his place. The initiates of both sexes, however, continued to dance throughout the night, with only manioc flour and water for refreshment. They danced as they had all day, either with downcast faces or looking straight ahead, very self-consciously. It was explained that, as during the isolation period, they might go insane if they looked about.

At dawn, the girl initiates were more elaborately decorated. Bird-down was glued on their arms and in their hair. A string band was placed over their foreheads and strings of yellow toucan feathers were fastened to it so as to hang down their backs. Members of their extended families lent them necklaces of glass beads. As soon as they were decorated, Ambrósio took them to dance by his side. Just as the boys had danced with women for the first time at sunset the night before, now for the first time the girls danced alongside a man. The dancing and singing was now more animated than at any other time during the rites. Even those few people who had elected to sleep now left their hammocks to take part in the singing and dancing which immediately preceded the feast of roast meat.

The meat, which had been collected in the cooperative hunts on previous days, had been boiled and roasted by the women of the various households. Now they brought it to Ambrósio's house and placed it in a large common pot. Some of it was broken into pieces, mixed with manioc flour, and offered on large flat baskets. Ambrósio sat down in front of the meat facing the girls. They approached him and formally asked him, "Grandfather, may we now eat meat from the hunt?" [17] Ambrósio took a small piece of meat to test it before answering. Then he said, "Yes, my granddaughters, you may eat." [18] The girls were given meat from the pot. This was the first time they had eaten the flesh of the taboo animals (see p. 79). The people fell upon the meat and within a short time it had disappeared. Much of it was eaten on the spot and much of it was carried home to be eaten during the day.

In general, by the time she reaches adolescence, a girl has acquired all the necessary knowledge and techniques of the adult woman. She may, in fact, already have been doing the work of a woman in many of the household tasks; thus she moves into her adult role easily. The young man, however, is an adult in name only immediately following the puberty rites. He must continue to work with his father in the garden, to collect *babassú* nuts or copaíba oil, to hunt or fish. Not until he is somewhat older will some man seek

[17] Ideally, the leader or patron of the ceremony should be the girl's grandfather, we were told, but Ambrósio, the leader of the extended family to which the initiates belonged, was substituted for the "grandfather." Normally, the grandfather would be the leader of the extended family and therefore the sponsor of the puberty rites.

[18] At this point, one of the young men by our side made a pun: "And they will soon be eaten," he said. In Portuguese there is a slang expression "to eat a young girl," meaning to have sexual relations with her.

him out as a son-in-law. Then even as a married man he continues under the domination of this father-in-law for at least a few years. The insecurity of Tenetehara men as adults can, perhaps, be partially explained by the position in which society places them during their early manhood.

MARRIAGE

The marriage of a Tenetehara woman is the concern of her extended family group, since the marriage brings an additional male worker into the group. Generally, therefore, the father of the girl, or even the leader of her extended family, takes the initiative in arranging a suitable marriage. The father looks for a good worker among the eligible young men of the village and among those who come visiting from other villages. Most people told us that a son-in-law from the same village is preferred, because he has no incentive to move away in order to live near his own relatives after the year or two he serves with his father-in-law.

Marriage is prohibited between near relatives; those whom a man calls *hehý* (mother), *heiýra* (mother's sister), *hereinýra* (sister or female cousin), *heratipéra* (sister's daughter; daughter of all those one calls "sister"), *hezaihé* (father's sister), *herazýra* (daughter, brother's daughter) and *heremiariró* (granddaughter) were all given as relatives whom one should never marry. Yet when these terms refer to distant classificatory kin, there is no ban on marriage and it does take place.[19] For example, Benedito who lives in Lagôa Comprida, was married to a woman he called *heiýra* (mother's sister) and Miguel at Januaria might have called his wife *hereinýra* (sister), but in both cases the relationship was very distant.

After the father has selected his candidate, he will call the young man, discuss the possible marriage with him, and ask if he is interested. Occasionally he asks the young man to work with him for a month or so in the garden to see how well he works. If the young man is satisfactory and if he agrees to the marriage, he simply moves his belongings to his wife's house. Many men remain with the wife's extended family group for many years or even become permanent members of it. Sometimes an ambitious man builds a new extended family of his own. In any case, the first year or two of the marriage—

[19] See Appendix for list of Tenetehara kinship terms.

until the first child is born—the young couple lives with the bride's extended family.

When we visited in the village of Januaria, the "daughter" (brother's daughter) of the family leader, José Viana, had already celebrated her puberty rites and had reached the age for marriage. José Viana told us that after discussing the matter with Pedro, an older man of his group, he selected two youths of the same village, Manuel Lima and Pirú. After discussing the subject with his adopted father, Manuel Viana, leader of another extended family of Januaria, Pirú agreed to the marriage. He moved his belongings to the house of José and began immediately to work with him in clearing the garden and in collecting *babassú* nuts.

This marriage followed the normal pattern among the Tenetehara. Frequently, however, a young man himself will take the initiative in looking for a wife. Less eligible young men, since they are not sought after by older men as husbands for their daughters, must court the girl as well as her father. One man explained to us that when a youth sees a girl he would like as a wife, "he works for a *civilizado* [a Brazilian] in order to buy presents to give to the girl's father" and he "asks the father if he can marry the girl." There are stories of young men courting a girl by whistling outside her house, which indicates that the desires of the girl are also taken into account. While most fathers consult the daughter upon making a choice for her, many override her wishes entirely in order to secure an able worker as a son-in-law.

It seems probable that Joana, the "daughter" of José Viana, was not consulted regarding her marriage to Pirú. She made her views felt very strongly afterwards, however, and it was she who decided whether or not the marriage would last. Pirú told us "she pays no attention to me." After two months the marriage had not as yet been consummated. She refused to cook for him. Her family put pressure on her to accept Pirú as a husband, as he was considered somewhat of a catch for the group. Her father went as far as to hide her hammock one night, thinking to force her to share Pirú's. Instead she sat up all night. Finally, Pirú returned to his own household for his meals and then, against the wishes of his in-laws, moved his belongings back to his adopted father's household.[20]

[20] The incidents are real but the names of the people involved are fictitious.

Although a few Indians and all local Brazilians identify the puberty rites with marriage there does not seem to be any marriage ceremony, as such. This confusion arises from the fact that girls are either married, or early marriages are consummated, immediately after the puberty rites.[21] Negotiations for marriage, however, may be made many years before the girl reaches puberty, when she is but eight or nine years of age. In a sense, the marriage often takes place when the girl is still very young. The father of a very young girl sometimes arranges a marriage for her with a youth old enough for marriage and for productive work. The youth moves into the extended family of his father-in-law as the husband of the pre-adolescent girl. The two refer to each other as *merikó-rana* (*merikó*, wife; *ana*, similar to) and *imén-ana* (similar to husband). He works with her father and contributes economically to the extended family group; she is said to do the housework for him, but actually the bulk of the cooking, preparing of manioc flour, washing of clothes, and other housework is done by her mother until she acquires the skill and strength to do it herself. Sexual relations begin only after the puberty rites. The Tenetehara told us that this type of marriage is generally successful. One old couple we knew were married this way. "Inácio married Maria when she was a small girl in order to raise her, to wait for her to grow," they told us. The common way of referring to this form of marriage is to "raise your wife." [22]

Gustave Dodt observed this form of marriage on the Gurupí River among the Tenetehara (Tembé) about the middle of the last century. He writes, "The Tembés (Tenetehara) have the custom of giving away their daughters still at a very tender age in marriage, which is naturally only nominal, for the daughter remains under her father's protection until puberty." [23] Few young men will, of course,

---

[21] Because of the ceremonial meal, the Brazilians of the region call the Tenetehara puberty ceremony "The Feast of the Roasted Meat" (*Festa de Moqueado*). On the Mearim River, the Brazilians call these rites the "Feast of the Oxen" (*Festa do Boi*), since, because of the scarcity of game in the region, a cow is usually killed by the Indians to provide meat for the occasion.

[22] A Tenetehara interpretation of the Christian story of the creation of woman— man's first wife—refers to this form of marriage (see p. 134). Tupan made woman out of the rib of a dog and gave her to man yet as an infant. Man was instructed to feed her until she is grown and then marry with her.

[23] Dodt (1939 ed.), pp. 202–203.

contract such marriages when older girls are available, and nowadays most marriages are contracted a few months before the puberty ceremony and consummated soon afterwards.

Young couples sometimes elope. Because the man owes his father-in-law service for the bride, elopement, or moving away with a bride within a short time after the marriage, is an offense against the girl's extended family. Such an offense is phrased as "stealing the girl." This was the situation when Manuel Viana forced Pedro to return his "stolen" daughter to the village at the Post. Although it was the second marriage for the girl, Pedro had not worked more than a month with Manuel. Fróes Abreu relates a similar case observed in the Mearim River region. Soon after their marriage, a young man moved away from his wife's village taking her with him. The father followed, took her from her new husband, and brought her back to his village. He threatened the son-in-law and "gave his daughter an awful beating," as punishment for leaving.[24] In all cases which were related to us of elopement or attempts at leaving the matrilocal household during the first months of marriage, the girl's relatives always made an effort to bring her back to their group.[25]

The rules of matrilocal residence and of service to the father-in-law limit the possibilities of having more than one wife. As we have already noted, in general those men who have more than one wife are leaders of extended families and their wives are relatives, coming from the same family group. Such marriages usually come about through a first marriage with a widow, followed by a marriage with her daughter or another near relative. At times, these marriages are partially motivated by a desire to keep a young girl in the family group rather than allow her to marry an outsider who would wish to move away with her after working for a time with the father-in-law. It would be almost unthinkable for a man to seek a second wife outside of his first wife's family group, since he would not be able to work for her family. It is also more advantageous to the family group to bring in additional young male workers by

---

[24] Fróes Abreu, p. 126.

[25] One Tenetehara told us that he "bought" his wife for 10 *alqueires* (300–400 kg.) of manioc flour. What he did was this: He made a bargain with her father not to hold him for the service of the girl. People thought this arrangement rather comical and many remarks were made regarding "buying a wife." Evidently, this was an unusual case.

marriage than for the leader to take on a second wife; for this reason
we heard criticism of the family leader Antoninho, because he had
taken two young women for himself instead of marrying them to
outsiders and increasing the manpower of the extended family.

Marriages are notably unstable during the first months of the
union, even until the first child has been born. Many Tenetehara
girls had taken several husbands, in quick succession, before settling
down with one. The uncertainty of the early days of a marriage is
reflected in certain Tenetehara folk tales; in one cycle of stories
the opossum (*mukwura*) searches for a suitable son-in-law; his
daughter accepts a series of men before one is so tricky that he causes
her father's death (see p. 151). In fact, whether or not a marriage
lasts depends as much upon the bride's family as on the young
couple. Several Tenetehara youths told us that they would not like
to marry a girl of a particular extended family because it was well
known that the family leader influenced the young women to abandon their husbands if other more suitable men were available. In
the village of Januaria, we observed one family group obviously
working to prejudice a young wife against the husband. She had
married with their approval only three months before, but they said
that her husband was lazy. As soon as the young husband left the
village on a short trip, the family leader arranged another marriage
for the girl. When the jilted husband returned, he sent a relative
to fetch his belongings. A girl or her family can easily make it clear
to a young man who is new to the household that the marriage is
not considered satisfactory.

The first few months of marriage are in reality only a period of
trial. The Tenetehara evidently do not set any great value on the
virginity of a bride and it is not a serious matter for a marriage to
break up before children are born. In fact, one young woman of
the village of Januaria, who was not more than fourteen or fifteen
years of age had been married in one year to four young men. When
we met her in 1942, she was the second wife of a family leader.
When we left Januaria in 1942, she had contracted a fifth marriage
which lasted until our return in 1945.

On the other hand, a girl's family sometimes puts pressure on the
girl to keep her young husband against her own desires, as in the
cited case of Joana and Pirú. We were told of one young woman

who became angry with her husband after two months of marriage. She threatened to leave her family and to run away to live with other relatives if they did not tell him to leave. The family was well satisfied with the youth and the girl's father gave her a beating for her trouble.

With the birth of the first child, however, marriage becomes stable. Although we were told of a few rare cases of men abandoning their wives after the birth of a child, we did not observe nor hear of one instance during our visits with the Tenetehara. The numerous joint obligations forced upon the couple during the pregnancy of the woman and also throughout the infancy of the child, and, of course, the added dependence of the woman on the man after the child is born binds the couple together. After the birth of the child, the husband is more or less free to leave and take his family back to his own family group, but in reality most young men by now have become accustomed to their new surroundings and have assumed an increasingly important role in the economic life of the wife's group. They therefore often find it convenient to remain. In such cases, the couple build their own residence near the wife's father's house; the men of the family cooperate in building the house in order to keep him with the group.

SEXUAL LIFE

Tenetehara men have an excessive sense of personal shame. Formerly men wore no clothing; the prepuce was tied over the glans penis with a piece of palm leaf.[26] Nowadays, however, they are very careful never to show themselves nude. Sometimes men work in their gardens with only a very carefully placed loin cloth, but if anyone outside the family of either sex approaches, they put on trousers immediately. Men bathing in a group shield their sexual organs with their hands as they enter the water. Men traveling with us would cross rivers wearing their trousers rather than follow our example and ford the river carrying our clothes over our heads. Man and wife sometimes bathe together in the river, but only after several years of marriage, during which the man has lost "his shame" with the woman.

The men are said to be timid in sexual contacts and therefore it

26 Pereira do Lago, p. 85.

is the bride who takes the initiative in the first sexual act of marriage. The groom is "ashamed" and ill at ease in the strange household. He brings his hammock and hangs it next to his bride's. During the first few days of marriage, they do not have sexual relations, we were told; soon, however, the girl becomes accustomed to having him sleep near her and she moves to join him in his hammock. If the girl has been married previously, she may approach her husband the first night and, in the case of a man who has "raised" his wife, he may take the initiative. Men assured us, however, that they were "ashamed" with their brides and were afraid to approach them for fear of being laughed at and in fear that they would be rebuffed.[27]

Our Tenetehara informants could not remember an instance of a frigid woman; yet, the same men related several cases of impotent men. In fact, while discussing the subject, one of them mentioned casually that he was impotent at the moment, and another remembered that he had been temporarily impotent twice during his lifetime. The former said that he had not been able to copulate for more than five months; recently he had felt sexual desire but could not have an erection. He stated quite frankly that his wife was complaining; she had called him "a woman" in front of other people. He was somewhat upset about the situation. Although the couple had two children, he feared that his wife would take up with another man. We were told of another case of an impotent man by one of his relatives. According to our informant, his relative had not had sexual intercourse with his wife for more than a year. Although the couple had one son, the wife was openly sleeping with another man. The husband continued to live in the house and the woman cooked for both men. "He does not mind," we were told, "because he does not want to copulate." The story was told, however, as a somewhat scandalous affair, and people seemed to be rather sorry for the impotent husband. Still the ménage was accepted by the villagers. The men know several remedies against impotency; a tea made from the bark of the catuába (Anemopaegma catuába) tree is thought to give temporary sexual stimulation and

---

[27] In regard to this passive attitude of the man, it is interesting to note that in the mythology the first Tenetehara woman is supposed to have carried on sexual relations with a supernatural, while the man was as yet innocent of sexual relations; only after a culture hero told man to kill the supernatural which was satisfying the woman did the woman teach the man to copulate.

some believe that it will cure impotence permanently. The dried skin of a male guariba monkey, an animal noted for its sexual prowess, soaked in aguardente, is taken by the Tenetehara on the Mearim and Grajaú Rivers for a similar purpose.

People told us of men who were well known for their numerous sexual affairs, yet we rarely heard a man himself recount his own sexual exploits. When the subject came up in conversation, the men would explain that they did not have affairs, or perhaps tell of the exploit of another man in another village. For example, we were told that Camirang sometimes took advantage of the absence of the young men of his village to cohabit with their wives and that he had constant extramarital affairs. Yet, despite considerable intimacy with Camirang and with the people of his village, both Camirang and the others of the village denied that this was true. In most of the stories related to us of adulterous affairs, the aggression was said to come from the woman. One young man told us that a married woman, whose husband was traveling, followed him when he went to the river to drink water and bathe and that she openly asked him to copulate with her. In telling the story, he said that he "was ashamed" and refused several times, but gossips related that he cooperated readily. Several Tenetehara told us that many women carry on affairs whenever their husbands travel, and they related several current instances. As a rule, adulterous affairs seem to be rare except in the case of widows and young women as yet without children, who are expected to indulge in them.

A widow usually does not remarry until about a year after the death of her husband. During this time she has considerable sexual freedom. She is in fact expected to have a series of affairs with eligible men so that she can select a satisfactory husband; yet actually a widow often carries on affairs with married men of the village. One informant told us that the deceased husband's brother had sexual rights over his brother's widow during the period and if he wished he might take her as his wife. The statements of others, however, as well as the facts, do not fully confirm his assertion. One woman whose husband had died just before we arrived in 1942 had affairs with more than eight men in eight months, and finally she settled with one man some years her junior. Another woman whose husband died in 1944 married again just two months after two short sexual affairs. In neither case did a brother of the deceased husband make any claim on the widow.

The Tenetehara have no institutionalized prostitution, although they know of it from their visits to Brazilian settlements. However, loose young women or widows who accept presents or even money in return for sexual favors are referred to by the Brazilian term for prostitute, but as an expression of opprobrium rather than in the exact meaning. Manuel Viana remembered that when he was a boy there were young girls who would live with men for a week and then take another companion. They were called *kuzareó* (crazy women) but he did not know if they received payments for their favors. Even today the instability of early marriages make a temporary wanton out of many young women.

Questions in regard to homosexuality brought to mind two stories to the Tenetehara—a myth in which a forest monster attracts a man deep into the forest and has pederastic relations with him; and a story of a Brazilian and a Tenetehara who had practiced pederasty because they were traveling far from home and had "been months away from women." In this latter story, the Brazilian, who was referred to as a "Cearense" [28] allowed the Tenetehara to take the active part the first night and the "Cearense" tried unsuccessfully to take the active part the second night "because the Tenetehara does not have a hole." No one could remember an actual case of homosexuality among the Tenetehara. It is evidently something that they have heard discussed by Brazilians but not a reality to be contended with in their own culture.

Tenetehara concepts of sexual behavior contrast strongly with those of the local Brazilians. Among rural Brazilians there is an exaggerated double standard of sexual morality. Men are expected to be sexually aggressive and to carry on premarital and extramarital affairs. Women must be shy and passive and they must remain virgin until marriage. If it is known that a Brazilian girl is no longer a *moça* (literally, a girl; but by connotation a virgin), marriage by civil or religious ceremony is generally out of the question. She must be satisfied with living with a man as a "friend" (*amigado*, in friendship). The Brazilians consider the Indians to be without sexual morals and they are especially shocked at the aggressive be-

---

[28] From the northeastern state of Ceará.

havior of Indian women. The few Brazilian men who are aware of Tenetehara male attitudes toward sex consider the Indian to be sexless. It is almost unbelievable to a Brazilian male that a man would openly admit his impotence.

Because relations between the Indian and the Brazilian are not intimate, however, their polar concepts of sexual morality seldom cause serious disagreements. In general, the two groups have always lived out their personal lives in separate towns and villages, and the relationship between the two cultures has not penetrated to the level of moral values and of intimate family affairs. For the most part, Brazilians are completely unaware of Tenetehara ceremonials, customs, marriage, and the relationship between the sexes. Only such overt practices as polygyny and the puberty rites draw the dispraisal of the "superior" group, and there is therefore a minimum of conflict in these spheres between the two cultures.

V · RELIGIOUS LIFE

IN SPITE OF more than three hundred years of intermittent contact with Christian missionaries, the Tenetehara have retained most of their aboriginal religious patterns. Yet from the missionaries they have learned much about Christian dogma and have integrated some borrowed elements into the framework of their own system. A few beliefs have been accepted despite the fact that they apparently conflict with corresponding native beliefs. The Christian concept of heaven has evidently been fused with the aboriginal belief in a "Village of the Supernaturals" where the souls of shamans live an ideal life after death. Although well-known native legends attribute the creation of mankind and the origin of fire, manioc, cotton, and maize to powerful culture heroes, many Tenetehara also speak of "Tupan (their name for the Christian God) who lives in the sky and who created all things." [1] There is no conflict between the two beliefs in the mind of the Tenetehara, for he is seldom called upon for philosophical discussion of the origin of man and of the world. The main body of Christian dogma, however, has been rejected. The Tenetehara is faced each day with such mundane matters as sickness, difficulties at childbirth, bad luck at hunting, and loss of crops, and for relief from these sorrows he never thinks to turn to Tupan. Instead, he attributes his difficulties to native supernaturals—to *azang*, the disembodied souls of the dead, to Ywan, a water diety, and to Marana ýwa, a forest demon. To control a multitude of dangerous and malevolent supernaturals, the

[1] Tupan is sometimes identified with Christ. In one story related to us, Zuruparí (the Devil) carried off Tupan (Christ) and caused his death. Tupan returned from the grave "and all the animals sang to see him alive again." In another story relating to Tupan's birth, José, his father, beat his wife when he returned from a long journey to find her pregnant.

Tenetehara turns to his native shamans. Modern Tenetehara religion contains a few accretions of Christian origin but the core of their religion has remained intact since aboriginal times.

Native ceremonials, on the other hand, tend to be neglected. Nowadays, the Tenetehara cannot afford to spend many days in preparing for and in celebrating lengthy festivals. The additional burden of growing crops and collecting forest products for market leaves little time for such activities. In the conflict between greater material desires and lengthy ceremonials, the ceremonials are losing out. A concrete example of this process occurred in a village on the upper Pindaré during one of our visits. One day the young men of the village began the dances of the Maize Festival. The village chief, Camirang, was angry. Once this dance was started, he explained, it must be performed each two or three days until maize is ripe (a matter of two months). If the dance is abandoned, dangerous supernaturals might send winds to destroy the gardens or bring sickness upon the people of the village. Camirang had planned to collect copaíba oil during this period for sale to Brazilian traders, and the time lost with the Maize Ceremony would make this impossible. Not one of the villages on the Pindaré River had celebrated the Honey Feast for a number of years for this same reason. Many whole days for several months must be devoted to collecting wild honey in preparation for this ceremony and the modern Tenetehara cannot afford the time. Yet, when the Tenetehara do celebrate a native ceremony, they take care to carry it out with respect and in the appropriate season. Despite his anger, Camirang was worried when the young men abandoned the Maize Ceremony before the maize was ripe, and the Indians of another village flatly refused to sing Honey Feast music for us during the rainy season even though we offered tempting payment. It was the wrong season, they explained, and singing such music without celebrating the entire feast might bring supernatural punishment. Native ceremonials are neglected not because people no longer believe in their power or because they do not find them attractive as amusement, but simply because the stress of modern economic conditions does not allow sufficient time for them.

TENETEHARA SUPERNATURALS

Although the Tenetehara constantly refer to all supernaturals by the generic term *karowára,* they recognize at least four distinct categories among them, namely: the creators or culture heroes, who are credited with creating and transforming the world; the owners of the forest and of the water; the *azang,* the ghosts of the dead; and the spirits of animals which inhabit the forest. While the culture heroes are supernaturals, they are not, however, deities which at present must be respected and placated by man; rather, they are creators whose legendary activities explain the origin of things and of human knowledge. Tenetehara mythology describes them as men with great supernatural attributes. They lived for a time on earth and then they left to live forever in the "Village of the Gods" (*Karowára nekwahdo*).[2] The culture heroes made man, equipped him with his knowledge and brought him the necessities of life. By now, however, they no longer control man nor the world in which he lives.

The most important figure among these heroes was Maíra.[3] According to legend, he came to the earth in search of the "Beautiful Land" (*Ywý poráng*). Once he located this ideal spot, he created man and woman. This original pair lived in peace under ideal conditions until Ywan, the water deity, surreptitiously began to have sexual relations with the woman. Man was innocent of sex until Maíra told him what was taking place and instructed him to kill the water spirit (see p. 131). Then, he taught man and woman to procreate and he said, "Now, you will make a child and you will die. Later, when your child has a child, he will die, too." [4] Maíra taught men how to plant manioc and how to make flour of it. At first, manioc planted itself and it grew and ripened in one day, but because mankind did not believe Maíra, he was angry and he made manioc grow slowly. Now mankind waits the entire wet season

---

[2] *Karowára nekwahdo* is also sometimes called *Tupanekwahdo,* the village of Tupan, and equated with the Christian concept of heaven.

[3] His name is sometimes used as a common noun to mean "a powerful shaman."

[4] The "Beautiful Land" has been a part of Tupí-Guaraní mythology since aboriginal times and the Tupí migrations and religious revivals which took place during the years following Portuguese colonization were motivated by a desire to reach this mythical land of the culture heroes (see Metraux, *La Réligion des Tupinambá,* pp. 201–224). The modern Tenetehara, however, have obviously merged the Christian idea of the Garden of Eden and the original sin of Adam and Eve with the aboriginal concept of the "Beautiful Land" and the creation of man by Maíra.

between planting and harvest of manioc, and men must perform the backbreaking task of planting and digging up the tubers. Maíra also brought cotton and taught people how to make hammocks; he stole fire from the vultures and taught men to roast meat instead of eating it dried in the sun. Soon, Maíra wearied of living with men and he retired to the "Village of the Gods"; there he still lives an ideal life with an abundance of food which grows without being cultivated. Before Maíra came to us, the Tenetehara say, "Men did not know anything. Only Maíra knew."

Another hero, Mokwaní, stole night from the Old Woman who lived in the forest so the Tenetehara would not have to sleep in eternal daylight. Still another, Aruwé, taught them how to perform the Honey Feast according to the ritual he learned while visiting the village of the jaguars. Second only to Maíra, however, as a culture bearer and creator is Tupan. Although the missionaries used this name for their Christian God, Tupan is also a native culture hero. He appears in myth as a great shaman and as "a companion of Maíra." The creation of the moon, the sun, the winds, the rain, the thunder, and the animals of the forest is said to have been the work of Tupan. Among the extinct Tupinambá of the Brazilian coast, who shared many of the same culture heroes, Tupan was a secondary supernatural whose principal function was to travel from east to west causing thunders and lightning, and he was not credited with the creative acts of the more important culture heroes.[5] Although we have no information as to Tenetehara beliefs regarding Tupan in premissionary times, it is probable that the equation of Tupan with the Christian God has tended to emphasize his importance as a creator and as a culture hero among the modern Tenetehara.[6]

Finally, while these are not ancestral culture heroes, the Tenetehara attribute to the forest demons called Zuruparí the creation of bothersome insects and reptiles—mosquitos and gnats, snakes, and

[5] Metraux, *La Réligion des Tupinambá*, pp. 52–56. Metraux points out that the early missionaries to Brazil used the word Tupan for the Christian God and it became the common translation for God in the "lingua geral," the form of Tupí language used throughout Brazil by missionaries and which was more commonly spoken than Portuguese in the Brazilian hinterland until the early nineteenth century.

[6] Other heroes appear in Tenetehara mythology (see Chapter VI), such as the twins Maíra yra and Mukwura yra, but they have the roles of powerful and astute men rather than creators or culture bearers.

poisonous spiders and centipedes. While these demons are thought to have lived contemporaneously with the great culture heroes, they also continue to live today, deep in the forest near a lake. They are described as small manlike creatures entirely covered with hair and completely invulnerable to a bullet or an arrow, except in the navel. The Tenetehara have obviously taken over these beliefs in Zurupari from their Brazilian neighbors. Just as Tupan was identified as God by the missionaries, Zurupari,[7] originally a native supernatural of the coastal Tupí, was equated with the devil. The Zurupari became an active figure in Brazilian folklore, and the Brazilian neighbors of the Tenetehara tell of the encounters of hunters in the deep forest with such demons. The modern Tenetehara identify them with the Christian devil and profess to be very much afraid of them, but in all stories of Zurupari told to us by Indians the victims were always Brazilians.

In contrast to the creator culture heroes, the Owner of the Forest (Marana ẏwa) and the Owner of the Water (Ywan) are active supernatural powers to be feared and respected. Both are malevolent and both punish offenders by causing sickness, bad luck in hunting and fishing, insanity, and general misfortune. Each is the owner and protector of its domain—Marana ẏwa owns the forest and all animals living in it, and Ywan owns the rivers and lakes and water life. They are therefore often referred to as *ywira zára* (*ywira*, forest; *zára*, owner) and as *y zára* (*y*, water; *zára*, owner). Both are described as male deities. In a legend, Ywan is described as a male spirit which rises out of the water to teach the first woman about sexual intercourse; [8] the Tenetehara describe Marana ẏwa as a small man with tangled hair and enormous testicles who lives deep in the forest. None of our informants had actually seen him, but several men had heard him shouting or singing in the distance and they were ready to tell us of the many instances when Marana ẏwa had punished one of their companions. For example, a young man who lived in the village of Jacaré killed a monkey one day when he was hunting. He already had more meat than he could use, but he decided to roast the monkey and take it back to his village. He noticed that the

---

[7] Especially in the Amazon region this demon is sometimes called Yurupari.

[8] Yet the local Brazilian identify Ywan with "the Water Mother," a water demon of local Brazilian folklore.

monkey jumped and jerked while it was being cooked. This was strange, but he paid little attention to the fact at the time. He remained in the forest for several days to hunt and then, suddenly, he came down with an attack of fever and could not find his way back to his village. Five days later his companions found him wandering half-crazed in the forest and had to drag him back to the village by brute force. "Marana ẏwa puts a piece of leaf inside one's body and one goes crazy," it was explained. "Only a shaman can bring one back to his senses."

Marana ẏwa punishes men for unnecessarily killing his animals and for wanton destruction of his forests. He is most frequently cast in the special role of the protector of wild pigs. A Tenetehara myth about this tells how Tupan transformed all the people of one village into pigs and put them under the care of his nephew, Marana ẏwa. He has always therefore given special protection to wild pigs, venting his anger on Tenetehara hunters who kill them in large numbers especially during the rainy season when large bands are trapped by the flooded low forests (see p. 57). Marana ẏwa also has a special predilection for the copaíba tree. When the trees grow dry with age, it is because Marana ẏwa has taken away the oil and placed it in a younger tree. He watches the men as they collect copaíba oil. If they cut too deeply into the bark when tapping the trees, he makes them fall ill or confuses them so they become hopelessly lost in the forest.[9]

The Owner of Water also punishes transgressors, even those who have offended unwittingly. A typical instance involved one of our Tenetehara companions during a trip up the Pindaré River in 1942. After killing and skinning a peccary, he went to a near-by stream to wash the blood from his hands. That evening he had a painful headache. It was obvious that Ywan had sent a foreign body [10] into

[9] The Brazilian neighbors of the Tenetehara identify Marana ẏwa with Curupira, a malicious goblin who haunts the forests and lures hunters from the path so they will be lost. Their description of Curupira differs from the Indian description of Marana ẏwa only in that Curupira's feet are said to be turned backwards on his body. The Brazilians believe in still another forest demon called *Kopé-lobo*. He, too, attacks lonely hunters in the forest, and he is believed to have the face of a jaguar and sharp spikes for arms and legs. All of these forest demons, Zurupari, Curupira, and Kopé-lobo of Brazilian folk belief were borrowed at an early period of Brazilian history from Indian religions, and in Marana ẏwa we have the Tenetehara aboriginal equivalent.

[10] See p. 110 for a description of such intrusive objects (*ymaé*) which the supernatural place in a person's body to cause illness.

the hunter's head as punishment for contaminating the stream. Although his headache was cured by a shaman in one of the upper Pindaré villages, he nevertheless suffered several months from bad luck in fishing because he had offended Ywan. The Tenetehara attribute illness to Ywan more than to any other supernatural, and at almost all shamanistic exhibitions and cures which took place in our presence this water spirit was invoked. Ywan is perhaps the most dangerous of all the supernaturals.

According to the Tenetehara, both men and animals have spirits which are distinct from the body and which live on after death. The spirits of human beings are called *ekwe* and the spirits of animals are referred to as *piwára*. After death of the body, both *ekwe* and *piwára* may become dangerous or malevolent supernaturals causing illness and death to the living Tenetehara. They must be controlled by shamans. Following a normal death, the *ekwe* of the human being is stated to live on in the "Village of the Gods" where the great culture heroes reside. There, the human soul or spirit follows a second life similar to that on earth, but in ideal conditions. Food is plentiful, there is no hard work, and no one is ever sick. This concept of an ideal afterlife is similar to the Christian idea of heaven and it is, at least partially, a belief acquired from Christian missionaries. The *ekwe* of people, however, who die from sorcery or who have broken tribal regulations such as those governing incest or birth, do not go to the "Village of the Gods." Instead, they become ghosts or errant spirits, called *azang* by the Tenetehara. Among other Tupí tribes there is a belief that shamans or other leaders go to live after death in a village where conditions are ideal, whereas the spirits of ordinary people become errant ghosts. In aboriginal times the Tenetehara probably shared this widespread Tupí belief that the dead become wandering spirits and that the ideal afterlife was reserved for shamans.

Such ghosts may be met in the forest. They prefer, however, to remain near cemeteries where their bodies were buried; thus the Tenetehara will never pass a cemetery after sunset if it can be avoided. In fact, the Indians do not like to leave the confines of the village after dusk at all, for fear of meeting the spirits of the dead. These ghosts, *azang*, are believed to be the owners of maize and to control the growth of maize. In mythology the twins Maíra yra and

Mukwura yra encounter a type of *azang* which have trailing hair, and others with sharp arms "like axes."

People frequently encounter ghosts and always become ill as a result. One man told us that one evening at dusk in the forest just outside the village he saw a short creature, entirely covered with hair. He was certain that it was a ghost. He was almost paralyzed with fear and for a moment was unable to run. As soon as he arrived home he felt ill. The shaman who came to cure him confirmed his suspicion—it was an *azang* that he saw in the forest. Another man, Raimundo, told us of an encounter with a woman ghost (*azang-kuzā*) who had red eyes that glowed like balls of fire. Raimundo, who was somewhat of a braggart, said that he was not afraid and ran after the ghost. According to his story, the ghost fled and nothing happened to him at all. Raimundo had often seen an *azang* in his dreams and he said they looked like people. Others, however, told us that *azang* were ugly and that most people are deathly afraid of them. One family rushed in panic from the "center" near the village of Januaria where they were preparing manioc flour because they heard groans coming from the direction of old house sites. The *azang* of the people who had lived in these houses and who had been buried near by were making the noise, they said. Women faint immediately when they meet a ghost and must be treated by a shaman without delay or they may die.

Azang sometimes appear to people in the form of animals.[11] Such animals cannot be distinguished from others except when a hunter's arrow or rifle shot fails to harm them, or when some strange occurrence warns the hunters that they have met a ghost, not an animal. One day, for example, João and Manuel Viana from the village of Januaria were hunting in the forest with dogs. The dogs took up the trail of a paca and followed it into its hole. The two hunters made a fire to smoke out the paca, but without success. Then they decided to dig the animal out, but after much digging they found only a dead forest rat. They were certain, therefore, that the dogs had seen

[11] Our informants disagreed somewhat regarding the transformation of *azang* into a toad, a deer, or a tapir. We were told by most informants that *azang* could appear in the form of any animal, and several incidents were related in which *azang* appeared specifically as a deer or as a tapir. Other informants, however, said that when the spirits of the *kururú*—the toad, the deer and the tapir—appeared to men as an animal, it was the spirit of the *animal itself*, not of a human ghost in animal form.

an *azang* in the form of a paca. On another occasion, a Tenetehara hunter dug an armadillo out of its hole and found a string of beads around the animal's neck. The hunter knew then that it was a ghost and left the armadillo where he found it. He ran back to the village in fear.

According to Manuel Viana, his brother-in-law once shot at a tapir from a distance of only three or four meters, but the animal ran off into the bush. Then he heard a voice moaning, "Oh! Do you want to kill me?" The man went home and lay in his hammock trying to imagine what had happened. He became sad and complained that he could still hear the moans of the tapir. He said he had shot a tapir that was like a Tenetehara. He came down with fever and a day or two afterwards he died. People whose death is caused by an encounter with an *azang* in animal form also become ghosts themselves. The Tenetehara told us of a young man who died of a lingering illness after an encounter with a ghost in the form of a tapir. Several months later his relatives saw his ghost when they passed by his grave late one evening. "His head was a man's and the body was that of a tapir," they said.

José Viana told us of an encounter with an *azang* which was part man and part animal. Many years ago, several men of the village had gone out to hunt. In an unusually dense part of the forest they saw a deer and heard a human voice. When they came closer, they saw that it was an *azang*. The body and feet had the form of a deer, but the upper parts were human. They returned to the village and told their story. The next day others from the village went to the same spot, out of curiosity. They, too, saw the *azang*, half animal and half man. On the third day, when the people went back again a deer was lying quietly on the spot. They left at once. It was an *azang* which had transformed itself, first into a half man–half deer, and then, completely into a deer.

Several Indians, who had been perhaps more exposed than others to Christianity, told us that one is more apt to meet *azang* during Easter week and that, therefore, it is better not to hunt during this period.[12] Miguel, however, who lived in the village of Januaria during our visit in 1942, paid no attention to this warning. He went

[12] Only a small number of Indians living in villages near Brazilian settlements had ever heard of Easter week; nothing is known of it on the upper Pindaré.

hunting during Easter week and shot a guariba monkey. He said
that he heard the monkey moan like a human being. "I felt my
head grow" (in fear), he explained, and he fled. He said that he
might have been attacked by the *azang* if he had stayed near by. For
some reason, unaccountable to Miguel, he was not sick as a result
of his encounter.

Piwára, animal spirits, also live on after their death. A few small
animals, such as the agouti, several of the smaller species of fish,
and small birds [13] are thought to be exceptions and do not have
piwára. Spirits of animals are malevolent toward mankind. They
protect their own species against hunters, causing sickness and other
harm to the Tenetehara. When a man or his wife breaks the regulations on hunting and eating of certain birds and animals imposed
upon them during pregnancy or during early infancy of their child,
the *piwára* may either make the parents ill or cause mental defi-
ciency or disfigurement in their offspring. Whenever a preadolescent boy or girl eats meat which is prohibited before the puberty
ceremony, the *piwára* may cause illness or insanity. The Tenetehara
relate numerous cases of the effects of these spirits on children. A
typical case was that of two young boys who became crazy and then
died because they had eaten meat of the mutum fowl before the
puberty ceremony.

In daily life, sickness is frequently attributed to the spirits of
animals, since hunters often involuntarily offend animals. It is not
difficult for the Tenetehara, or for their shamans, to determine
which animal spirit has caused the illness, since each manifests itself
in a special manner. For example, the *piwára* of the jacamin fowl
places the seed of the *babassú* palm in the body of the victim; the
tapir spirit places a *bacuri* nut in the lumbar region or in the thorax
of the victim. The spirit of the tree sloth places a leaf in the knee
or the foot of the sick person. The toucan spirit places a *jussára* seed
in the head and one species of the hawk sends the tail of small lizard
to enter the body.

Some animals have particularly strong and malignant *piwára.*
Among these are the tapir, the *kururú*-toad, the hawk, and the
jaguar. For this reason, the Tenetehara do not as a rule kill hawks.

[13] The *sabiá* (*Turdida*) is an example of birds which do not have spirits, and the
piranha (*Serrasalmo*) and the *piau* (*Leporinus frederici*) of fish.

Sabino killed one and told no one what he had done. The next day he became ill with a high fever. A shaman was called and he tried to cure Sabino, but without success. Finally, when it looked as if the young man would die, he told one of his relatives what he had done. Then he became delirious and in his delirium he kept saying that he saw the *piwára* of a hawk sitting near his hammock. Another shaman who was able to "call" the hawk spirit was asked to treat Sabino. He was able to extract the object which the hawk spirit had put into Sabino's body, and Sabino recovered.

The jaguar spirit seems to have unique powers; it is said to enter into other animals, which then have the strong supernatural force peculiar to the jaguar. The animal thus entered is said to take on some morphologic characteristics of the jaguar. A tapir, for example, with the jaguar spirit (called a *tapiíra-zawáre* by the Tenetehara) has "legs like a tapir, feet of the jaguar and the *piwára* of a jaguar." Like the *azang*, the jaguar *piwára* often appears to hunters in the form of another animal. José Viana told us the following incident: "My father told me that one time he was deep in the forest with several companions collecting copaíba oil. They made camp early and the group went out to hunt. My father's brother-in-law saw a guariba monkey. He climbed a tree to get near to the monkey and shot it with his rifle. The monkey was wounded and it began to moan like a man. It put his hands over his head and suddenly it disappeared all at once." The hunters went back to the camp. "In less than one day my father's brother-in-law died." José explained that this was a guariba monkey with a jaguar *piwára*. One of the hunters noticed that it had especially feline facial characteristics. Another hunter told us that he had encountered a coati with "a face of a jaguar." He told that he did not try to kill it because he recognized it at once as a *coati-zawáre* (coati-jaguar). Our informants were not especially clear as to how it came about that the jaguar *piwára* enters into and takes on the forms of animals. They were certain, however, that such animals exist, and certain of great dangers to the hunters who chance to encounter them.

SHAMANISM

The power and importance of a Tenetehara *pazé*, or shaman, is in direct relation to the number of supernaturals he is able to control, that is, the number of spirits he is able to "call." A shaman "calls" a supernatural by dancing and singing the songs distinctive to that supernatural and as he dances and sings, he smokes tobacco in a large tubular cigar. Finally the spirit comes to him and is said to enter into the body of the shaman. While the shaman is thus possessed by the supernatural spirit, his reactions are characteristic of that spirit. Yet he is not completely in its power; rather, the shaman controls the supernatural during this time and is able to cure the disease provoked by it and to protect the people against any evil result it may cause.

The supernaturals most commonly "called" by Tenetehara shamans nowadays are Ywan, the water spirit; *azang*, the ghosts of the dead, and the spirits of such animals as the monkey, the opossum, and the deer. Only a few shamans are able to "call" such strong spirits as the hawk and *kururú*-toad; so far as we know, there are no modern *pazé* so powerful as to be able to "call" Marana ýwa, the Owner of the Forest, or the spirit of the jaguar. The *piwára* of almost any animal may be "called" by shamans. Each shaman knows the songs and the dance and is able to "call" a series of supernaturals. The shaman Joãozinho, for example, one of the most famous on the middle Pindaré, was able to "call" the spirit of the lizard, the opossum, the butterfly, the *kururú*-toad, the hawk, Ywan, and *azang*. Massa, the strongest shaman in the village of Januaria, was able to enter into rapport only with Ywan, *azang,* and the spirit of the opossum; while an old and powerful shaman who lived on the upper Pindaré was able to "call" *piwára* of many animals, including the deer, the *kururú*-toad, the hawk, as well as Ywan and *azang.* Young men who had been shamans only a short time have only one or two spirits which will come to them at their bidding.

Although theoretically both men and women may become a *pazé* among the Tenetehara, there were no female shamans in any of the Pindaré villages. Few adults had ever seen one, and one who lived on the Gurupí River was said not to be particularly powerful. On the other hand, almost all Tenetehara men attempt at one time or another during their youth to acquire the powers of shamanism. Only a few, however, show aptitude, and very few ever acquire the ability to "call" and to be possessed by the supernatural. A young man who wishes to become a shaman must learn from a recognized

shaman. He assists the older man during cures, learns the songs of
particular spirits by singing with the shaman, and if he shows any
aptitude, the spirits "called" by the older man often possess the
novice also. Because it is difficult to find a shaman who controls a
large number of spirits and who is willing to teach his songs, many
young men travel to distant villages, attracted by well-known prac-
titioners who will agree to accept them as novices. Mature and experienced Tenetehara shamans remember the famous *pazé* from
whom they learned to "call" each specific supernatural, and they
tell of their travels from village to village acquiring control over
additional spirits. At the time of our visits only two shamans in the
entire Pindaré region were able to "call" the spirit of the *kururú-*
toad; any young man who wished to learn the appropriate songs
and dance had to travel to their villages. Novices do not pay their
teachers, but merely by promising to teach young men, well-known
shamans draw workers into their extended family groups.

CURING

The Tenetehara believe that all misfortune, illness, and death
have supernatural causes. Respiratory diseases, malaria, and hook-
worm are known to have been acquired through contact with Brazilians and, therefore, not to result directly from supernatural
actions; yet when death results from one of these diseases, the Tenetehara feel certain there must have been some supernatural reason
as well.[14] In general, all other diseases are thought to be punishment
even for such unconscious and involuntary offenses as seeing a dead
hawk. If one glances at a dead hawk, the spirit may well follow the
unfortunate individual, causing his illness or even his death. Such
illness results directly, according to the Tenetehara, from an extraneous object or thing, called *ymaé,* which the supernatural places
in the body of the victim. *Ymaé* are of a wide variety of forms and

[14] At the Indian Post and in all the villages on the Pindaré, the Indians asked for
medicine (quinine, purgatives, and vermifuges) yet this did not prevent them from
calling on their shamans at the same time. Shamans told us that medicines help cure
unimportant illnesses. Even the shamans themselves took the medicine we gave them.
On one occasion, the stepfather of a young boy who was suffering from pneumonia
asked us for medicine and arranged for the *pazé* to treat the boy the same night. He
explained that the medicine might help cure the boy, but unless the shaman took out
the supernatural cause of the illness the medicine would be of little use.

substances and each is distinctive of the supernatural from which it originates. Such objects as seeds, forest fruits, pieces of bone, pieces of wood, splinters of glass, and long ribbon-like fabrics are the characteristic *ymaé* of certain spirits. Also, depending upon the particular supernatural, the *ymaé* enters into the body of the victim at specific points. The *ymaé* of the Owner of Water, Ywan, is a bit of ribbon-like fabric, and it always enters into the head of the person.

Since a shaman can only cure an illness caused by a supernatural which he is able to "call," he will usually attribute a mild disease to one of these. In order to discover which supernatural it is, he questions the patient carefully as to his activities during the last few days. From what the patient tells him, he is sometimes able to identify the spirit and to discover how and when the patient offended it. Obviously the cure will be unsuccessful if an incorrect diagnosis has been made and the shaman has not "called" the right supernatural.

Unless the patient is seriously ill and needs immediate attention, a Tenetehara shaman performs his cure at night, after the day's work has been done and when, incidentally, he will be assured of an audience. He begins his cure by singing the songs of the appropriate supernatural, beating out the rhythm with the rattle. He dances as he sings and the family of the patient as well as any bystanders who are attracted by the music sometimes dance with him. He stops from time to time to take deep drags on a long cigar made of native tobacco rolled in *tawari* bark. He soon becomes intoxicated from the smoke combined with the rhythm of the song and the dance. This process is known as "calling" the spirit. The spirit responds only to its distinctive songs and he himself is only prepared to receive the spirit after gulping large quantities of tobacco smoke. Suddenly the shaman staggers back a few steps, sometimes grasping his chest to indicate that the spirit has come to him and has entered into his body. Under the influence of the spirit, the style of dancing changes. When a shaman is possessed by the spirit of the opossum, for example, he jumps about with his feet together in a hopping motion. During this time the "spirit is strong" and the shaman goes into a trance; sometimes the spirit is too "strong" and he falls unconscious to the ground. During the trance, while he is possessed by his spirit, the cure, properly speaking, takes place.[15] Under the influence of Ywan, for instance, a shaman can extract the *ymaé* introduced into the victim's body by Ywan.

A description of a typical cure will perhaps give a better picture of the process. The patient sat on a bench. The *pazé*, once he was possessed by the spirit, blew smoke over his own hands and then over the patient's body. Then, kneeling down, he massaged the patient's chest and throat toward a point near the thorax region, as if bringing together or collecting something in one point. Again he blew smoke over his own hands, and then squeezed his own fingers toward the extremity as if trying to draw out some substance from them. He then lifted the patient's arms, embraced him, and rubbed himself against the patient's body, as if seeking to draw the extraneous object into his own body.[16] He was not successful in extracting the *ymaé* in this manner, so he began to massage again, and bending over the patient he began to suck violently on a spot on his shoulder, stopping now and again to puff on his cigar. Suddenly he stood up and tried to vomit. After repeating this process several times, he cleared his throat violently and he spat something into his hands. He had been successful in extracting the "object" and the cure was a success. In none of the cures which we witnessed did a shaman actually show the "object" that had been removed. In each case he simply explained to the audience what he had extracted from the sick man's body and everyone seemed satisfied with his statement. Powerful shamans, however, are said to show the *ymaé* to the people, and several people have "objects" which shamans are supposed to have taken from their bodies during an illness.[17]

The shaman often describes his own reactions during the cure for

[15] An old man told us that in former times a few shamans were able to cure without calling a spirit, merely by blowing smoke over the patient.

[16] We were warned that the shaman would not attempt to take the *ymaé* into his body if the patient was seriously ill. On another occasion, during the dance of the Maize Festival, we saw two shamans hold a sick child between their bodies so that the *ymaé* would pass into one of them. One of the shamans fell to the ground unconscious from the *ymaé* which had entered his body. The other shaman returned the child to its mother and staggered and fell unconscious too. This is considered a very dangerous method of treatment.

[17] We were told that the woman *pazé* who lived in one of the Tenetehara villages on the Gurupí River did not use sucking to extract the *ymaé*. She blew smoke from a cigar, sang, was possessed by the spirits, and massaged the *ymaé* to one point on the patient's body. Then her husband, who was also a shaman, sucked out the object. It was not clear whether or not this was the usual practice for a woman shaman.

the benefit of the audience and, if it is a successful cure, he retells it many times. Joãozinho was proud of his successful treatment of Sabino and told of it with considerable pride. "One puffs hard on a cigar," he explained, "forcing smoke deep into one's stomach. When one smokes a great deal on the cigar, one becomes weak and cannot sing any more. Next day I do not feel sick because I vomit all the smoke out of my stomach. If any smoke remains in my stomach it is bad for me. When I have many people to cure, I do not eat much, I only drink water. When I cured Sabino, I ate only early in the morning. When one eats in the evening [before the curing session], one's mouth is bad for the cigar." Continuing his explanation, Joãozinho told us "the *karowára* [supernatural] had covered his [Sabino's] head with a substance which only I could see. Did you not see me ask him, 'Who am I?' Many people asked him if he recognized them. He [Sabino] could see nothing. He did not recognize anyone." Joãozinho explained that he first removed this invisible substance by massaging it away, for it "was very dangerous" and if he had not removed it, the patient might have been left insane. Then, says Joãozinho, "I sucked until the *ymaé* entered into my body, then I vomited the *ymaé* from my mouth. I held it with my hands, then I threw it away like this [gesture of rubbing one hand against the other] and no one saw it."

Sometimes a shaman finds that he had made an erroneous diagnosis and cannot extract the "object" under the influence of the supernatural he has "called." He then sings, sending the first spirit away and calling another. At one curing session at the village of Camirang, we watched a shaman call and be possessed with several spirits—the opossum, the porcupine, Ywan, and, finally, a ghost. He called all of these in an effort to cure one patient. Also, frequently the supernatural becomes too powerful for a shaman and he falls inert to the ground and another shaman must be called to send his spirit away by blowing smoke over the unconscious body of his companion. All Tenetehara shamans claim that they remember nothing of such trances.

Cures are frequently performed by several shamans and for the benefit of several patients at the same time. At the village of Januaria, the two principal shamans, Massá and Inacinho, frequently worked together, on one occasion curing four patients in the same evening. Early in the evening they began to sing together, seated side by side on a log and stamping out the rhythm with one foot. One of them kept time with a rattle. Finally, after a good-sized audience had gathered, they lighted their cigars and stood up facing the group. They inhaled deeply until they coughed violently, suffocated by the smoke in their lungs. They began dancing and singing the songs of Ywan, the water spirit. The audience joined in the chorus. After about an hour and a half of singing and smoking, Massá indicated that he had received the spirit. He suddenly staggered backwards, putting his hands to his chest, then continued his song. "Now it is not the voice of Massá singing; it is the voice of Ywan," we were told. Massá, obviously in a trance state, began to rub the glowing end of his cigar over his chest and arms, scattering sparks in all directions. As soon as he smothered one cigar in this manner, his wife brought him a freshly lighted one. Soon Inacinho was also possessed by Ywan. Patients were brought forth and Massá, the stronger of the two shamans, went from one to the other blowing smoke over their bodies. One by one he massaged their heads and finally sucked on the neck, slightly below the chin, of each patient. The other shaman continued singing and dancing while his companion worked. Then Massá moved away from the group, rubbing his hands together as if he were throwing away the *ymaé* extracted from the patient's body.[18]

Several other curing sessions which we witnessed in the upper Pindaré villages were primarily exhibitions of power and prowess on the part of the shamans and were only secondarily for curing. On such occasions, four, five or even six shamans sang and called their spirits, and young novices danced and sang alongside them attempting also to call the supernaturals. One such session took place late one night at the village of Camirang. Two shamans began calling the opossum spirit, while another seated near by marked time for them with the rattle. Within a short time, most of the villagers had gathered around them in the open plaza.[19] The women formed in

[18] One of the women treated at this time was not herself ill; it was explained to us that she was taking the place of her ailing infant son who was too young to be treated himself. (See p. 63 for physiological tie between mother and father and young children.)

[19] In general, shamanistic cures take place inside of a house, but when more than one or two shamans take place, it is customary to move out of the house into the open plaza.

a group separate from the men, sitting on mats on the ground. The men sat alongside the shamans on a long bench. A line of men kept time to the song by stamping out the off beat. The shamans rose and began dancing and they continued for over an hour, stopping now and again to puff deeply on their cigars. While doing so, they faced away from the audience, holding the cigars to their mouths with both hands and taking in great gulps of smoke. Then, suddenly blowing instead of drawing on the cigar, they sent streams of sparks into the night. Soon, both shamans were possessed by the opossum spirit. They rubbed the burning ends of the cigar over their arms and chests with such vigor that live embers showered their entire bodies. A third shaman joined the dance, and then a fourth stood up and joined them. Several young novices formed a group and accompanied the shamans in singing. Each novice began to swallow smoke from large cigars handed him by the dancing shamans. The novices drew in and blew out on the cigars and in a short time they were all unsteady on their feet, in a very receptive condition for a spirit; but on this particular evening none of them were possessed. During other sessions which we attended, however, novices were possessed by the spirits which the shaman had "called."

Antonio, the shaman who had joined the session somewhat late, suddenly received the spirit of the opossum. He began to dance violently in short hops, his torso bent forward, and his knees together—a style typical of the opossum spirit. He interrupted his dancing several times and ran quickly from one side of the plaza to the other as if he were trying to escape something. Suddenly, he fell unconscious to the ground, his arms extended, his fists closed and his body rigid. No one went to help him; his wife rescued his cigar which had fallen several feet away from him. After some fifteen minutes, he slowly regained consciousness and stood up and began to dance again. Soon the spirit left and there was a short pause in the session.

After a few minutes' rest the shamans began to "call" other spirits. In quick succession, they were possessed by the spirits of the porcupine, of the rat, and of Ywan. While the other shamans were singing for the rat spirit, Antonio received without warning the spirit of the capuchin monkey. The audience knew at once which spirit had possessed him because he began to dance with his arms hanging loosely from his shoulders and from time to time emitted a strange, shrill laugh in imitation of the call of the capuchin monkey. Finally, he fell to the ground in a deep trance. "The supernatural was too strong for him," we were told. After a few minutes, he struggled to get to his feet but he was only able to support himself in a sitting position. He sat there weaving back and forth, but continuing to sing the song of the capuchin monkey. A young novice brought him a new cigar. After a while, the song of the capuchin monkey died away and Antonio was able to stand up. During this portion of the session, the attention of the audience was focused on Antonio and the other shamans abandoned their songs to join him in the song of the capuchin monkey.

Soon another shaman, Inácio, began to call *azang* and after a few minutes he put his hands to his chest to show that the spirit had entered his body. He increased the rhythm of his song and began to dance in a circle, which indicated that the spirit was an *azang*. He rubbed his chest and arms with the burning end of the cigar. Then a woman approached Inácio with a gourd filled with raw tapioca flour mixed with water. Holding the gourd in his hands, he danced in circles and finally stopped in front of the audience. A man stepped out from the audience and blew tobacco smoke over the gourd and the tapioca flour. Then Inácio noisily drank down the contents of the gourd without pausing for a breath. Raw tapioca, it was explained, is the food of the *azang*. The *azang* which possessed Inácio was hungry and had called for food.

Following this performance there was an intermission. It was midnight, and many people in the audience wandered to their houses to drink *chibé* (manioc flour mixed with water). Fresh cigars were prepared and the shamans sat on the benches resting. Soon one of them picked up a rattle and, without singing, began to beat time. The villagers returned to the plaza to watch. Then, a shaman began slowly to sing the songs of the water deity, Ywan. Two other shamans and several novices joined in and the audience took up the chorus. During the early part of the evening, the audience had simply kept time to the music while sitting by, stamping with one foot. Now the men stood up and formed in a line. They danced to the music, stamping heavily with the right foot. The women danced in pairs, more or less in a line facing the men. The shamans danced between the two lines, which moved back and forth, enclosing and then withdrawing from the shamans. Suddenly a shaman was possessed with Ywan and fell unconscious to the ground. The dancing continued. No one bothered to help him. After a few minutes he regained his feet and continued singing to Ywan. He danced toward a woman who was sitting in the plaza holding her sick two-year-old child in her arms. He stopped near her, blew smoke over the child, and began to suck on the child's chest. Then he vomited into his hands and danced facing the river, throwing away the *ymaé* that had caused the child to be ill.

During this session, which lasted at least five hours, several cures were performed. Now and again the shamans stopped singing and blew smoke over someone to cure minor pains or sores. It was obvious, however, that the principal motive of the evening was not to cure but to exhibit their powers. Through such exhibitions a shaman increases his prestige by showing the number of spirits which he controls.

Because there were only two shamans in the entire Pindaré region able to "call" the dangerous spirit of the *kururú*-toad, we did not have an opportunity to see it done. The *kururú*-toad spirit and the jaguar spirit are said to be the most dangerous of all supernaturals, and no modern shaman controls the jaguar spirit. When a shaman is possessed by the *kururú*-toad, he dances over burning coals, holds glowing coals in his hands, and sometimes swallows them. H. E. Snethlage describes a "festival of the *kururú*" witnessed in a Tenetehara village on the Grajaú River in 1925. This was without doubt a shamanistic exhibition during which a powerful shaman "called" the spirit of the *kururú*-toad. Snethlage writes:

Among the dances I want to describe in more detail is the *kururú* dance which I witnessed in the village of the Guajajara [Tenetehara] on the Grajaú River. The chieftain and I were conversing sitting on a tree trunk in front of a hut. Around us there were men and women and children of the small village. The night was clear and starry; the moon had just risen, throwing over us its silvery beams. My neighbor [the chieftain] began to sing, beating time with his feet to the rhythm of the music and other voices joined in the music which increased and decreased in intensity. A pause. The song began again; when it grew in intensity the chieftain stood up and danced several steps and sat down again. Then they brought him an enormous cigar from which he took several puffs. Following this he repeated his dance with more vivacity while I took the opportunity to try out the cigar. I did not like it very well. The nerves of my vocal cavities became insensitive. The chieftain, however, took advantage of each pause in the dance, which was becoming wilder each moment, to smoke intensely. He needed this, as will be shown by what followed. He stirred up the fire around which the dark, misty figures jumped in complete intoxication. Suddenly, the chieftain fell on his knees and with a hu! hu! hu!, imitating the frog, he jumped into the fire from several directions. Picking up a burning coal and blowing on it he swallowed it slowly. This was one [high point] but not the culminating point of the festival because this continued almost without interruption during the night, repeating again and again the swallowing of the burning coals.[20]

Shamans are said not to be harmed by these burning coals while possessed by a spirit, and we frequently saw them rub the burning end of their cigars over their bare chests and arms. They professed not to feel it at all.

In spite of his great powers and his great prestige among his people, the Tenetehara shaman lives in the same manner as any other man, working in his garden, hunting, fishing, and building his own house. Payments for successful cures are given as gifts; there is no stipulated price, nor, strictly speaking, any obligation to pay. A grateful patient simply gives a shaman a pair of trousers, a piece of cloth or a dress for his wife, in appreciation for what he has done. Manuel Viana told us that he gave one *pazé* a pair of trousers and a shirt as well as a dress for the shaman's wife, after the shaman had extracted the *ymaé* of Ywan which had caused Manuel to be ill. The *pazé* Joãozinho told us that a shaman should be given "a little something," because he must furnish tobacco to make cigars and because he suffers in curing. When people do not offer gifts, he explained, then the next time they call for a shaman he will not come. Thus, well-known shamans do collect considerable personal property from such voluntary gifts, and because the Tenetehara depend so heavily on them to control dangerous spirits, a shaman is a valuable individual to count among one's extended family. Formerly, powerful shamans were leaders of extended families, for both

[20] H. E. Snethlage, "Reise durch Nordoslbrasilien," pp. 468–469. Translated by the authors.

H. Snethlage and Raimundo Lopes [21] describe shaman-chiefs. At present, however, only a few men can boast of filling both roles, but these few are the men of greatest prestige in this society.

SORCERY

Tenetehara shamans are believed to be able to manipulate their familiar supernaturals not only for curing illness but also to cause illness in others. While a shaman is possessed by a spirit, he is able to place the *ymaé* of that particular spirit into the body of a victim, even though the victim is at the moment in another village some distance away. All the shamans we met, however, maintained that they themselves had never caused illness to others in this manner. Sometimes when they diagnosed the sickness before a cure, they accused another shaman of the practice, but in doing so did not name the sorcerer. Instead, they simply announced that the illness resulted from the activities of another shaman, leaving it to the patient or to his family to decide who it might be. One *pazé*, who was widely reputed to be a sorcerer himself, told us that no experienced shaman would ever send illness to other people. Illness, he stated, resulted from the activities of novices, who through their lack of experience offended the supernatural by breaking taboos. One or two shamans did admit that they had the power to send illness, but at the same time denied ever having used it.

At first, therefore, Tenetehara shamans led us to believe that they were always the victims of unjust suspicion of sorcery. During our second visit in 1945, however, we became convinced that a few shamans do consciously attempt to manipulate their supernatural controls with evil intent. We learned that shamans own small "objects" which they firmly believe may be used for sorcery. One of our informants, a shaman of limited powers, showed us one day two pieces of wood, which he called *ywirá maíra* (*ywirá,* wood; *maíra,* shaman), to be used in sorcery. They were oblong in shape and were tied together with a string. He also owned another "object" shaped like a top, small enough to fit into the palm of the hand. All these objects were coated with a rosin having an odor of which the supernaturals are said to be especially fond. With some

21 Snethlage, "Unter nordoslbrasilianischen Indianer," p. 129, and Lopes, "Os tupis do Gurupí," pp. 162–163.

hesitation he explained that a shaman who knows how to "soften the wood" (as he expressed it) cups one of these objects in his hands, calls his familiar spirit at the time naming his victim, and blows smoke over the object until it disappears. It then enters the body of the individual named, where it causes illness or even death. Other Tenetehara shamans own *ywirá maíra* but they keep them hidden from the laity.

Tenetehara shamans explained that pieces of glass may be used the same way as the especially prepared *ywirá maíra*. A small piece is made to enter the body of the victim; it lacerates the intestines and the victim dies in agony. A shaman may also rub a piece of string or vine in his hands and with the aid of his spirit send it into the body of a pregnant woman. It wraps itself around the foetus, tying it in her womb and causing a difficult delivery or even the death of the woman during childbirth. Shamans know how to fashion minia-ture bows and arrows, and, while possessed by a spirit, shoot the arrow in the general direction of the victim to cause him violent pains. Not all shamans are able to perform sorcery. Artur Vaqueiro, for example, told us that he did not know how to work sorcery by any of these methods, but admitted that he had made arrangements to learn how to do so from the shaman Pedro who lived in Lagôa Comprida. He would have to pay Pedro and buy *ywirá maíra* from him.

The Tenetehara fear this evil sorcery and the shamans who are believed to use it; they are certain it is rampant among them. As a shaman increases his number of familiar spirits, he is able to per-form a large number of cures and he gains fame, but his great power and the resulting fame often bring suspicion of sorcery. People of other villages are the first to accuse him of causing illness and once suspicion is directed toward him, proof of his guilt grows. People mourning a dead relative remember some incident that may have made the shaman sufficiently antagonistic toward the deceased or to have desired his death. An epidemic in a village is certain proof that a shaman is working against the people of that village. In 1942, for example, Joãozinho, who lived in the village of Ilhinha, was widely suspected of being a sorcerer. He had been called several times to Januaria village to cure and he had been remarkably suc-cessful. Then three people died suddenly in Januaria, and people began to gossip about Joãozinho. They remembered that he had moved to Ilhinha from the upper Pindaré region several years before and they decided that he had left his upriver village in fear of the revenge of the relatives of people he had killed by sorcery. Although Joãozinho was a village chieftain and generally well liked in his own village, his power was obviously being undermined by the reputation he was gaining in Januaria.

Sometimes the relatives of a deceased person attempt to murder the shaman believed to have caused the death. In most instances, however, he hears of their threats and is put on his guard. Because suspicion grows slowly, he usually is able to escape to a distant village. Furthermore, the anger of the would-be assassins is tempered by the belief that a sorcerer becomes an *azang* after death and as such might well revenge himself. In general, therefore, attacks on a suspected sorcerer stop short of murder. A year before our first visit to the Tenetehara, Miliano, a shaman who lived in Januaria village, was suspected of causing the death of his own father-in-law. The family attacked him but he took refuge in the house of a Brazilian who lived at the near-by Indian post. He was wounded, but the next night under the cover of darkness he escaped to another village. Pedro, a well-known shaman of Lagôa Comprida, was also attacked by irate villagers who accused him of bringing about a series of deaths among them. He arrived late one night in Januaria village with a deep knife wound in his head. His evil reputation followed him, and after a time Pedro was forced to move on to a more distant village. By 1945 the anger of the people of Lagôa Comprida had evidently calmed down, for he had returned to live there. He was still feared, however, as a dangerous sorcerer.

On rare occasions the killing of an evil shaman is thought necessary for the public good and he is put to death in cold blood. Zapu, a shaman who lived in the village of Tawari Queimado, was believed to have caused the death of a large number of people in his own village. Finally the village chieftain, the leader of a large family group, decided that Zapu must die. He called together a group of men and told them of his decision. That same night, the men surrounded Zapu's house and when he tried to escape they clubbed him to death. Zapu's wife was also badly beaten but she was allowed to flee to Lagôa Comprida, where she was living with relatives in

1942. As a rule, the shaman's wife is executed, too, because she is often the instigator of his evil actions. The children of such a couple, if they are small, should never be told how their parents died for fear that they might become shamans and take revenge on the executioners. Our informants were naturally somewhat reserved about giving names and details regarding the execution of shamans for fear of incriminating the Indians concerned, but they did relate enough cases out of the past to make it clear that the execution of sorcerers is a traditional culture pattern.

CEREMONIALS

As we have already said, the pressure of modern economic life leaves the Tenetehara with little time for lengthy ceremonials. They have not forgotten their ancient ceremonies but they hold them less frequently and with less elaborate preparation. The two most important are the Honey Feast, which comes to its climax in the dry season, and the Maize Festival (*awachíre wahuháwo*) which occurs traditionally in the rainy season. Puberty rites are carried out in the rainy season as part of the Maize Ceremony.

The Honey Feast.—This is without doubt the high point of Tenetehara ceremonial life. They speak of it with pride as the most festive occasion they remember, and the festal songs are considered by the people themselves to be the most beautiful of all in Tenetehara music. Although the Honey Feast is spoken of as a gay occasion, it is more than a secular festival. Its origin is explained in mythology. Aruwé, a culture hero, saw this ceremony for the first time in the village of the Jaguars and learned the songs from them. Upon his return, he taught the songs and ritual to the Tenetehara. The songs refer to birds and to the animals of the forest, and the Tenetehara say that the Feast insures an increase among the birds and animals and brings success in the hunt.[22] They are not able to explain the correlation, but they insist that each year the Honey Feast was performed they were remarkably successful in the hunt.

The Honey Feast proper should take place in the late dry season

[22] Barbosa Rodrigues interpreted these songs as the "achievements of their ancestors," while Gustave Dodt (1939 ed.), p. 198, wrote that there are different songs for different animals and "they tell how one hunts, chases, and finally kills the animal."

in September or October, and it lasts only a few days.[23] Preparation
for it often takes as much as six to eight months. During this period,
beginning in the late part of the rainy season in March or April,
groups of men collect wild honey, storing it in gourds which are
hung from the rafters of the Big House erected in the village plaza
for this purpose.[24] Each time the men return with a gourd of honey,
they enter the village dancing and singing. For an elaborate Honey
Festival from one hundred and twenty to one hundred and sixty
gourds of honey (each holding more than a liter) are necessary. Even
a small village will collect "five or six lines"—a "line" being the
number of gourds which a rafter will hold, namely six to eight.
Each night while the honey is being collected, the villagers gather
in the Big House to sing the songs of the Feast. On these occasions,
the women sing inside the house under the honey and the men sing
outside on the dance ground.

The initiative in collecting honey and in organizing the feast is
taken by "the Owner of the Honey Feast." [25] This is generally a
man of considerable prestige who knows the songs of the ceremony
and who sings well. It is not quite clear how this man is selected, but
in the village of Januaria, our informant, João Bochecha (see p. x)
was an "Owner of the Honey Feast." João was not an extended
family leader nor was he a shaman. He did, however, sing ex-
ceptionally well and was greatly respected for this gift, as well as for
his industry in economic pursuits. He told us that he had learned
the songs and how to perform the ceremony from Mariano Kururú,
an old man who had been "Owner of the Honey Feast" in Januaria
village many years ago. Mariano was not João's close relative nor
was João selected by the villagers. It seems that Mariano decided to
teach João because the young man showed aptitude and appreciation for music.

[23] "It is a habit among them [Guajajara-Tenetehara of the Mearim] to hold a
Honey Feast each year in September" (Fróes Abreu, p. 130). The Indian Service officers
told us that the Honey Feast is seldom performed nowadays in the Mearim villages.

[24] Barbosa Rodrigues (p. 32) when he visited the Tenetehara (Tembé) observed:
"Several large gourds, covered with a net of cotton strings, were tied to the roof beams
of the chief's house. These were the containers of tucanyra [honey], their favorite
drink, which was prepared for the festival."

[25] In Portuguese of the region this man is called "the master of the Honey Feast"
(*maestro*), but the Tenetehara expression, *zemuichioháwo zare*, translates clearly as
"owner of the Honey Festival."

The Honey Feast is an important factor in cementing good inter-village relations. As soon as sufficient honey has been collected, the Owner sends out messengers inviting the chiefs of neighboring villages to come with their people. When the village of Januaria celebrated the Honey Feast for the last time, the Owner sent his nephew to invite the people of Lagôa Comprida. The chief of Lagôa Comprida offered to send messengers to carry the invitation to the more distant villages of Jacaré and Contra Herva. Without a formal invitation, the people of a village will not attend a ceremony even though they know that it is taking place. Invitations are sent only to a limited number of villages, since a large number of guests would be too great a burden for the host village. Large supplies of manioc soup and flour must be prepared and the men of the village must hunt several days before the beginning of the feast so as to provide food for the guests. The "Owner of the Feast" and the village chief, especially, "have many expenses" during a Honey Feast.

The guests from each village arrive in a separate group, pausing outside the host village to announce their arrival by blowing on a trumpet made of cow's horn. The host villagers immediately go out to meet them; singing, blowing on trumpets, and shouting, they accompany their guests into the village. When the people from Lagôa Comprida came to the feast given in Januaria, they paused on the far side of the river and gave the signal that they had arrived. The Honey Feast had already begun, but the singing and the dancing ceased while the people of the host village went to meet their visitors. As soon as the guests entered the Big House where the honey was kept, all fell silent. The men formed in lines, according to villages, each of which was headed by the village chief or leader of an extended family. Picó, who was chief of the guest village, was the first to take up the song. He sang alone; when he finished the song was repeated by the next man in his line until all had sung it. Manuel Viana, chief of the host village, then began to sing and each man in his line in turn took up the song. When there are guests from more than one village, the men of the host village are always the last to sing. During the singing, the honey is taken down from the rafters of the Big House and mixed with water in a large pot. After each man sings, he is given this mixture of honey and water to drink from a decorated gourd vessel. After all the men have sung, many voluntarily sing and dance again. The women join the solo singer in the chorus.

In the afternoon, the dancing and singing follows a different style. The men join hands, forming a large circle in the village plaza, and the women form a still larger circle surrounding the men. They now sing in chorus. Between each two songs honey and water is passed around. Singing always ends at sundown. The feast continues for as many days as the supply of honey holds out. During the morning of the last day there is a communal hunt and in the afternoon meat is roasted and distributed to the people. On this same afternoon the singing and dancing grow to an animated climax. The next morning the guests leave for their own villages.

The Maize Festival.—Like the Honey Feast, the Maize Festival is nowadays rarely performed by the Tenetehara. According to the Tenetehara, it should be carried out annually to insure the growth of maize and to protect the maize against the *azang,* the ghost "owners of maize." The ceremony should begin in January when the first sprouts appear and end in March when maize is harvested. Ideally, the dancing and singing of the Maize Festival takes place each day, but our informants assured us that even in the old days it was danced only every other day. Once begun, the festival must be carried on throughout this season; if abandoned, the *azang* will destroy the maize crop and cause sickness among the people of the village.

The Maize Festival seems to be primarily an opportunity for the Tenetehara shamans to exhibit their power in controlling the dangerous *azang.* The celebrations which we witnessed took place during the day. The whole population of the village participated, singing and dancing while their shamans called and were possessed by an *azang* and other spirits. Each day, the session was begun by one of the shamans. One of the sessions at which we were present started about nine o'clock in the morning. The shaman stood in the village plaza and began to sing, marking time with his rattle, and to smoke a cigar, calling an *azang.* Gradually, a few at a time, men and women of the village gathered about him and joined in his song. The men had painted their faces with *urucú* and genipa and had glued white breast feathers of the hawk in their hair. The women had decorated themselves by tying feathers in their hair and sticking white hawk breast feathers in stripes over the upper portion of their bodies. At first the men remained seated as they sang, keeping time with one foot, and the women either sat alongside them or danced about casually in pairs. After a while, however, the shaman and the assembly moved under a house roof and began to dance in a circle in the manner already described for the morning portion of the puberty rites.

The shamans are the principal figures in the Maize Festival, and on this day, several days after the puberty rites were held, the shamanistic exhibitions were particularly noteworthy. Six shamans and several novices performed. Two shamans, André and Inácio, fell simultaneously into a trance, possessed by *azang*. Inácio fell hard to the ground. His body was rigid; his arms were thrown open and his fists tightly closed. He remained unconscious for more than thirty minutes. Finally he seemed to pull himself together and struggled to his knees. He smoked again on his cigar and then stood up joining the others in the dance, still obviously under the influence of *azang*. André was less spectacular. Possessed by an *azang*, he fell several times but each time he quickly regained his feet. He danced stumbling about as if he were blind, bumping into people and now and again holding onto a house post for support. Both Inácio and André danced in a style different from the others, leaning forward from the waist, holding their arms open, and hopping with their knees together. While they were possessed by *azang*, women brought each of them a gourd filled with tapioca and water. They gulped down this mixture, because the *azang* "wanted to eat." At one time or other during the day, each of the six shamans was possessed by an *azang* and all called various other spirits as well. Caetano, for example, was possessed by Ywan, the water spirit. He danced in the manner of this spirit, and opening his shirt he rubbed the lighted end of his cigar over his chest and arms repeatedly. Finally when he could no longer stand on his feet, he knelt, weaving about, with his head almost touching the ground. While he was in this condition, a woman brought him a piece of raw sweet manioc which he chewed and swallowed with apparent disgust and pain. We were told that he did not want to eat it—in fact, raw sweet manioc would

make any man deathly ill—but his spirit wanted to eat.[26] Throughout the day *azang* was the spirit most often called. At sundown the
festival was over for the day. It should have been continued again
the next day, but at the village of Camirang in 1942 it was not performed again until three days later and finally after several irregular
performances it was abandoned before the maize was ready for the
harvest. Contrary to expectations, the harvest was not a failure that
year, but any minor damage to a maize field was attributed to the
neglect of the festival.

Shamanistic activity is the main attraction of the Maize Festival.
During this festival the shaman is assured of a good audience and
he exhibits his control over as many spirits as he knows how to call.
Azang are the ones most frequently invoked, but it is not unusual
for a shaman to call several spirits during a day of the festival just
as he often calls several to effect a cure. On this occasion, the
shamans work for the benefit of the village, not for an individual,
protecting maize and the people against harm. For this reason the
exhibitions during the Maize Festival are traditionally more elaborate and more spectacular than during an evening of curing. Because
the shamans call their whole retinue of spirits during this festival,
it is said to be a very propitious occasion for young novices to become possessed for the first time and to show aptitude for shamanism.

26 During another session of the Maize Ceremony which took place several days
later, Inácio was possessed by the *arapohá azang* (deer ghost spirit). Under the influence of this spirit he danced out of the house to a near-by garden where he stuffed
his mouth with manioc leaves, because, we were told, "the deer [spirit] likes to eat
manioc leaves."

VI · MYTHOLOGY AND FOLKLORE

MODERN TENETEHARA oral literature reflects the mixed origins of the contemporary culture. Many stories which are aboriginal American Indian myths contain, as told today, elements of Iberian and African derivation. Entire European and African stories have been borrowed from Brazilians; and these are flavored with many Indian details. For example, in the well-known European tale, Beauty and the Beast (No. XXXVI), the husband becomes an alligator and the wife, who loses him by looking upon his face, goes in search of him to the house of the Moon, the Sun, and the Wind. Cinderella (No. XXXVII) is aided by Zuruparí, a forest demon, rather than by a fairy godmother, and her sisters are jealous of her because a shiny moon appears on her forehead and sparks issue from her mouth when she talks. Instead of attending a ball where she dances with the Prince, in the Tenetehara version she rides off on a horse to attend a church festival and marries a soldier, an ideal ending from the point of view of the simple rural Brazilian from whom the Tenetehara must have learned this story.

The majority of the stories which follow are aboriginal. A few of them—such as the Twins (No. XIV) which is so common in South American Indian mythology—remain fundamentally faithful in their main episodes to versions of the same stories recorded in the sixteenth century among the coastal Tupí and, more recently, among other Tupí tribes of the Brazilian hinterland. Details of many native stories, however, have been modified to conform to present-day conditions. The story of the Origin of Agriculture (No. II), for example, agrees in certain basic incidents with corresponding stories reported for the coastal Tupí. As it is told by the modern Tenetehara, however, it mentions axes and bush knives, objects

clearly acquired from contact with Brazilians, as being part of agricultural paraphernalia in a mythical time in the distant past when
the culture hero, Maíra, lived on the earth. In several stories involving aboriginal culture heroes, Biblical themes are developed, as a
result of Christian influence. Thus, in the story of the Creation of
Man (No. I), the creator, Maíra, punished man and woman for the
"original sin" by making them procreate and then die; and, in a
conflicting story (No. VII), Tupan creates the first woman from the
rib of a dog.

Many of the stories regarding animals which follow are part of
the national folklore of Brazil, and various versions are told by
Negroes, by *caboclos,* and even by urban Brazilians. Like the stories
of Br'er Rabbit introduced into the folklore of the United States
by Negro slaves, some of them, such as the Rabbit and the Jaguar
(No. XXXII) were brought to Brazil by Negroes. The origin of
other animal stories, such as those involving the Brazilian *jaboti* (a
land tortoise) poses a more difficult question. Cycles of stories in
which a turtle is cast in the role of an astute trickster are reported
from West Africa, the region from which most Brazilian slaves were
transported, and they have been recorded by several writers among
Brazilian Indians who had little or no contact with the outside
world.[1] It is quite probable that in such stories as the race between
the Tortoise and the Deer (No. XXVIII) we have tales common to
the aboriginal cultures of both continents.[2] Escaped Negro slaves,
however, lived with, and established communities near, Indian
tribes in the deep interior of Brazil during the colonial period, and
they undoubtedly introduced African stories among the Indians
even before Portuguese or Brazilian contact. Since the Tenetehara
have had contact with Negroes from the coastal regions, they probably received many of these animal tales either directly from
Negroes or indirectly through the local Brazilians.

Irrespective of origin, however, the stories which follow fall into
three categories in terms of their function in contemporary Tenetehara culture. Myths of culture heroes (Nos. I–XIX), treating as they

[1] See Ramos, pp. 169–182.

[2] Tortoise myths were collected by Charles Hartt (1875) for the Indians of the
Amazon in the 19th century; by Couto de Magalhães (1876); among the Indians of the
Rio Negro, Tapajoz, and Juruá in the 19th century; by the present author among
the Tapirapé of central Brazil; and by many others too numerous to mention here.

do of the origin of things and the creation of man and of natural phenomena, are in a sense both sacred and philosophical. They have the same function as the Biblical stories in Christian cultures. A second category of stories (Nos. XX–XXV) as well as the stories of European origin (Nos. XXXVI–XXXVII) generally point out a moral to the Tenetehara—even though that moral is not always readily apparent to the outsider. In the story of the Rolling Head, the hunting party has offended the Owner of the Forest by killing more animals than they can use for food and all are killed except a man and his wife. The dramatic plots and episodes of these stories as well as the narrative style in which they are told incites interest, but their primary function seems to be to point out a moral lesson rather than to entertain. Finally, stories of animals such as Opossum Takes a Son-in-Law and the tortoise cycle (No. XXVI through XXXIV) seem to be told primarily for entertainment, even though they also sometimes teach a moral lesson. They are comical and people laugh at them no matter how many times they have heard them before.

All these myths and tales are told with a distinctive narrative style. Dialogues between the characters are introduced and the sounds of animals are mimicked with accuracy and sometimes with satirical exaggeration. The stories which are recorded here, however, are freely transcribed for their content alone. We have tried to remain faithful to detail and to episode but we have not attempted to transmit any of the colorful Tenetehara narrative style. The stories were related to us freely in the native language and translated into Portuguese for us either by the narrator himself or by an interpreter. A few stories were taken down at dictation in the Tenetehara language, but this method was so slow and painful to our informants that they tended to omit many important details and even whole portions of a story.

Finally, although thirty-eight stories are presented here, it must be said that to our knowledge no individual Tenetehara knows as many as this. Most adults know ten or even fifteen, and Manuel Viana, who was an excellent storyteller, told us more than twenty. Furthermore, we feel certain that the stories here recorded do not represent the entire body of oral literature of Tenetehara culture; with longer residence among these people, one would undoubtedly be able to collect many more. Yet, at the end of several months among the Tenetehara, the anthropologists found themselves in the strange position of knowing with the aid of writing more stories (at least the bare plots) than any native. The people themselves made no great point of knowing all the stories. The interest of the good storyteller lay not in the size of his repertory but in the skill of delivery and presentation.

1. THE CREATION OF MAN

Maíra traveled on the earth and wanted to create mankind. When he found the Beautiful Land (*ywý poráng*) he decided that it was a good place to make mankind. He made a man and a woman. Tupan prohibited them from having sexual intercourse. Without knowing why, the first man always had an erect penis. The first woman went to wash Maíra's clothes in a stream and the Water Spirit (Ywan) appeared and courted her, finally copulating with her. The woman liked her experience and each day from then on, she went back to the stream; she tapped on a gourd vessel which she placed on the surface of the water, calling the Water Spirit who appeared at once and lay down with her.

Maíra knew what was taking place and he told the man. He showed the man how the woman called Ywan. Then the man went to the stream and called Ywan who appeared by showing his erect penis above the surface of the water. The man quickly cut off Ywan's penis. The next day, not knowing what had taken place, the woman returned to the stream and called Ywan, but the spirit did not appear and never appeared again.

During all this time, the man had been pouring a manioc beverage over his penis in an effort to soften it, but without success. Now, the woman was not able to withhold her sexual desire and approached the man while he was pouring the beverage over his penis. She told him that she would teach him how to soften his penis; she sat on top of him and taught him how to perform sexual intercourse. Later, when Maíra saw the man with a flaccid penis, he asked what had happened and the man explained. Maíra was angry and said, "Henceforth your penis will be soft, you will make children and then you will die; later when your child grows, he will make another child and in turn he will die."

II. THE ORIGIN OF AGRICULTURE

When Maíra lived on this earth, the Tenetehara did not have to work in their gardens. Their axes and bush knives would work at clearing the garden plots by themselves, and manioc shoots went to plant themselves in the gardens. They planted themselves on one day, and manioc was ready for harvest the next. Maíra told his wife to harvest the manioc which had been planted by itself the day before. She always found an abundance of manioc and brought it home, making a manioc beverage for her husband.

When his old wife became ill, Maíra took a younger wife. As usual, he sent her to harvest the manioc which had planted itself the day before, but the new wife doubted that it could be ready for harvest so soon. Maíra was angry with her and said, "Now you henceforth will have to wait the entire winter [rainy season] for manioc to grow." Since then, the Tenetehara plant manioc and wait until the end of the rainy season to harvest it.[3]

III. THE ORIGIN OF MANIOC FLOUR

A long time ago, the Tenetehara did not have fire or manioc. Maíra sent his wife and son to collect *kamamô* (*Solanacea*, a forest fruit). He remained behind in his hammock and Tupan brought manioc flour for him to eat. One day his son found crumbs under his father's hammock. He tasted them and he took some to his mother. He told her that his father had been eating this new food, but she answered that this was impossible, because Maíra was not eating anything. He was sick. The next day and for several successive days Maíra complained that he was sick and said that he did not want to eat anything. Each day his son found crumbs under his hammock. One day, his wife became suspicious, so she and her son

[3] In another version of the same story, the origin of work is attributed to Tupan and not Maíra. In this variation, men sharpen their axes and order them to go to the forest to clear garden sites. Manioc shoots are tied in bundles and ordered to go plant themselves. Tenetehara men made baskets and these were sent to the gardens to harvest and carry back manioc to the village. Women were prohibited from seeing this operation, but one day several women hid in the forest to see the carrying baskets go by. When the carrying baskets passed before their eyes, all the manioc spilled to the ground and the baskets became limp. Tupan was angry. He told the women that from now on they would have to carry the manioc back from the gardens, soak it in water and roast it in order to make flour. For this reason, women have the great burden of preparing flour for their families.

returned from their collecting early. They surprised Tupan sitting by Maíra's hammock. Tupan fled but left a gourd vessel full of manioc flour which they ate. Tupan left a stalk of manioc, and Maíra sent the manioc to plant itself. The next day, Maíra asked his wife to harvest the manioc planted the day before and when she arrived she was surprised to find it grown so high. She took many roots home, and from the tubers she made flour. It was in this same way that Tupan brought sweet potatoes, and yams.

IV. THEFT OF FIRE

A long time ago, the Tenetehara did not have fire. Meat was cooked in the sun, which at that time was closer to the earth. The vultures were the owners of fire, which they themselves used to roast the meat which they ate. Maíra decided to steal fire from the vultures. He transformed himself into a dead deer and the vultures were attracted by decaying flesh. They brought fire along with them to roast the meat. When they were very close, Maíra jumped up quickly and attempted to snatch the fire, but the vultures flew away, taking the fire with them.

Then, Maíra transformed himself into a dead tapir. The vultures came and made a fire near by. Maíra patiently let them peck at him and the vultures were certain that the tapir was dead. When the fire came near his arm, Maíra suddenly grabbed a burning coal. The coal burned Maíra's hand, so he quickly hid it in a stick of *urucú* wood (*Bixa orellana*), so that when a man needed fire he would know where to go. Therefore, nowadays, when people need to make a fire when they are in the forest, they use sticks of *urucú* wood to create sparks to make a fire.

V. ORIGIN OF HAMMOCKS

One day, Maíra collected together some cotton and took out the seeds. Then, he spread it out in a thin layer over the ground. Then, he tied it with two pieces of vine to the house supports. He asked a man to lay down upon it, but the man saw that it was weak and refused. Maíra was angry, and he said, "I wanted to teach you how to make a hammock to sleep on. Now you will have to make your hammock the hard way." Now, people have to spin cotton cord and then slowly make hammocks by tying strings strung between two posts.

If they had not doubted Maíra, there would not be so much work involved nowadays in making a hammock.

VI. CREATION OF WILD PIGS

Tupan traveled on this earth accompanied by his young godchild. One day, they came to a large village where several relatives of his godchild lived, and Tupan left the child with these relatives, instructing them to treat him well. They did not, however, care for the boy, and on Tupan's return the boy complained of the bad treatment he had received. Tupan was angry. He told the boy to gather all the bird feathers he could find and to spread them around the edge of the village. Then, Tupan set fire to the feathers and the entire village was surrounded by a wall of fire. The inhabitants ran from side to side, but they were unable to escape the walls of fire. Little by little their cries became lower until they were transformed into the grunts of wild pigs; at the same time the people began to take on the form of peccaries and wild pigs. A few of them escaped into the dense forest, and the wild pigs which inhabit the forest today are their descendants. Tupan made his godchild, Marana ẏwa, the owner of wild pigs.

VII. TUPAN CREATES WOMAN

The first man did not have a wife and thus could not have children. Tupan decided to make a woman and to give her to the man as a wife. Tupan took a rib from the dog, rolled it in a banana leaf which he covered with clay, and spent a long time working the material into a mass. Soon the man heard the cry of a baby coming from inside the banana leaf and soon Tupan gave him a baby girl. Tupan told him to give the baby a bath and to care for her until she grew. After a time she grew to be a woman and was ready to marry with the man. Their first child was a Brazilian (*karaẏ* a white or European), and the second was a Tenetehara. There were many children and Tupan had them marry among themselves, so nowadays there are many Tenetehara and many Brazilians.[4]

[4] This story was told by a *mestiço* informant who, however, had lived most of his life in the upper Pindaré region. It obviously conflicts with the story of the creation of the Tenetehara by Maíra. Although it contains aboriginal elements, such as the fact that the first Tenetehara raised his wife until she was old enough for marriage, the story itself is an interesting modification of the Biblical story of the creation of woman from the rib of man.

VIII. CREATION OF THE MOON

Formerly the nights were pitch dark, since there was no moon to light the sky. The Tenetehara asked Tupan to make night less dark, so one night Tupan made the moon. He asked the Tenetehara where he should place it. They asked him to leave it on the ground, but they soon saw that from the ground it did not illuminate the night very well. Then they asked Tupan to place the moon higher, and he placed it in the sky so it would light up the earth at night.

IX. THE STAR WHICH FOLLOWS THE MOON

A star wanted to marry the moon, and she went to ask the moon's mother to help. She said that it was sad that the moon went through the sky alone each night. Moon's mother warned the star that she would have to prepare his meals, and said that she would consent if Moon liked the star. Moon accepted. He liked the food his new wife prepared and Moon's mother left, leaving him to his new wife's care. Thus, nowadays, we see a star which follows the moon each night on its long road through the sky.

X. ORIGIN OF CANOES

A long time ago, the Tenetehara knew very little and Tupan helped them. Little by little, he taught them how to live. When the rivers were swollen during the rainy season, the Tenetehara were forced to remain on small islands of high ground and were not able to hunt. For this reason they sometimes were hungry. Then Tupan decided to teach them how to make canoes so they could cross rivers and so they could travel during the rainy season. He selected a large and straight *jatobá* tree and taught the Tenetehara how to remove the bark without breaking it. He showed them how to loosen the bark by inserting wedges slowly between it and the trunk. When the bark was removed, Tupan told the Tenetehara to make a fire and to suspend the sheet of bark over the fire so as to soften it. Then he showed them how to form it into a canoe. After a long time the first canoe was ready. Thus, the Tenetehara learned how to construct canoes from the bark of the *jatobá* tree so they might hunt and travel during the period when the rivers flood the forests.

XI. TUPAN BRINGS RAIN

One time all the streams dried up and many people were dying of thirst. A Tenetehara who was hunting water in the forest met Tupan. Tupan told him, "See what has happened to mankind, because they are always speaking badly of me." The Tenetehara protested that such was not the case and said that if Tupan would bring water, he would never do anything to anger him. Tupan sent him back to his village and when he arrived rain began to fall in torrents. Streams began to run again and the manioc which had been dying for lack of water came to life again. Men slaked their thirst and no longer died of it.

XII. THE VOICE CONTEST

Tupan went on a trip with jaguar as a companion. One evening in front of their other traveling companions, they began to argue as to which of them had the strongest voice. The jaguar roared as loud as he could, but his traveling companions were not afraid. They gathered near the place where the jaguar and Tupan were camped to watch the contest. Then Tupan gave forth thunder of the type that brings rain, and the travelers ran away to untie their hammocks and to find shelter. The jaguar was so afraid that he ran to hide in a hollow tree trunk. Tupan was the winner of the argument, and he continued on his journey alone.[5]

XIII. TUPAN AND THE HALF-WITTED CHILD

There was a father who did not like his son because the boy was half-witted. The grandfather, however, was sorry for the child and took care of him. At that time, people did not have manioc flour, but Tupan sent manioc flour for the boy and his grandfather. When the boy died, he went to live in the "Village of the Gods," where he became a great favorite of Tupan. The boy remembered his grandfather and continued sending flour to him. The evil father found a

[5] In another version of this story, Tupan asks a group of animals which of them has the strongest voice. Each one tries to out shout the others. Then, one of the contestants, the land tortoise (*jaboti*) retires into another room and has sexual intercourse with his wife, during which he cried louder and shriller than any of the others. Nowadays the tortoise during coitus cries loud enough "to frighten anyone walking in the forest." After all had demonstrated the strength of their voices, Tupan caused thunder which made all of them tremble with fear, thus winning the contest.

few crumbs of flour and asked the old man where it came from. As soon as he learned, he wanted to go live with his son but the grandfather told him that he could not do so until he died. Soon the half-witted boy came to take away his grandfather. The two climbed a ladder into the sky to live with Tupan. There they lived with abundance of food.

XIV. THE TWINS: MAÍRA YRA AND MUKWURA YRA

Maíra left to travel and never returned. He left his wife behind and she was pregnant. His unborn son suggested to his mother that they go in search of his father. The mother complained that she did not know the way, but Maíra yra (*yra*, son) told her that he would tell her the way. So they began their journey in search of Maíra.

Once, when they were going through a forest, Maíra yra (still in his mother's womb) asked his mother to pick a flower for him. She reached for the flower, but in so doing a wasp stung her stomach. Trying to kill the wasps, she slapped herself across the stomach, thereby hurting Maíra yra who was in her womb. He was angry and refused to give her directions any more. She lost her way and took a trail which led to Mukwura's [6] house. Mukwura heard her story and invited her to spend the night in his house. The woman hung her hammock in one corner of his house. Mukwura made a hole in the roof directly over her head and during the night it rained as she slept. The poor woman got wet because rain came through the hole in the roof. Then Mukwura urged her to move her hammock near his own since that part of the house was dry. After she had moved near to him, he convinced her that she should not sleep in her wet hammock but should share his. She moved to sleep with Mukwura and he left her pregnant with a second child, Mukwura yra. Maíra's son was angry because now there was another child in the womb with him.

The mother continued to travel until she arrived at the Village of the Jaguars, where an old jaguar woman (*zawarehu-zarýi*) invited her to stay in her house. The jaguar woman hid Maíra's wife under a large pot so that her jaguar son would not eat the guest.

---

[6] *Mukwura* is the opossum or *gambá* in Portuguese (*Didelphis marsupialis*); however, in this story the name seems to refer to the culture hero rather than to the animal itself.

When the jaguar son arrived, he suspected that a stranger was present, and he hunted throughout the house. He discovered Maíra's wife under the pot, but Maíra's wife transformed herself into a doe and fled. The jaguar son and his dogs chased her and finally killed her. When they opened up her stomach they found twins, Maíra yra and Mukwura yra, alive. The jaguar wanted to eat them, but when he tried to roast them, they jumped aside and the jaguar plunged his hands into the hot coals trying to catch them. Then, he tried to string them on a sharp stick so he could roast them over the fire, but they jumped aside again and the jaguar stuck himself with the sharp stick. He tried to boil them in water but they made him spill the boiling water over himself. Then, the old jaguar woman asked that she be allowed to raise the twins. She put them to sleep for the night in an old utensil. The next morning they had been transformed into young macaws and the jaguar woman was happy. She fed them well. The next day they appeared as two small parrots, and each day for several days after that as different animals. Finally, they became human beings again and the jaguar woman took them as her own grandchildren.

With time the twins grew to be strong young men. The jaguar woman told them to stay near the house each time she went to walk in her garden. One day, however, while Mukwura yra was picking lice from the old jaguar woman's hair, Maíra yra said that he could pick them better. He asked the jaguar woman to hold her head up higher and then, instead of picking lice, he pulled her head from her body. He threw the head to his brother and they spent some time playing, throwing her head back and forth. Then, Maíra yra placed the head back on the body and blowing over the jaguar woman brought her back to life. The jaguar woman opened her eyes and told them that she had been asleep.

The next morning, when the jaguar woman went to her garden, the twins escaped and went into the forest. There they met a gigantic *jacú* (a forest fowl), who told them the story of how their mother had died. They cried, and when they returned the jaguar woman noticed that their eyes were swollen. They lied and said that they had been bitten by wasps, but the jaguar woman would not believe them. Maíra yra put together leaves and clay to look like a wasp's nests. He threw the nests at the jaguar woman, and wasps came out of them to sting her.

Then the twins decided to revenge their mother by killing all the people of the jaguar village. They built a bridge over a dry swamp. Maíra yra stamped on the ground and the swamp was filled with water. Maíra yra sent his brother to fetch straw with which they made fire fans. They grew these fans into the water and immediately each turned into a carniverous piranha fish. Maíra yra threw a monkey into the water and the fish were slow in eating it so he made more fire fans. He threw these into the water, until there were so many piranha that a second monkey thrown into the water was devoured at once. The twins returned to the village of the jaguar people with a load of fish and said that they had caught them in the swamp. The jaguar people organized a fishing party and Maíra yra guided them to the swamp. Maíra yra asked Mukwura yra to lead the people across the bridge. As soon as Mukwura yra had crossed, he jumped aside and each brother took hold of one end of the bridge and turned it over, throwing all the jaguar people into the water. The piranha fish devoured them immediately. The skull of the jaguar man who had killed the mother of the twins came floating to the surface. Maíra yra transformed himself into a small insect, flew to the skull and took away the jaguar spirit. He placed it in a bamboo container.

After traveling for many days, the twins encountered Maíra and gave him the jaguar spirit closed up in the bamboo container. Maíra, however, asked for proof that they were his sons. He asked them to kill a female ghost (*azang kuzã*) and showed them where to encounter the ghost. This ghost had long hair which trailed behind on the ground. The twins set fire to her hair and when the ghost ran to a near-by lake to extinguish the fire, Maíra yra caused the lake to dry up. The woman ghost ran to another lake and still another, but each time Maíra yra had taken the water from the lake. The ghost died when the flames reached her head and the twins returned to Maíra.

Then, Maíra sent them to kill a male ghost (*azang awá*). They found one in the forest cutting down a tree. They approached him and, calling him "grandfather," asked him what he was doing. He replied that he was making a bow and arrow with which to kill all animals. They argued with him that they knew better how to do it. Then, taking the ghost's arm, which was sharply pointed, they thrust it into the log so deep that he was unable to pull it out. They left him there to die with his own arm stuck into the log. They told Maíra of their new victory.

Maíra sent them to kill another ghost. This time, it was a fishing ghost. They saw him sitting on the river bank fishing with a hook and line. Maíra yra dove into the water and transformed himself into a large *surubim* fish. Maíra yra stole the bait from the ghost's hook several times. Then, he told his brother to become a fish and to do the same thing, but Mukwura yra was slow and was caught. The ghost took the fat *surubim* fish (Mukwura yra) home and roasted it over the fire. Maíra yra went to save his brother, but when he arrived the ghost had already eaten the *surubim* fish and only the bones remained. Maíra yra asked the ghost if he might have the bones of the fish which he had just eaten. The ghost gave him the bones of his brother. Maíra yra placed the bones in the leaves of the *sororoca* plant and began to pat them gently. Little by little the bones began to grow flesh and soon his brother returned to life. Maíra yra scolded his brother for his lack of care and for his lack of wit. They returned to Maíra, who this time accepted them as his sons.

Then Maíra yra challenged his father to sink an arrow into a rock. Maíra shot his arrow against the rock and it broke into pieces. Maíra yra shot his, and it entered firmly into the solid rock. In this way, he showed his great strength to his father. Maíra and his sons still live on in the "Village of the Gods," where there is an abundance of everything.

XV. ADVENTURES OF WIRAÍ

In the days when animals could still speak, Wiraí, a small boy, went with his mother to the garden. He wandered deep into the forest chasing a night hawk and lost his way. Suddenly, a river divided its course, isolating him on a small island. There was no way for him to reach the near-by shore. When a night hawk came by, the youngster asked it to carry him to the opposite shore, but the night hawk flew on, saying that the boy was too heavy. Then he asked the same of a woodpecker. The woodpecker let the boy get on his back, but found that he could not fly because the boy was too heavy. Then Wiraí asked the alligator to transport him to solid ground. The alligator agreed, stating that he had "a large canoe" (wide shoulders) which would support the weight of the boy. Wiraí climbed onto the back of the alligator and they began to cross the river. Halfway across the alligator began to weave, trying to make Wiraí lose his balance and fall in the water so the alligator could eat him. Wiraí knew what the alligator was trying to do; he remained quiet and did not fall. Near the bank the alligator submerged, leaving Wiraí in the water. A *socó* (water bird) who was fishing near the river bank dove into the water and quickly swallowed Wiraí. The alligator was angry and accused the *socó* of eating Wiraí but, to prove that it had not, the *socó* vomited the fish which it had kept in its pouch. When the alligator went away, the *socó* vomited up Wiraí and set him free.

Wiraí wandered in the forest looking for a place to sleep. Finally he curled up underneath what he thought was a large rock. It was a gigantic *kururú*-toad, and early the next morning the toad began to sing, "Get out from under me—I am not a rock." Wiraí was afraid and ran away.

He traveled all day through the forest until night. Then he saw a fire in a clearing in the forest. Around the fire a group of humming birds were dancing and singing, "His head is mine to make a gourd vessel." Wiraí made a loud noise, and, frightened, the humming birds flew away.

Then Wiraí came to the house of the great snake, Moizuhú, who invited the boy to enter. The snake intended to eat Wiraí, but Wiraí began to sing a song which he had learned from the hawk. "The hawk eats the eyes of the snake." The great snake was so afraid that he went away to hide. Wiraí fled through the forest.

He slept under the gigantic *kururú*-toad again. During the night, the toad began to sing, "Sleep on the other side, sleep on the other side." Each time he sang Wiraí moved to a different side of the toad and in so doing he found a hidden trail. The next day he followed this trail until he reached a large *sapucaia* nut tree and gathered enough nuts to satisfy his hunger. That evening he found a *najá* tree (a forest fruit) and decided to make camp there. He ate so many *najá* that his hair began to fall out. He met a peccary who also slept under the *najá* tree and the two traveled together the next day. The peccary took him to a garden where they could eat yams, but the people of the village chased them. The peccary escaped, but a man caught Wiraí. It was his own father, and he immediately recognized his son. He took Wiraí back to their village, and he was received with a great festival. When Wiraí met his mother, they embraced so strongly that they could never be separated again.[7]

XVI. THEFT OF NIGHT

A long time ago, the sun was continually in the sky. There was no night and the Tenetehara slept in full daylight. Deep in the forest an old woman kept Night closed up in several vessels. Mokwaní, a young man who could run extraordinarily fast, decided to go to steal Night from the old woman. He went to her house and calling her grandmother, he asked if she would give him Night. She showed him the vessels and asked him to choose one. He picked a small pot. He broke it open and out came darkness with owls and bats. Mokwaní ran as fast as he could, back to the village, followed by the darkness, but by the time he arrived the darkness had disappeared and it was daylight again.

He told the people what he had seen and done. They suggested that he return to the house of the old woman who was the owner of Night. This time when she asked him to choose, he picked a larger pot. He broke it and more darkness came out. He began running back toward the village, but Night overtook him and he was transformed into a night bird whose sad song people can still hear during the night from deep in the forest.

XVII. THE GREAT FIRE

A great fire destroyed the forests, the plains, and the gardens. The Tenetehara fled in all directions and most of them died. Only a few arrived safely in the house of the tree sloth—the only spot which the fire did not destroy. As the fire approached, the tree sloths began to sing and they sang until the fire went out. Their songs held

---

[7] In one version we were told that it was necessary to call a shaman to separate them. In another version, "Wiraí was a shaman," and because he was, he and his mother could not be separated.

back the fire and it did not destroy the village. Of all the animals of the forest, only a small guariba monkey escaped. After the fire was extinguished, the monkey went in search of his relatives. He knew only the song his parents had taught him. He met another small monkey and asked him, "How do my parents sing?" The monkey began to whistle, so the guariba monkey knew that he was not his relative. He met a deer and repeated his question. The deer sang a strange song, and thus the small guariba monkey knew that the deer was not of his people. He met many animals and none could sing the song he knew. Then, when he came to the house of the tree sloth, in answer to his question, the tree sloth sang the song his parents had taught him. So he remained with the sloth until he grew up and then he went to live with other guariba monkeys.

XVIII. ORIGIN OF THE HONEY FEAST

One day, Aruwé, a well-known Tenetehara hunter, found a spot where many macaws came to eat seeds from a tree. He climbed into the tree, built a hunting blind and waited. He killed many macaws. When he climbed down from his hunting blind at the end of the day, however, he saw jaguars approaching. He hid again and saw that they came to this tree to collect wild honey. When they left, he returned to his village with the macaws which he had killed. He spent the next day hunting from the same tree and with the same excellent luck. He waited until after the jaguars had come and gone before leaving his blind.

One day Aruwé's brother asked him to teach him where to hunt. His brother wanted tail feathers from the red macaw to make decorations for a festival. Aruwé told him where to find the tree and instructed him not to climb down until after the jaguars had gone. The brother spent the day hunting from the tree and killed several macaws. He saw the jaguars coming to the tree and, against the advice of his brother, decided to try to kill one. His first arrows missed, and the jaguar climbed the tree and killed the brother.

Aruwé waited all one day and all one night for his brother to return. When he did not return, he was certain that his brother had been killed by the jaguar. He returned to the spot and saw signs of the battle. He followed the jaguar's tracks, which were marked with his brother's blood, until they disappeared at the opening of an anthill. Aruwé was a shaman so he lighted his cigar and began to "call the supernatural." He transformed himself then into an ant and entered into the hill. Inside he saw many houses; it was the Village of the Jaguars (*zawarehú nekwaháo*). Aruwé changed himself into a man again and entered the village in search of his brother. He saw a jaguar woman there who appealed to him. He went with her to her father's house and married her. It was her father who had killed his brother and the father explained how the brother had provoked the jaguars. Aruwé lived with the jaguars for a long time.

Aruwé watched the jaguars leave the village each day for many days and return each day with gourd containers full of wild honey which they hung to the rafters of a house. At night the jaguar people gathered near the house where they hung the honey and sang beautiful songs unknown to the Tenetehara. When many gourd containers had been accumulated, the jaguar people decorated themselves and began the great Honey Feast. The songs began at sunrise and ended at sundown. The dancers drank a mixture of wild honey and water between songs. Aruwé learned the dances and the songs.

Soon afterwards, Aruwé was homesick to see his Tenetehara wife and son. He asked the jaguar people to let him go back to visit them. They agreed on the condition that he take his jaguar wife with him. The couple left by the same anthill and returned to the Tenetehara village. Aruwé asked his jaguar wife to wait outside while he told his Tenetehara wife of his arrival. The Tenetehara wife was happy; she made him a soup of manioc, and he stayed a long time. When he went back to the anthill, his jaguar wife had gone, and she had filled in the entrance of the anthill after her. Aruwé returned several times, but he never again found the jaguar village. Then, he taught the Tenetehara how to celebrate the Honey Feast. The Honey Feast as it is celebrated nowadays was taught to the Tenetehara by Aruwé.

XIX. ORIGIN OF BEANS AND MAIZE

A Tenetehara girl was decorated and placed in an isolation hut with strict orders from her parents to stay there. She became hungry and left the hut. She went to a neighboring garden, where she dug up a yam and made a fire to roast it. While she was doing this she heard the song of a hawk. Then she said, "If it is a man, then come eat yam with me." The hawk heard and immediately changed himself into a young man. He joined the young girl and the two ate yams.

The next day the girl's mother asked her to go to the garden with her, but the girl refused; she waited in the hut for the visit of the youth. He visited her several days and one day her mother surprised them lying together in the same hammock. The girl then said that she was going to marry the youth and finally her father gave his consent. The hawk-youth came to live in his father-in-law's house and worked with her family in the garden. One day after he had returned from the garden, he asked his wife to take out two splinters in his foot. She extracted two objects and the hawk husband instructed his wife to keep them and plant them. This is how the Tenetehara received beans and maize.

XX. THE ROLLING HEAD

Once a group of Tenetehara hunters killed more animals than they could use and much of the meat spoiled. One of the hunters, however, had killed practically nothing. While he was away his wife was working on a hammock. As she worked a man arrived at the camp, whom she recognized as Marana ýwa, the Owner of the Forest. He told the woman that as soon as her husband arrived, they should leave the camp. He left two watermelons. The woman told the men what had happened and warned them not to eat the watermelons, but they would not listen. She was able, however, to persuade her husband to leave the camp with her. As soon as the hunters had eaten the watermelons, they retired to sleep. Then swarms of owls and vampire bats arrived and killed them all. The couple who had left heard the cries of agony of those who had remained behind.

The husband was curious and decided to return to the camp. There he found a head without a body. The head spoke to him and asked him to put it in his carrying basket and take it along back to the village. The man was afraid, but did as he was told. On the road the head fell from its place in the carrying basket several times, but each time the man picked it up and traveled on. At last he lost patience and spoke to the head telling it to wait on the trail while he went into the bush to defecate. He left the head on the trail, slipped off into the forest to defecate, and then continued on his way with his wife, leaving the head behind. The head cried out, calling the man, and the man's feces answered. The feces told the head the direction the man had taken and, rolling along, the head followed the couple. Finally, the head caught up with them and the husband was angry. He put the head back in his carrying basket and proceeded along the trail. Again he put the head down on the ground, this time saying that he was going into the forest to urinate. The head waited. When the man did not return, the head called out and the urine answered. From the urine the head picked up the man's trail again and followed the couple by rolling along the ground. When the man discovered that the head was following them again, he asked his wife to make a pitfall. The head came rolling along the trail and fell into the pitfall; it could not get out and the couple went on to their village.

The couple told the people in the village what had happened to them and the next day the villagers went to the pitfall. They heard shouts coming from it and were afraid to go near. On the second day, however, the shouts ceased and the villagers looked into the hole. The head had disappeared. They decided that the head was a ghost (azang). Soon afterwards, a group of hunters became lost in the forest and never returned; this ghost had caused their death.[8] Then the men of the village hid in the forest waiting for the ghost to appear, and one of them killed it with an arrow.

XXI. THE MAN WHO MARRIED HAWK'S DAUGHTER

A man discovered a hawk's nest and he invited his brother to go with him to rob the nest. The next day they returned and constructed a ladder (mutakwára)—a series of poles tied to a thick tree to make it possible to climb. The man suggested that his married brother climb up to the nest first. He remained below with his brother's wife and, while the husband was climbing, the wife made sexual approaches to her brother-in-law. The husband was angry

---

[8] See Nimuendajú (p. 290) for a version of this story collected among the Tembé (Tenetehara). In this version, the man is warned to leave the camp by his son—not his wife. The head turns into a gigantic hawk—not a ghost—and the hawk is killed by a strong shaman.

and coming down out of the tree, he told his brother to climb ahead of him. He was very angry. After they reached the hawk's nest, the jealous husband began to descend and as he climbed down he cut away the poles lashed to the tree trunk, isolating his brother high in the top of the tree in the hawk's nest. He went home, leaving the brother to die.

The brother cried. Soon the hawks returned with a tree sloth which they had killed to feed their young. The poor man told the hawk father what had happened and the hawk father was sad. He called his wife and they decided that the man should stay with them and should raise their daughter to marry her. They brought him a guariba monkey and showed him how to open the flesh so the hawk daughter could eat, but since he did not have a beak or claws, he was not able to tear apart the meat brought him to eat. Then, the hawks began to beat their wings around him and he was transformed into a hawk. He was able to hunt and to feed his young wife. When she grew older, he married her. The hawk parents flew off high in the sky to the hawk village.

One day, the man was flying with his wife and, by chance, they flew over his old village. He remembered his brother who had left him stranded in the hawk's nest and he decided to take revenge. He changed himself into a small hawk and sat on a post in his brother's garden. His brother's wife saw the small hawk and called her husband to shoot it. The husband shot but missed, although he was well known as a marksman. Then the small hawk suddenly became a gigantic hawk and, swooping down, caught up the brother in his claws and flew off with him. He gave his brother to his hawk brothers-in-law, who tore the brother to pieces and dropped the bones back into the poor man's village. The parents of the two brothers were sad because they thought they had lost both sons. So the hawk brother transformed himself back into a man and returned to visit his parents. He invited them and the villagers to go away with him. He began singing early one morning and asked all to sing with him. Only his old parents sang with him and when the sun was down, their house began to rise from the ground. They went off with their son to the hawks' village. The village they left behind was destroyed by a flood and the people were turned into small birds which are preyed upon nowadays by hawks.

XXII. THE CANNIBAL HUSBAND

A young Tenetehara girl went on a hunting trip with her husband only a few days after they were married. The husband spent the first two days hunting. Each day he returned with large quantities of meat for his wife, but he never ate any of the meat himself. Finally, on the third day, he asked his wife to pick the lice out of his hair and while she was doing so he killed her. Then he ate her. The husband returned to the village in tears. He asked if his wife had returned and he said that she must be lost. He pretended to return to look for her. Since she never returned, her relatives soon gave him a younger sister as a wife. Again he suggested that his new wife accompany him on a hunting trip and he killed and ate this second wife. He returned again crying and pretending that his wife had gotten lost. Then he was given a third wife. He took her hunting with him as he had the other two, but she was suspicious. One day, when he left their camp to hunt, she discovered a hole where the husband had buried the bones of the two previous wives. She hid near by in the forest. When the husband had returned and called his wife, she did not answer. Soon he was tired calling and became very hungry. He began to cut pieces of flesh from his own legs to satisfy his hunger. Afterwards he tried to stand and found that he had eaten his own legs. As soon as she saw that he could not move, the young wife came out of her hiding place. He was angry and accused the wife of causing him to lose his legs. She killed him with a club and returned to the village where she told her story. Several men from the village went to the hunting camp to verify her story, and they set fire to the hut built there.

XXIII. THE WOMAN WHO MARRIED A TAPIR

A long time ago, a young Tenetehara woman met a tapir in the forest. The tapir suddenly changed into a handsome young man and began to court her. The young woman liked her lover and she returned often to the forest where she called her lover by beating on the trunk of a tree. The tapir would appear and change into a man. Soon her father and her brothers became suspicious. One of them followed her one day and saw how she called her lover. The next day, they went to the forest and called the tapir by beating against the tree. When the tapir appeared, they killed him with an arrow. They cut the tapir into pieces and brought the meat back to the village to be roasted. They gave the penis to the unsuspecting girl to eat. When she learned what had happened she was very sad. She went to the river bank. She threw her brothers and father into the water, and then she followed them. All of them became fish.[9]

XXIV. THE WOMAN WHO MARRIED A SNAKE

A young Tenetehara woman met a snake while she was walking through the forest. She returned frequently to the forest to make love to the snake. He built a house where they could lie down together. Finally she became pregnant. Since her family did not know about her lover, she did not tell them that she was pregnant. One day she gave birth to a son; he was already a youth when he was born and he went at once to the forest where he spent the day making arrows for his mother. At sundown each day he returned to his mother and reentered her womb. After several days, the girl's brother discovered her secret. He waited until after Snake's son had left for the day, to talk with his sister. After hearing her story, the brother advised her to let the youth leave her womb next day and, while he was away, to hide. Her brother helped her hide a great distance away. When Snake's son returned that evening to enter his mother's womb, she could not be found.

The snake son immediately went to talk with his snake grandfather who advised him to hunt for his father. Snake's son did not wish to do this, so that evening, transforming himself into a ray of lightning, he climbed into the sky carrying with him his bow and arrow. As soon as he arrived he broke the bow and arrow in pieces and they became stars in the sky. Everyone was asleep and no one except the spider saw this take place. For this reason, the spiders do not die nowadays when they get old but simply change their shells. Before this, men and animals also changed skin when they were old, but from this day until now they die when they are old.

[9] In another version, she fell into the water with her children. They became Ywan, spirits of the water.

XXV. THE MAN WHO MARRIED THE VULTURE

Once a Tenetehara man who had no wife found a small female king vulture (*Gypagus papa*) as he walked through the forest. He took it home with him and raised it. After it was grown, he remarked one day that if only this bird were human, it might cook for him and his meals would be ready when he returned from the garden. The vulture heard him, and that evening when he returned from his garden, he found his meal ready for him. After this had happened several times, the poor man suspected who was cooking for him, so one day he said as he left for the garden, "Today, I shall return late from the garden." Then, instead of leaving, he hid himself in the forest and saw the vulture take off her feather garments and become a beautiful girl. He watched her prepare his food. Then he stole into the house and took away her feather garments so she would remain a beautiful girl. Then she explained to him that because he had been good to her when she was small, she wanted to be good to him after she was grown. They were married.

After a while, the husband suggested that they visit her relatives, but the young wife did not want to do so. She said that her father, the king vulture, was very dangerous. The husband insisted, so one day when there was little wind, they went off together into the sky. When the girl took her husband to her father, the king vulture asked his son-in-law to build a canoe the next day. The Tenetehara knew that he would not be able to build a canoe in one day, but he decided to begin anyway. He sat on a log in the forest complaining of the impossibility of his task, and suddenly a woodpecker flew down to his side. He told the woodpecker his sad story and the woodpecker offered to help him. A great band of woodpeckers came and within a short time the tree had been hollowed out and the canoe was ready. The Tenetehara took the canoe to his father-in-law, who was indeed very much surprised.

The next day the father-in-law asked the young man to clear a large garden in one day. Again the woodpeckers came, and with their help the job was finished by sundown. After several days the father-in-law decided to burn off the clearing. He asked the Tenetehara to start a fire in the middle of the clearing. While this was being done, he sent his sons to set fire to the edges of the clearing so that the Tenetehara was surrounded by the fire. The Tenetehara was afraid, but a spider suddenly spoke to him. The spider told the Tenetehara to come with him below ground and to share his house with him. They went below ground and the fire swept over the clearing but the Tenẹtehara was safe in the spider's house. When the fire was over, the Tenetehara went to the house of the hawks and asked their aid. He told them that his father-in-law wanted to kill him and asked their help to get his vulture wife and their child back. The hawks flew to the house of the king vulture. Everyone was afraid of them. They took the Tenetehara's wife and child back to their village where he was waiting for them. He continued to live in the village of the hawks with his wife and children.[10]

XXVI. OPOSSUM TAKES A SON-IN-LAW

The opossum [11] had a daughter old enough for marriage and he wanted a son-in-law to help him work his garden. One evening the woodpecker walked round and round the opossum's house singing to let the girl know he wished to marry her. Opossum called his daughter and sent her to find out who was singing. She was pleased with the suitor and soon they were married. Opossum sent his son-in-law to make a clearing for a garden. In a short time the woodpecker had cut down many trees by pecking with his beak. Opossum's daughter went home and told her father how her husband had worked. Opossum decided to try his remarkable son-in-law's simple way of cutting down trees, so the next day he went to clear a garden site himself. He beat his nose against the trees as his son-in-law had done until it became sore and swollen. He went angrily home and told his daughter, "That man is not a good husband for you. No one can possibly work in such a manner." He sent his son-in-law away.

Soon the hawk came to court the opossum's daughter. The girl

[10] In a variation of this story told to us by a Tenetehara man who had lived many years with Brazilians, a Negro marries a parrot. He returns to discover that she has become a white girl and they are married. One day he takes her to a festival and a white man tries to take his wife away from him. The white man says, "Negroes should marry with Negroes."

[11] The *gambá* (*Didelphis marsupialis*). In Tupí, the opossum is called *mukwura*, the name of a character in the story of the Twins.

was delighted with the hawk as a suitor. Opossum gave his consent and the hawk came to live with them as the opossum's son-in-law. Opossum asked this son-in-law to make a garden for them. The hawk replied that he did not know how to make a garden, but that he was an expert hunter. So opossum sent his new son-in-law hunting. The hawk went to the forest, seated himself in a high tree and waited for game to pass. When an animal appeared, the hawk swooped down from the tree and killed it. The hawk returned with two forest fowls and an agouti. Opossum's daughter explained to her father how her new husband hunted. Opossum was delighted and decided that the next day he himself would hunt the same way. Opossum laboriously climbed a tree and waited. Soon a coatí appeared and opossum swooped down—but since he did not have wings he fell to the ground, bruising himself badly. He tried again and again and each time he fell heavily to the ground. He was angry. He went home and sent this son-in-law away.

A few days later, another man came singing near his house and opossum sent his daughter out to see who it was. She returned and said, "It was a man with a beautiful skin." It was the otter,[12] and opossum consented to the marriage. Otter came to live with them. The otter explained to his father-in-law that he was an expert fisherman, and opossum sent him to fish for them. Otter built three fires on the river bank; then, with a sack in his hands he rolled through the fire into the water and when he appeared on the surface his sack was full of fish. The daughter explained to opossum how her husband fished. The next day opossum went to the river to fish in the same manner as his son-in-law. He built three fires and rolled through them, burning himself badly. Annoyed by his failure, he sent otter away.

Then another suitor came to opossum's house. This time it was the *juriti* (a dove or pigeon, *Leptotila rufaxilla*), and opossum took him as his son-in-law. *Juriti* said that he knew only how to fish, so opossum sent him fishing. *Juriti* went to a small lake; he walked along the edge of the lake and drank so much water that the lake was soon dry and all he had to do was to collect the fish and take them home to his father-in-law. After his daughter had told him how her husband fished, opossum decided to fish the same way.

[12] *Lontra* in Portuguese.

Opossum drank so much water that he was ill and still the lake did not dry up. He sent *juriti* away, and again his daughter did not have a husband.

Kingfisher appeared courting the daughter and opossum accepted him as a son-in-law. He too said he was an expert fisherman and opossum sent him to fish. Kingfisher seated himself on a branch overhanging the river and waited, but no fish came. Then kingfisher spat in the water and immediately a fish came to the surface and kingfisher swooped down and caught the fish in his beak. Using this method, he soon filled his sack. The daughter explained to opossum how it was done and the next day opossum seated himself on the same branch. He spat in the water and when a fish appeared near the surface, down went opossum after the fish, but since he did not have wings, opossum splashed into the water. The fish escaped, and opossum almost drowned. He told his daughter that kingfisher would not do as a son-in-law, and she sent him away.

Then he took the wood tick (*carrapato* in Portuguese) as his son-in-law. The wood tick told his father-in-law that he could neither make a garden, fish, nor hunt, but that he could gather *sapucaia* nuts. The wood tick climbed to the highest trees and threw the nuts to the ground. As soon as he had collected enough, the wood tick seated himself on a leaf and floated gently to the ground. After opossum had been told of this, he decided to do the same. He climbed the trees laboriously and after he had thrown the nuts to the ground, he caught hold of a leaf on which to float down. But opossum was too heavy for the leaf; he fell to the ground so hard that he was knocked senseless. He sent the wood tick away.

His daughter again did not have a husband, so she was very happy when the handsome forest fowl called *jacamin* came to court her. For all his colorful feathers, *jacamin* was not able to perform any useful task so opossum would not give his consent. He sent *jacamin* away. Then the honey monkey arrived, and since he could collect honey for them, opossum accepted him as a son-in-law. The honey monkey walked through the forest and sucked up honey. When he arrived at home, he asked his father-in-law for a knife, and punching a hole in his throat he filled up a gourd vessel with the honey which flowed out. This looked easy to opossum and he decided to do the same. He drank honey until he was full. Then, returning home, he took a knife and punched a hole in his throat. Opossum bled to death because he did not have a sack in his throat as the honey monkey does. Opossum died and the honey monkey lived on with the daughter.

XXVII. THE TORTOISE AND THE OPOSSUM

Tortoise [13] and opossum had an argument as to which could go the longest without eating. Tortoise challenged opossum to a contest. As agreed, tortoise entered a hole and opossum covered over the entrance. Each day, for more than two moons, opossum returned and asked tortoise if he had eaten anything and if he wished to continue the contest. Each day tortoise answered with a strong voice that he had not yet eaten and that he did wish to continue. Actually, tortoise had discovered another entrance to the hole and each day he left by the other entrance to eat and returned the same way. Finally tortoise came out and now it was opossum's turn. He entered the hole and tortoise covered the entrance. Tortoise had cleverly closed the second entrance. Opossum became very hungry but he still wished to win. He held out for ten days and then died of hunger. Tortoise called his friends to eat what was left of opossum.

XXVIII. TORTOISE AND THE DEER

Deer wished to marry tortoise's daughter. Tortoise agreed to the marriage on condition that deer must prove he could run faster than tortoise. They arranged a race. Deer was certain of winning, for it is well known that a tortoise cannot run fast. Deer ran so fast that he soon left tortoise far behind, so he slowed down his pace. Suddenly, out in front deer heard tortoise say, "Look, *compadre,* you don't know how to run." Deer was surprised, but he increased his pace and soon he was certain that he was far ahead again. Then again he heard tortoise speak ahead of him, "Oh, *compadre,* you can't run very fast." Deer ran faster; each time he was sure he had outdistanced tortoise and was surprised to hear tortoise still ahead. Finally deer felt exhausted. After he had rested many hours he went on to the spot marked to end the race, and there was tortoise waiting for him. Tortoise told him that he had lost and could not marry his daughter. Deer did not know that the tortoise had posted his

---

[13] The *jaboti* in Portuguese (*Testudo tabulata*).

brothers along the course of the race and each of them cried out in turn, making deer think that tortoise was ahead of him.

XXIX. TORTOISE TRICKS HIS BROTHERS-IN-LAW

Tortoise had been hunting for many days without killing anything. His daughter was hungry, so he cut a piece of meat from his own leg and gave her the meat, telling her that he had killed a tapir. His brothers-in-law were also very hungry, and they made him promise to take them to the spot where he had killed the tapir. There they discovered the truth and they were angry with the tortoise. His brothers-in-law decided to kill him and roast him over a fire. They prepared a big fire but tortoise said, "Don't put me in a fire. You cannot kill me that way. Fire is my father. Place me in the water, in the near-by river, and I will drown." His brothers-in-law believed him and threw him in the river. Tortoise dove beneath the surface and swam away singing, "Ton! Ton! Ton!" [14]

XXX. TORTOISE AND THE JAGUAR

Tortoise saw a band of monkeys feasting on *najá* fruit. He stood under the trees and asked them to throw a few down to him; instead the monkeys invited him to come up into the tree with them. He explained that he could not climb but insisted that he wished to eat fruit, so finally one of the monkeys carried tortoise into the tree. He ate his fill and only then did he notice that the monkeys had gone off leaving him stranded in the tree. He shouted but no one heard him, so he settled down to wait until some animal passed which would be able to help him down. First the peccary passed by, but the peccary explained that he did not know how to climb, and went on. Then the jaguar came by. He agreed to help tortoise down but asked tortoise to throw down a few *najá* fruits first. Tortoise threw some fruit and then jaguar told tortoise to jump. "I have strong arms and I will catch you," said jaguar. When tortoise jumped, jaguar missed and tortoise fell full on jaguar's nose and knocked

[14] The Tenetehara told us another version of this story. According to the other version, tortoise marries a young girl. He has a reputation as a great hunter because he has found a band of peccaries trapped in a hole. Each day he takes one back to his brothers-in-law, until all the peccaries have been eaten. Then, to retain his reputation he cuts meat from his own leg to prove that he can kill a tapir. He is discovered, but escapes after his brothers-in-law are persuaded to throw him in the water.

jaguar unconscious. Tortoise was delighted and walked away singing, "I hit jaguar on the nose! Ha! Ha!" Jaguar gained his senses and heard this song. He was angry and ran after tortoise. When jaguar caught him, tortoise swore that jaguar had not heard correctly. Tortoise said he had sung, "I hit deer on the nose! Ha! Ha!" Jaguar was satisfied and let tortoise go, but no sooner had jaguar moved out of sight than tortoise sang his original song. Jaguar heard it clearly this time and caught tortoise again. Jaguar was angry and said that he was going to copulate with tortoise in his anus. Tortoise then persuaded jaguar that they should take turns. Tortoise asked to be first, claiming that he had a very small penis. Jaguar agreed. Tortoise took hours before he had an ejaculation and his penis is very large. He hurt jaguar. Now it was jaguar's turn, but tortoise said that they must select a clean part of the forest. They walked until tortoise saw a hole and he tried to escape into the hole. Jaguar was quick and caught hold of his leg. Tortoise laughed. He told jaguar, "You have hold of a root, not my leg." Jaguar turned his leg loose. Tortoise climbed deep into the hole and began to sing again, "Ha! Ha! I hit jaguar on the nose!" Jaguar stayed in front of the hole four days and died of hunger.

XXXI. THE VULTURE'S PARTY

The vulture wanted to have a festival. He came down to earth to buy the necessary coffee, sugar, manioc flour, tobacco, and so on, and to invite all the animals to come. He met the *kururú*-toad but he did not invite the toad because he could not fly. He invited only birds who could fly to his house, but two uninvited guests came. The *kururú*-toad liked festivals and was sad. He went from one bird to another asking them to take him along, but no one offered to do so. So while the vulture was not looking the *kururú*-toad took his *cavaquinho* [15] and hid himself in vulture's sack among the supplies for the festival. As soon as he arrived at vulture's house he came out and began to play the *cavaquinho*. Vulture was not angry because the toad played the *cavaquinho* well. The white water bird came bringing the tortoise.

The next day the festival was finished and the birds began leaving. The *kururú*-toad hid again in vulture's sack, but vulture discovered

[15] A small stringed instrument, about the size of a ukelele.

him and turned the sack over. The toad fell hard to the ground. He was very sick from his fall but after a time he got well, but since that time the toad, who was formerly tall, has been short. The water bird forgot and left tortoise behind when he returned from the festival. Tortoise went to the door of vulture's house and called for help. No one came. He lost his balance and tumbled down to earth. The fall broke his shell into many small pieces. Tupan was sorry for tortoise, and he collected all the small parts of his shell and put them back together. Even today, the design on the shell of the tortoise shows the cracks ·between the pieces placed together by Tupan.

XXXII. THE RABBIT AND THE JAGUAR

Jaguar met rabbit in the forest one day; rabbit had a vine rope. Jaguar was curious and asked what rabbit intended to do with the rope. Rabbit explained that a tremendously strong wind was approaching which would carry off all the animals of the forest. He said that he planned to tie himself to a strong tree. Jaguar was impressed and afraid. He asked rabbit to tie him to a tree. Rabbit selected a strong tree and tied jaguar securely. Rabbit went away. After considerable time had passed and nothing had happened, jaguar began to suspect that he had been tricked. Jaguar waited for someone to pass to untie him. A woodpecker flew by and jaguar begged to be released but the woodpecker refused to come near. Woodpecker was afraid that jaguar would eat him. Deer came, but he was also afraid of jaguar. All the animals were afraid and passed on, leaving jaguar tied to the tree. Finally, a red monkey untied jaguar and jaguar grabbed at him, pulling off part of his tail as the monkey climbed back into the tree. Jaguar had been tied to the tree so long without eating that now he was starving.

Jaguar was making a garden and rabbit, who was hiding near by, watched until jaguar left; then rabbit worked on the garden at night. The next day jaguar saw that someone had been helping him and was naturally happy about it. For several days jaguar worked in the daytime and rabbit helped with the garden at night. Finally one day rabbit stayed until the jaguar arrived. Jaguar was friendly and asked rabbit to come live with him. Jaguar had three children and needed someone to take care of them while he worked in the garden and hunted. Thus, it was understood that rabbit would care for the children. One day there was no meat in the house, so rabbit killed one of jaguar's children and served it for dinner. Jaguar ate and complimented rabbit for being such a good cook. The next day rabbit cooked a second child and after the meal jaguar asked rabbit to bring out the children for him to feed them. Rabbit brought out the only one left and jaguar fed it. Then, he took the child back and brought it out again saying, "Look, the second is fatter than the first." He took it back after it had eaten and brought it out again. "Look," said rabbit, "the third is fatter than the second." Jaguar was suspicious because the second and the third did not have good appetites, and went to see the three together. As soon as he saw there was only one left, he knew that rabbit had killed two of them. Rabbit ran far away, happy because he had tricked jaguar.

Jaguar wanted revenge and he hunted for rabbit many days. Finally he found rabbit, but rabbit quickly jumped into a hole and jaguar mounted guard over the entrance. Jaguar called vulture and asked vulture to watch the entrance of the hole while he went to get digging instruments so they could dig rabbit out. Soon as jaguar had left, rabbit called to the vulture and vulture stuck his head inside the hole to look for rabbit. Rabbit asked vulture to open his eyes—"so you can see me." When vulture did this, rabbit threw dust in vulture's eyes and quickly ran out of the hole and escaped. Jaguar returned and asked the vulture if rabbit was still in the hole. Since vulture had not seen rabbit leave, he said "Yes." Then they both began to dig and after much work found only the empty hole. Jaguar was angry and wanted to kill vulture, but vulture flew away before jaguar could catch him.

Jaguar continued to hunt rabbit. He met tortoise, who told him that every night rabbit came to drink at a certain water hole. Tortoise agreed to help jaguar. That night tortoise hid under the water and when rabbit stood in the water to drink, he grabbed rabbit's leg in his mouth. Tortoise tried to call jaguar, but still holding on to rabbit's leg, he could only call faintly. Rabbit laughed and said that jaguar would never hear him. "If you want him to come," said rabbit, "you must open your mouth to shout." Tortoise released his hold on rabbit to shout, and rabbit escaped into the forest.

Jaguar continued to wait for rabbit at the water hole; all the other drinking places in the region had dried up. The *saúva* ant warned rabbit. Then rabbit asked the *saúva* ant to carry him to the water hole in a gourd vessel. When the ants came near, jaguar asked them what they were doing with the gourd vessel. The ants replied that they were collecting water, but at that time the vessel turned over and rabbit fell to the ground and barely escaped the clutches of the jaguar.

Rabbit met a man who had a bottle of honey in his pack. Rabbit smeared honey over his whole body, then rolled on the ground so that leaves and dust would stick to him. Thus, disguised as a *saúva* ant he approached the water hole to drink at the place where the *saúva* ants were accustomed to drink. Jaguar was suspicious. Jaguar asked, "What is your name?" and rabbit responded, "My name is *Cirrupira.*" Jaguar came nearer and rabbit stood up and ran off with jaguar after him. They ran far and the jaguar the next day was ill with sore feet. Jaguar soon died.

XXXIII. JAGUAR AND THE SLOTH

The tree sloths (*Bradipus tridactylus;* the *preguiça* in Portuguese) were playing; they went to a high limb of a tree and dropped to the ground. They laughed because the fall did not hurt them. Jaguar came by and asked them how to play this game which seemed to be so much fun. The tree sloths explained and jaguar was envious. He asked them to allow him to take part in the game, and they agreed to let him join, warning him however that he might hurt himself. Jaguar would not listen; he was certain that he could do whatever the tree sloths could. He was arrogant and he climbed to the highest spot in the tree and dropped to the ground. Jaguar landed hard on some rocks and was killed. Looking at his body, the tree sloths said, "Look, we told you that you would die."

XXXIV. JAGUAR AND THE ANTEATERS

One time jaguar met two anteaters; they were rubbing their faces into a mass of thorns to see if this might punch open their eyes. Jaguar asked what they were doing and they explained. He asked if he might do the same. They warned him, but the arrogant jaguar stuck his face, which is flat, into the mass of thorns. The thorns tore his face and made him blind. He ran screaming through the forest.

Another time, the jaguar and the anteater were arguing which of them could kill the most animals. Anteater said each should show what he had killed and eaten by his excrement. Anteater challenged jaguar to a contest. Each would defecate with his eyes closed. They began and after a time jaguar asked anteater if he was ready to open his eyes. Anteater asked jaguar to keep his eyes closed a while longer. While jaguar had his eyes closed, anteater changed excreta with him. When jaguar opened his eyes he saw a large pile of excreta near anteater and a small pile near himself. They looked at jaguar's pile. "Oh!" said anteater, "you evidently eat only ants. Look at my excrement, I eat many animals." Jaguar went away ashamed and sad. He soon died of shame.

XXXV. BEAUTY AND THE BEAST

There was a young girl who wanted a husband and one night a young man appeared and asked the consent of her father to marry her. They were married. The new husband appeared at his wife's house each night after dark and each morning just before it was light he left. The young wife was anxious to see her husband's face. She spoke to her mother, saying that she had never been able to see him. Her mother advised her to take a burning stick from the fire and while her husband was asleep to illuminate his face. That night she followed her mother's advice and discovered that she was married to an alligator man. A spark from her fire fell on his face and he waked up angry with her. He went away at once. After many days had passed she missed her husband, even though he was an alligator; he had brought her presents and had pleased her as a husband. She decided to go out into the world and seek him.

She traveled far and wide and finally arrived at the house of the Moon, where she was received by Moon's mother. She was told to wait until Moon arrived; perhaps he would have news of the alligator husband's whereabouts. But Moon did not know where the husband was. So the wife traveled many days again until she came to Sun's house. Sun's mother asked her to wait until Sun arrived; perhaps he would know something of her husband. But Sun did not know. The wife then went to Wind's house, and Wind's mother asked the woman to wait until Wind returned; perhaps he would know. Wind arrived and said that he knew where the alligator husband was living, but the place was far away and impossible to reach

by walking. Then Wind offered to take her there on his shoulders
and the woman accepted. Wind carried her very far away near the
edges of the earth where there were but a few islands. Wind left the
woman on one of these islands, and there she saw her alligator husband, sunning himself as alligators customarily do. The woman
came close to him and spoke. He did not answer her and quickly
slid off into the water. She waited and the next day he appeared
again. For four days he would not come near his wife, who each
day begged him to come back to her. Finally on the fifth day he
came to the island, embraced his wife and took her with him below
the surface of the water. The woman and her alligator husband
were never heard of again.

XXXVI. CINDERELLA

A girl named Maria lived with her parents who owned many cattle and Maria was treated with great affections. After a time, however, Maria's mother died and her father began to mistreat her. He
soon married a woman who had other daughters, and Maria's life
became one of suffering. Her stepmother and sisters mistreated her
and made her do all the household tasks. They would not buy her
new clothes when her clothes became old and ragged.

One day her stepmother gave her a very large amount of cotton
and demanded that she spin all of it in one day. Maria knew that
this was impossible and she was afraid because she knew that her
stepmother would beat her. She began to cry and went to see her
good friend, a small lamb with which she often played. She told the
lamb why she was sad and the lamb spoke to her and told her not
to worry. The lamb swallowed all the cotton and that afternoon,
cotton threat issued from the lamb's mouth. Maria rolled the thread
in balls and took it back to her stepmother. The stepmother was
amazed when she saw how much the girl had spun. The next day
the stepmother gave her more cotton to spin than the day before
and the lamb did all the work, but one of Maria's stepsisters saw
her taking thread from the mouth of the lamb and told their mother.
Their mother insisted that the lamb be killed, and because the
mother was pregnant, the father agreed. The lamb heard what was
said and told Maria not to worry after it was dead. The lamb said
that she should wash off the intestines and keep a piece of arrow

which she would find in them. Maria did as she was told and put the arrow in a small basket. Each time her stepmother asked her to spin cotton she would put the cotton in the basket with the arrow and by afternoon it would all be spun.

One day Maria remembered that the lamb had told her that she should go to an isolated house deep in the forest and that if she found it dirty and unkept, she should clean it up. Maria found the house; she filled the pots with water, swept out the house, brought firewood, and built a fire for cooking. When she heard the owner arrive, she hid. The owner was Zurupari (the forest demon) and he was delighted with the way he found his house. Soon his companion arrived and Zurupari said that beautiful sparks would henceforth issue from the mouth of the good person who had cleaned his house, and his companion added, "and she will have a shiny moon on her forehead." The two Zurupari left to bathe and Maria escaped, running all the way back to her house.

When she arrived home everyone was surprised at her beauty. She had a shiny moon on her forehead. They were even more surprised when bright sparks came from her mouth when she talked. Her stepsisters were jealous and made her tell what she had done. Maria in revenge told them that they should dirty up the house of the Zurupari. The next day the stepsisters went to Zurupari's house and instead of cleaning it they broke the pots and scattered everything about. Zurupari and his companions were very angry when they arrived. One of them said, "Whoever did this will have a tail on her forehead," and the other added, "and excrement will come from the mouth of whoever did this when she talks." When the stepsisters arrived at home they had tails on their foreheads and when they opened their mouths to talk, excrement came out.

Each day Maria had to prepare the meals for the entire family. One day she remembered the piece of arrow that she had kept in her basket. She asked the arrow for a beautiful dress and a horse, both of which appeared at once. She mounted the horse and went to the near-by town where a church festival was taking place. Everyone saw the beautiful girl enter the church but no one knew who she was. Even the stepmother saw her and did not recognize her. As soon as the ceremony was over, Maria got back on her horse and hurried home. She found the meal ready, prepared by the magic arrow, and when her stepmother and stepsisters arrived she was able to serve dinner to them. Maria then began to go to church for vespers every day, always attracting attention by the elegance of her appearance. One day a white soldier [16] saw her and fell in love with her. When she left he tried to catch her but she escaped. When she jumped on her horse, her shoe dropped off and the soldier found it. He went through the whole region trying to find the girl whose foot fitted the shoe. Finally he came to Maria's house and her stepsisters tried the shoe; they liked the soldier and tried to show that the shoe was theirs. Then the soldier asked the mother if she had another daughter and she said that she did not. Maria heard the conversation; she went to take a bath in the stream and asked the magic piece of arrow to bring her the dress and shoes she had used at the church. She dressed and returned to the house and claimed the shoe. Then Maria married the representative of the government.

XXXVII. BABES IN THE WOODS

A poor man had many children and he was not able to feed them, since his gardens were small and hunting was bad in the region. One day he asked two of his children João and Maria, to go with him into the forest to collect honey. The daughter took an ear of corn with her and dropped grains of corn from it as she walked, so that she might find her way back in case they got lost. Deep in the forest the father left the two children and said that they should wait for him at that spot. He told them that he would signal to them now and again by whistling. Then he hung a gourd in a tree so it would make a whistling noise when the wind blew, and he took off for home, leaving the children to die. They waited a long time and then the children went to seek their father in the direction they heard the whistling. They discovered the gourd in the tree and they knew then that they had been abandoned. They cried all night.

The next day they tried to return home following the grains of corn which Maria had dropped, but they lost their way. They wan-

---

[16] The Tenetehara make a distinction between the Negro (paranã) and the white Brazilian (karaý) whom they prefer. In the telling of this story, the soldier was described specifically as white to show that he was a man of prestige. The Tenetehara are aware that the majority of government officials and people of prestige among Brazilians are European, not Negroes, and for that reason, perhaps, they look upon the European Braizilians with more favor.

dered several days in the forest, living on seeds and wild fruit. Then they came to a house. João went near to see who lived there. He saw several hot manioc cakes in the kitchen and he stole them. After he and his sister had eaten they came near the house. They saw an old woman. The old woman was angry and was scolding her cat for stealing her manioc cakes. The children approached her and she invited them to come in. They stayed to live with her and she gave them a bath and fed them well. Each day, however, after they had eaten she asked them to put their fingers through a small hole in the wall to see how fat they were getting. João was suspicious so each day the two children put the tail of a rat through the hole and the old woman fed them more because she thought they were very thin. Maria lost the rat's tail and the next day they had to put their fingers in the hole and the old woman saw that they were getting fat. Then a small forest bird came and told them that the old woman planned to eat them. The bird told them that she would dance around the fire before roasting them and that they must push her into the fire as she danced.

One day the old woman sent them to gather wood, and when she had made a large fire she began to dance. João did as the bird had told him and pushed her into the fire. As the old woman burned, she called for water. João brought her oil instead. As soon as the fire had burned to ashes, João spread a blanket over it and the next morning when he took away the blanket he found four small dogs.

João and Maria wandered into the forest. They found the village of Zurupari. It seemed empty, so João left his sister and went collecting *bacaba* (fruit). Maria was curious. She entered one of the houses and saw a group of people—half of their bodies were hanging on one side of the house and half on the other. They begged her to cut them down and bring their halves together so they could become people again. She did so and a handsome young man appeared before her. She liked him and they had sexual intercourse. She did not know that he was Zurupari. Then the Zurupari said they must kill her brother so she could live on there with him. João appeared and his four dogs killed the Zurupari and Maria, who was a traitor to her brother.

João traveled on alone, accompanied only by his four dogs. He wandered for more than two moons. Then he came to a house where a girl was crying. She told him that she had been left there to be eaten by a large snake. She warned him to leave because the snake would come and kill him. João lay down beside her and asked her to pick lice from his hair. As she did so, João went to sleep. As the snake approached, the girl began to cry and João was awakened by her tears falling on his face. João released his dogs and they killed the snake. João cut out the snake's tongue and gave it to his dogs to eat. He left the girl, telling her that he would come back for her later.

A Negro had been hiding in the forest and had seen all this take place. He cut out what was left of the snake's tongue and took it to the girl's father, saying that he had saved the girl's life. When the girl arrived home, the father had already agreed that she should marry the Negro. She refused and in time João arrived at her village. He went to speak with the "government" (authorities) and proved that it was he who had killed the snake and that the Negro was an imposter. The "government" was angry and had the Negro tied between two horses which were whipped into running in opposite directions, tearing the Negro in half. The girl was married to João. His dogs were very sad at this and they said that they would go away. The noise of thunder would announce their arrival in the sky. That night João and his bride heard the noise of deep thunder in the sky and they knew that his faithful dogs had arrived. Thunder is the howling of these dogs, who are homesick for their owner.

VII · A CULTURE IN TRANSITION

UNDER THE influence of various forms of Brazilian-Portuguese culture, Tenetehara culture has undergone many changes since the seventeenth century. Precisely how extensive this process has been, or in other words, precisely how modern Tenetehara culture differs, from the aboriginal Tenetehara way of life, is difficult to ascertain. When the earliest accounts of the Tenetehara were written in the nineteenth century, much change had already occurred, and even these accounts are disappointingly fragmentary. Lacking direct information, however, we may draw upon our knowledge of other Tupí-Guaraní tribes who inhabited the Brazilian coast from the Amazon to São Paulo, as well as great portions of the continental interior. Although it is known that the culture of numerous Tupí-Guaraní-speaking tribes differed in many details, the tribes are also known to have shared a common body of custom. The Tupinambá, one of the most populous of these tribes, inhabited the entire coastal region of Maranhão, where they had some 27 villages with a total of approximately 12,000 people. They had also a number of villages along the lower reaches of the Pindaré, Itapecurú, and Mearim Rivers.[1] Fortunately, early writers described the culture of these coastal Tupí in considerable detail before their disappearance under the impact of Portuguese rule.

These coastal tribes and the aboriginal Tenetehara cannot of course be assumed to have had identical culture patterns. The Tupí were unabashed cannibals, for example, and there are no indications that the Tenetehara ever resorted to cannibalism. If an element reported for the aboriginal coastal Tupí is lacking from present-day Tenetehara life, we cannot infer that it has been dis-

[1] Abbéville, pp. 139–145, 209.

carded since aboriginal times or replaced with a Brazilian element. Yet, with some precaution, a comparison between the modern Tene-tehara and the aboriginal coastal Tupí culture as reported by the French and Portuguese chroniclers does allow us to point out cer-tain basic changes which have occurred and certain specific spheres in which Tenetehara culture has remained stable.

As among the aboriginal Tupinambá, the economic life of the Tenetehara is still based on the cultivation of manioc, corn, beans, yams, peanuts, squash, and other native plants, and the system of cultivating the soil is essentially the same.[2] They have acquired new plants such as sugar cane, bananas, rice, papaya, and hashish from the Brazilians, and iron tools have been substituted for the aborig-inal stone implements, making larger gardens possible. They have learned to keep a few chickens, not for the eggs, which they do not find palatable, but for food. Some villagers have domestic pigs, guinea fowls, and even goats. The meat of these animals, although consumed on occasion, is not especially liked, and domestic animals are kept mainly as pets rather than as a steady dependable food sup-ply. Pets such as pacas, wild pigs, macaws, and talking parrots are common nowadays in Tenetehara villages, as they were in the vil-lages of the extinct Tupinambá. The Indians still depend upon hunting and fishing for their basic source of meat. The general pat-terns of food-getting have been left essentially unchanged.

However, the Tenetehara are nowadays a part of the Brazilian commercial system and have acquired from the Brazilians new tastes for many material objects which have acquired the rank of absolute necessities. While they formerly went nude,[3] they now need clothes. Men feel that they must have at least two pairs of trousers and a shirt, and women wear European-type skirts and blouses and need at least one change. Even more, clothes have become an item of dis-play, and a man of prestige likes to own a complete suit with trousers and a sack coat. Women have learned to sew and therefore need manufactured thread, buttons, scissors, and steel needles. Most

[2] *Ibid.*, pp. 226, 242. Even in aboriginal times, Tupinambá villages customarily moved their location each five to six years in search of new and more fertile garden sites (*ibid.*, p. 222).

[3] The men wore "a ring called *tocanhoba* made of a palm leaf over that part of the body which natural shame requires" to be hidden, and the women wore "only a leaf." (Pereira do Lago, p. 85). The Tupinambá were nude. See Claude d'Abbéville, 1945 ed., p. 216.

Tenetehara families use kerosene lamps for light. All of them purchase salt, and many have developed a taste for coffee and brown sugar. Men make their gardens with purchased axes, bush knives and hoes; they hunt with muzzle-loading rifles and fish with fishhooks. Like the Tupinambá before them, most Tenetehara still sleep in hammocks woven by their women from native cotton, but there are many who prefer machine-made hammocks instead. Most Tenetehara women cook in metal pots manufactured in southern Brazil or abroad rather than in large clay pots of the type manufactured by the Tupinambá. Although the Tenetehara are not fervent drinkers, many of them have acquired the taste for sugar cane *aguardente,* which is produced throughout the interior of Brazil. All these items and many others must be purchased from Brazilian traders.

While the system of food-getting has been only slightly modified, the orientation of economic patterns has changed from one of production entirely for consumption to one of production for consumption and for sale. One way of purchasing manufactured articles is by producing a surplus of garden products which can be sold on the local market, and the resulting "commercial" farming has induced several changes in the organization of agricultural production. More and more, in order to have the right to sell the surplus, men are planting individual gardens rather than working along with their extended family group. Agriculture has become therefore almost entirely a man's occupation. Formerly women played an important role in planting and harvesting certain food crops, but now gardening is a commercial undertaking, and thus a man's job. Since an important item of trade is manioc flour, men are replacing women in the work of manufacturing the flour. In the past, men would have lost face had they taken over these traditionally women's jobs. Another way of purchasing manufactured necessities is to collect the native products of the tropical forest for sale to Brazilian traders. On the upper Pindaré River, the Tenetehara collect copaíba oil; on the middle portions of the river they collect *babassú* nuts; throughout the region they collect wild animal pelts —in order to be able to buy manufactured objects.

The price paid to them for these products, as well as the price paid by them for manufactured articles, depends upon world conditions and on the markets of São Luiz, Rio de Janeiro, London, and New York. The Tenetehara do not understand commerce. Trade was not highly developed among the Tupinambá and does not seem to have been important in the Tenetehara aboriginal economic system. Even today, buying and selling in units of money is not quite comprehensible to even the more sophisticated among the Tenetehara. They find it strange and unjust that prices fluctuate. They are easily cheated. The Indian Service attempts to protect them from exploitation by controlling trade with the local merchants, but because the Service tries also to control what they purchase, the Indians frequently trade without the knowledge of the Indian Officers. With no background in their culture for trade and no real understanding of commerce, the Tenetehara naturally suffer from their contact with a commercial system.

The Tenetehara have lived for more than three hundred years under foreign administrative jurisdiction, no matter how loose the controls have been—first of the Jesuit missionaries, then of Colonial and Republican administrators, and finally of the Indian Service. Inevitably, outside political control has resulted in basic changes in their political and social organization. The aboriginal kinship system, which was evidently shared in its essential patterns by the coastal Tupí tribes, as well as by other Tupí-Guaraní tribes as far apart as the Brazilian frontier with Paraguay and northern Mato Grosso,[4] and the matrilocal extended family group, which is also common to other Tupí tribes, are still the basis of Tenetehara social organization. The real leaders of modern Tenetehara villages are still the heads of the extended family groups. Nowadays, however, each village has an appointed chief whose qualifications for the position are mainly his ability to speak Portuguese and to get on amicably with the Brazilian Indian Officers. The Tupinambá are said to have had chiefs whose authority was sometimes subordinated to a village council,[5] and some Tupinambá villages seem to have had two, three, or even four chiefs.[6] Such chiefs were men of great power in war; they had magical power, and they were often shamans. It was important for them to have many relatives and to

[4] Wagley and Galvão, p. 20.

[5] Abbéville writes (1945 ed., p. 140) that one Tupinambá chieftain was not only the most powerful man of his own village "but also of the entire Island." There were four chiefs in one Tupinambá village.

[6] *Ibid.*, pp. 255–256.

be well liked "so that they would have people who were willing to help cultivate their plantations." [7] If the Tenetehara ever had a village chief of the type described for the Tupinambá, or a village council, the rule has now been supplanted by a secular chief with few powers imposed by outside administrators. The Tupinambá chiefs with large families who worked with them in their plantations would seem to correspond to the Tenetehara leaders of extended family groups. But in reality the power of the latter is based less on any magical powers than on their capacity to organize the group to produce for sale to Brazilians and on their astuteness in dealing with the Brazilians. Only in rare cases among the modern Tenetehara does a man have the combined powers of magical and secular leadership as did the Tupinambá chiefs.

The Tupinambá lived in large communal dwellings housing many families. Such houses had a rectangular floor plan and an arched or vaulted thatched roof which carried down to the ground to form the walls. There were no internal walls marking off the quarters of the individual families. [8] This type of house is also found among the Tupí-Guaraní speaking Tapirapé and each communal dwelling ideally houses a large extended family group. The house of the modern Tenetehara corresponds in form to that of the local Brazilian population. In general they are single-family dwellings, but are close to the houses of others of the extended family group. We cannot say with certainty whether or not the Tenetehara ever had large communal dwellings like those of the Tupinambá and of other Tupí-Guaraní-speaking groups, but if they did, they have been supplanted by the Brazilian single-family house. It is considered preferable for each family to have its own home, and a multi-family dwelling is regarded as a temporary and crowded arrangement.

In personal appearance, the Tenetehara might easily be mistaken for the Brazilian *caboclos* (Indian-white mixtures) who form the basic population of the region. All Tenetehara wear clothes. Both men and women cut their hair in European style. Although many of them file their teeth, a few *caboclos* in the Pindaré region also follow the same practice. The Tenetehara no longer perforate

7 Soares de Souza (1946 ed.), p. 246.   8 Abbéville (1945 ed.), p. 222.

the lower lips and ears of young boys,[9] nor do they practice scarification. Many Brazilian *caboclos* of the region have approximately the same skin coloring as the Indian, since many of them are, at least in part, descendants of Amerind stock. Such similarity ends in outward appearance. The Tenetehara have retained many traditional ceremonies, beliefs, habits, and behavior patterns which the *caboclo* finds strange and exotic, since they are so different from his own patterns.

The birth of a child among the Tenetehara still involves prenatal and postnatal restrictions on both parents. The birth is performed in a native manner and they observe a modified form of the couvade.[10] While there is a tendency in some villages to use Christian names, all children are given a native name as well. The general methods of educating children, with early responsibility for girls and delayed responsibility for boys, are singularly Tenetehara. Their preference for daughters because they attract men to the extended family is in sharp contrast to the ideal of the local Brazilians who prefer sons over daughters and share the old European idea that children should help—even support—their parents. The passage from adolescence to adulthood among the Tenetehara is still marked by puberty rites for both boys and girls, although the ceremonies are nowadays performed in a slightly attentuated form.[11]

As among the Tupinambá, marriage is still, in general, matrilocal in residence, and young men are obliged to work with their fathers-in-law for several years after marriage.[12] In spite of the prohibitions of the Indian Service, men of prestige among the Tenetehara still practice polygamy as did the Tupinambá chiefs.[13] Notably lacking, however, in Tenetehara culture is the preferred marriage of a man with his sister's daughters as reported for the coastal Tupí, to whom the custom may well have been peculiar, since it is lacking

---

[9] The Tupinambá pierced the lower lip of boys when they were five or six years of age. Abbéville (1945 ed.), p. 214.

[10] The Tupinambá father remained in his hammock for a few days after his wife gave birth, and until the child's navel cord fell off he was not allowed to do any heavy work and had to refrain from certain foods. Metraux, *La Réligion des Tupinambá*, pp. 100–101.

[11] The Tupinambá practiced isolation of girls after their first menstruation and girls were tattooed with a sharp rodent tooth.

[12] Soares de Souza, II, 248.   [13] Abbéville (1945 ed.), pp. 222–223.

also among at least two other Tupí-Guaraní tribes.[14] The custom of betrothing immature girls in "marriage" to adult males seems to be an old custom, since it was reported for the Tenetehara by Gustave Dodt in the nineteenth century, and it is reported that Tupinambá chiefs took infant brides.[15]

Tenetehara customs in regard to mourning and burial have been greatly modified. The formal patterns of burial among the Tenetehara follow closely those of the local Brazilians. The corpse is rolled in a mat or placed in a wooden box to be buried in a prone position in the near-by cemetery of the village. The Tupinambá either wrapped the body in a hammock, or squeezed the body in an urn for burial. The grave was often dug in the house floor.[16] Evidently the Tenetehara once shared the custom of burial in the house floor. since it was reported by Pereira do Lago.[17] The Tenetehara nowadays build a small shelter over the grave, contrary to Brazilian custom. This may have been an alternative pattern of burial in aboriginal times, for the practice was reported also for the Tupinambá.[18]

While the formal pattern of burial has changed, the attitudes and associations concerned with death and burial are similar to those reported for the Tupinambá. The Tupinambá were said to have been terribly afraid of spirits and to have buried their dead in such haste that often the dying man was still alive when placed in the earth.[19] The modern Tenetehara are very negligent of their dead, and few people will consent to participate in the burial. At one burial we witnessed, only two or three people accompanied the body to the cemetery; most villagers—even the close relatives of the deceased— made some excuse for remaining away. There was practically no mourning. People seemed to wish to forget. In this respect the Tenetehara differ from the Tupí-Guaraní-speaking Tapirapé and from the Tupinambá, who are said to have wailed for the dead for many days. During mourning, Tupinambá men allowed hair to grow on their shaven foreheads, the women shaved their heads, and both

[14] See Wagley and Galvão. This marriage is not found among the Tapirapé or the Cayuá.

[15] Dodt (1939 ed.), p. 200; Soares de Souza, II, 248–249; Abbéville (1945 ed.), p. 223.

[16] Soares de Souza, II, 285; Metraux, *La Réligion des Tupinambá*, pp. 116–118.

[17] Pereira do Lago, p. 86.

[18] Dodt (1939 ed.), p. 184, and Metraux, *op. cit.*, p. 118.

[19] Soares de Souza, II, 287–288; Metraux, *op. cit.*, p. 116.

sexes among the Tupinambá painted their bodies black with genipa
dye.[20] We have no way of knowing just what the aboriginal patterns
of mourning and burial were among the Tenetehara; yet while they
bury their dead much in the same manner as do the local Brazilians,
the attitudes they hold toward death are certainly different from
those of the local Catholic Brazilians, who are singularly shocked by
the behavior of Indians in this respect. The present patterns would
seem to be the result of a merging of the attitudes of extreme fear of
the dead similar to those of the Tupinambá with the formal methods
of burial borrowed from the Brazilians. The Catholic attitudes and
beliefs regarding death are hardly compatible with Tenetehara culture.

In spite of the pressure of Christian missionaries, beginning as
early as the seventeenth century with the Jesuits, it is in the realm
of religion that Tenetehara culture seems least modified. Their religion is still based on the control of the native shamans (pazé) over
a series of dangerous supernaturals. Each village has several shamans
and several young novices. These modern Tenetehara shamans act
as intermediaries between the people and the supernatural in much
the same manner as did the Tupinambá shamans who called the
spirits to help them divine, call rain, and heal the sick. Possession
by familiar spirits, as it occurs among the Tenetehara, has been reported widely for American Indians and is no doubt aboriginal.[21]
Tupinambá shamans used tobacco as do the Tenetehara nowadays.[22]
Tupinambá supernaturals correspond closely to those of the Tenetehara. They believed in ghosts comparable to the Tenetehara
azang; the Tupinambá concept of the demon Curupira seems to be
the equivalent of the Tenetehara Marana ýwa, the Owner of the
Forest; and several ancestor culture heroes of the Tupinambá, such
as Tupan and Maíra, have their Tenetehara equivalents.[23]

There are, however, several specific differences between Tenetehara and Tupinambá religion. For example, among the Tupinambá, gourd rattles were highly sacred objects and were believed
to contain a powerful spirit attracted into them by a shaman;[24] and
Tupinambá shamans were said to shut themselves for a period into

[20] Metraux, op. cit., p. 119; Soares de Souza, II, 287.
[21] Stewart (1946), pp. 323-339.   [22] Metraux, op. cit., pp. 79-93.
[23] Ibid., pp. 3 ff., 31 ff., 52 ff.   [24] Ibid., pp. 74-84.

a secluded cabin and to drink beer prepared for them by virgins, during which time they sought interviews with their familiar spirits and made offerings to effigies which appeared during ceremonies.[25] While the Tenetehara shamans use decorated rattles when they call their spirits, there is no indication that such rattles were ever considered sacred in the Tupinambá sense. The séances with spirits in a secluded cabin and the offerings to effigies do not appear in any report for the Tenetehara, and may again have been culture traits limited to the coastal Tupí.

Certain concepts of modern Tenetehara religion, however, do seem to be due to acculturation. Both the concepts of "good" and "evil" and the belief, even though vaguely held, that "good" people lead an ideal life after death are at least partially borrowed from Christianity. The Tupinambá believed in a paradise in the west where shamans and gallant warriors who were killed in battle or who were eaten by cannibalistic enemies went after death to live with their ancestors,[26] similarly, the Tenetehara told us that their shamans live in an ideal village with their ancestors after death. There was a basis, therefore, in the aboriginal culture for the understanding of the concept of a Christian heaven, and it was accepted by the Tenetehara and fused with the native belief in an ideal afterlife limited to shamans and men of great prestige. It is significant in this respect that the companion Christian concept of a burning hell, which has undoubtedly been described to the Tenetehara many times by missionaries, evidently made no impression on them and was rejected.

The influence of Christianity is also felt in the equation of Tupan, a minor culture hero among the coastal Tupinambá, with the Christian God or with Christ, and of Zurupari, a forest demon, with the devil. These beliefs are maintained separately with corresponding and sometimes contradictory aboriginal beliefs. There has been no attempt to make them consistent with the main body of religious concepts. For example, the same man who told us that Tupan (in this case, the Christ or God) made mankind and then told us a myth in which the creation of mankind was attributed to the culture hero Maíra. Another man told us that a deceased

[25] *Ibid.*, pp. 71–72.   [26] *Ibid.*, pp. 121–123; Abbéville (1945 ed.), p. 252.

relative "had gone to live with Tupan" (that is, in the Christian heaven), yet he consistently refused to go near the cemetery for fear of the *azang* of this same relative. It was significant that he obviously believed more strongly in the relative's ghost than in the Christian heaven. Such inconsistent beliefs, however, do not result in emotional conflicts within the individual, for as yet the belief in Tupan as a supernatural protector and the belief in heaven have not penetrated to the level of influencing behavior. In any specific situation involving the supernatural, the Tenetehara follow the dictates of the native religious system. They stay away from the cemetery and they call upon the shaman to protect them from the dangerous spirits.[27]

In contrast to religious belief, native ceremonials, as we have already said, are neglected primarily because of the time involved in preparing for and in celebrating them. While both the Honey Feast and the Maize Festival had important sacred functions, namely the increase of animals of the hunt and the protection of the maize, both also provided entertainment and amusement for the people. With the loss of these two ceremonials, present-day Tenetehara life is certainly more monotonous than it must once have been. Adults who remember the time when these ceremonies were more frequently celebrated describe them as gay and exciting occasions— the high points of the year. At present, in many Tenetehara villages Brazilian style dances have filled the gap and many young Tenetehara say that they find these dances more entertaining than the old-style ceremonials. For them, singing of native music is something to pass the otherwise dull evenings "when there is nothing else to do," while they look forward with great eagerness to a *festa* (a Brazilian dance). Such dances take place generally on Saturday night, as they do in near-by rural communities. Indians have learned to play the Brazilian bamboo flute and the *caixa* (a type of drum), and sometimes a group of villagers will hire Brazilian musicians to come to

---

[27] Ralph Linton, pp. 273–287, has pointed out that all societies contain such "alternative elements" and beliefs. "The average individual can hold a whole series of conflicting beliefs as long as the behavior patterns which are related to these beliefs do not themselves involve direct conflict" (*Ibid.*, p. 362). The process of culture change involves new ideas and patterns which often exist as alternatives, side by side with the old, until they finally displace the old or until they are themselves discarded.

play the accordion and the violin for their dances. They dance in couples to Brazilian *marchas* and *sambas* and the "ladies" sit passively on a bench waiting for the "gentlemen" to invite them to dance.

In modern Tenetehara culture, individuals are frequently exposed to the behavior patterns and social values of the rural Brazilians of the region. The Brazilian considers the Indian a savage and holds Indian customs in complete disparagement. This feeling of superiority is reflected by the Indians themselves. A few of them now and again express actual shame in being Indians and decry their own cultural traditions. Our repeated question as to their way of doing things was often answered: "Just as the 'civilized' do." Several Tenetehara told us that they were "raised together with 'civilized,' " thinking in this way to gain prestige in our eyes. One young Indian who had lived for a few years with the family of the Brazilian administrator at the Indian Post and who spoke excellent Portuguese, told us that he did not want to be an Indian. He said that he was "forced to live" temporarily in the Indian village, but that he hoped soon to move away and marry a *civilizada*. He refused to work with us as an informant and refused to tell us Tenetehara myths, which he admitted knowing, because, as he said, "they are nothing but the stupidity of the Indians." One family leader and village chief, for example, constantly imitated Brazilian behavior and we met several village chiefs who boasted of having Brazilian ancestors. The Indian believes that this proves that he knows the Brazilian way of life and gives him prestige over other Indians in the eyes of the Brazilians.

It is common to see Brazilian modes of behavior imitated in Tenetehara villages, sometimes so imperfectly as to be ludicrous, and to hear vocalizations of Brazilian values by Indians who consider themselves progressives. In rural Brazil, as in all Latin America, there is a warm and respectful relationship between a baptismal godson (*afilhado*) and his godfather (*padrinho*); and there is a relationship of mutual respect and cooperation between the godfather and the godson's father (*compadre*). Tenetehara "progressives" are impressed with the attitude of respect shown in the external behavior forms between Brazilian *compadres* and between *afilhados* and *padrinhos,* and they imitate this behavior in situations calling for respect.[28] Frequently in the village of Lagôa Comprida, for example, we heard Tenetehara fathers remind their children to "ask for the blessing of your godfather," referring to an older man of prestige. In another village, two family leaders, although conversing in their native language, constantly called each other *compadre*, and upon taking leave of each other embraced in Brazilian style.

Even some Brazilian moral values have been at least superficially accepted, but it is interesting to note that such values seldom serve as a basis for overt behavior. Several men told us that if they found their wives in adultery they would kill both the wife and the adulterer. Most murders and the majority of physical encounters among the Brazilians of the region arise from sexual affairs of this kind, yet we never heard of such a murder taking place among the Tenetehara. The Tenetehara husband, usually living in the midst of his wife's relatives, would not dare to resort to such violence. Furthermore, Tenetehara males are rather passive and timid in sex affairs as compared to the Brazilian *caboclo;* and the Tenetehara women, who are often the aggressors in sex, are brazen as compared to Brazilian women. The Indians repeat Brazilian expressions, but such braggadocio is completely out of keeping with Tenetehara behavior patterns. Somewhat similar is the Tenetehara use of *amigado* (in friendship), a term used by Brazilians of the region to describe the relationship of a couple living together without the benefit of a church or civil marriage. The Tenetehara use the term to indicate an unstable and temporary affair; no moral or emotional overtones are implied.

Yet the core of Tenetehara culture is still alive and vigorous. Despite numerous modifications in the aboriginal patterns, they still constitute a society and a culture distinct from rural Brazilians. Tenetehara beliefs, values, emotional responses and behavior patterns as well as institutions form a functioning cultural configuration which seems to have provided them at least for the time being with a satisfactory adjustment to their new social environment. There is a minimum of conflict with the rural Brazilians of the re-

[28] Levi-Strauss has drawn attention to the early adoption of the *compérage* or *compadre* system by the Tupinambá: in aboriginal times a parallel form existed among the Tupinambá and other Brazilian tribes; unrelated individuals, even strangers, were brought into a "brother-in-law" relation in order to amalgamate family groups and insure intermarriage (p. 407).

gion. Relations with them have not been intimate, and although Brazilian culture is considered "superior" by both peoples and a few Indians are ashamed of being "savages," the majority of the Tenetehara are satisfied to live as Indians according to the values and patterns of their own present-day culture. Only a few wish to "pass" into Brazilian society, and on internal evidence it would seem as if Tenetehara culture might resist such assimilation and survive as a distinct culture for several generations. But external factors make it quite certain that the Tenetehara will soon be overwhelmed by rural Brazilian society. Modern technology with modern means of communication is bound to penetrate the area, and as a result of the phenomenal growth of the Brazilian population [29] the movement of Brazilians inland and upriver from the coast which began after the middle nineteenth century will normally gain in velocity. It is only a question of a generation or so until the Tenetehara as a distinct tribe with a distinct culture will disappear.

The Tenetehara have been able to achieve a modified cultural integration and they have been able to survive as a distinct tribal group into the twentieth century not because they have been more conservative than other tribes or because of any special quality in the culture that enables it to resist change. On the contrary, as compared to other tribal groups such as the Canella and Apinayé who inhabit the steppe regions of Maranhão, the Tenetehara seem to hold less firmly to their old customs and to be relatively eager to accept new ideas and techniques. In fact, their flexibility and readiness to accept change has probably been a major factor in their survival. Furthermore, history seems to have treated them gently. In the seventeenth and eighteenth centuries, Jesuit control over their territory protected them from slave raiders. Although only a few Tenetehara were settled in mission villages on the lower Pindaré, those who remained in their native villages on the upper reaches of the river were theoretically under Jesuit rule. After the expulsion of the Jesuits in 1759, the Colonial Government and then the Brazilian Empire set up Indian colonies on the Pindaré. Very few Indians were attracted to the colonies themselves, but during this period few people seemed to have traveled up the Pindaré River. It

---

[29] From 1890 to 1940, the population of Brazil increased 192 percent. The population of the state of Maranhão has increased 188 percent during this same period.

was not a main road of penetration into the interior of Maranhão and the dense tropical forest did not attract settlers from the coast. Not until late in the nineteenth century, when rubber and other forest products began to attract a few Brazilians into the headwaters of the Pindaré and when the Brazilian settlements on the middle river grew in size, did the Tenetehara enter into continuous and face-to-face contact with a large number of people of Brazilian culture. Although early casual and intermittent contacts with colonial and Brazilian administrators, with missionaries, and even with bands of explorers and escaped slaves brought many changes in Tenetehara culture, only in the last half century have they been under the direct impact of Brazilian culture.

This Brazilian culture is not an imported form of modern Western civilization. It is a peasant culture which has derived many patterns from the Portuguese, from African slaves, and from various aboriginal peoples of Brazil. In the first years of colonization, the Portuguese depended upon the Indians for labor and learned from them the techniques and knowledge necessary for adaptation to the new environment. In the sixteenth century throughout Brazil there was considerable miscegenation between the Amerinds and the Portuguese, and the Indian exerted a decisive influence on early colonial life. The tribes who inhabited the coastal regions, however, soon died from enforced slavery and foreign disease, and their remnants fled into the interior. The numerous African slaves imported into Brazil in the seventeenth and eighteenth centuries replaced the aborigines in the rich plantation regions of the northeast coast. In the south, where the climate and physical character of the country attracted many European colonists, Indian influences were soon submerged. In north Brazil, however, both in the arid *sertão*, the desert-like region which lies inland from the northeast coast, and in the Amazon tropical forest, the Indian continued to be a basic element of the population and to play an important role in cultural development. Neither of these northern regions offered profitable conditions for plantation agriculture. Few Negro slaves were imported and African influences were therefore not as strong here as in the plantation areas along the coast.[30] The *sertão* developed a

[30] The coastal region of Maranhão centering around São Luis received a large number of Negro slaves during the colonial period, and there is a numerous Negroid

grazing economy and the Portuguese landlords used the Indians to care for their herds. The Amazon region attracted relatively few European settlers, who depended almost entirely upon Indians to work their agricultural properties and to collect the natural products of the tropical forest. A mixed Indian-white population soon developed in the Amazon basin, as well as in the tropical forest areas of Maranhão, and a folk culture was developed with a strong residue of Indian traditions.

The three principal racial components (Iberian, Negro, and Indian) are present in the area, but the so-called *caboclo* (Indian-white mixture) forms the basic population, especially in the rural areas. These northern *caboclos* are Brazilians. They do not think of themselves as Indians, nor even as *mestiços* (Indian-white mixtures), although it is obvious that many of them are of predominantly Indian ancestry. They are neither ashamed nor proud of their Indian heritage. The northern *caboclo* plays *futebol* (soccer) which is Brazil's national sport; he plays at "the animal game" (*jogo do bicho*), the favorite form of gambling throughout Brazil; he discusses local and national politics, and he celebrates the Seventh of September, Brazil's Independence Day, as well as the pre-Lenten Carnival, the most popular festival throughout the country. Yet, the culture of the Amazon *caboclo* retains many aboriginal elements. His basic subsistence methods are essentially derived from the Indian. He has a few domestic animals such as cows, chickens, and pigs, a few plants such as rice and coffee, and he has iron tools of Old World origin; but his basic food crops and his inefficient agricultural methods—called the *roça* system—are of native American origin. He plants beans, maize, cotton, peanuts, tobacco, squash, peppers, yams, and manioc in the same manner and at the

element in the modern population. The strong survival of culture elements of African origin in São Luis and the coastal zone has been described by Octavio da Costa Eduardo. During Colonial times escaped slaves formed small communities in the interior and a few are reported to have joined Indian villages. Some Negroes migrated inland and mixed with the *caboclo* population of the lower Pindaré region; they must certainly have influenced the local variety of *caboclo* culture which they adopted. A few elements in modern Tenetehara culture, such as pointed incisors, some animal myths, hashish, and certain mechanical methods of making black magic, may be attributed to Negro influences which came to them indirectly through the local *caboclos*. Negro influence on modern Tenetehara culture, however, is slight when compared with the influence of *caboclo* culture, basically of mixed Indian-Iberian origin.

same time of year as the Tenetehara Indians, and the *caboclo's* staff of life is manioc flour, as is theirs. He prepares it with the same instruments and the same methods. The *caboclo* fishes with a bow and arrow and with the poison of the *timbó* vine (Indian methods) as well as with a net and a steel hook. He hunts with a gun, but he builds hunting blinds (*tocaia*) and uses a fund of knowledge in hunting which he owes to his Indian cultural heritage.

Although the *caboclo* is a faithful Catholic, he believes in numerous supernaturals of Indian origin. The water spirits mãe d'agua or Yara, the forest demons Zuruparí and Curupira, as well as Cobra Grande (a gigantic snake whose shining eyes appear in the dark to frighten travelers) and the spirit of the *bôto* (the fresh water dolphin) which appears in isolated villages as a young man to seduce local virgins, are modified versions of Indian supernaturals in which the *caboclo* believes as strongly as he does in the powers of the Catholic saints. Throughout the entire Amazon region, and specifically along the Pindaré River, there are medicine men, or *pagés,* as they are called by Brazilians, in almost all rural districts. The *caboclo* medicine men perform cures by massage and sucking, they use tobacco as a stimulant, they dance to the rhythm of a gourd rattle, they call their supernaturals in song, and they are possessed by supernaturals in the manner described for Tenetehara Indian shamans. Their supernatural familiars, however, are both Christian saints and such pagan spirits as Zuruparí.

Until the middle of the last century, even the language of the interior of north Brazil was derived from the Indian. In many parts of the Amazon Valley, until recently, the *caboclo* spoke *lingua geral,* a modified form of Tupí-Guaraní, rather than Portuguese. Although at present this language is spoken only in certain isolated spots of north Brazil, the Portuguese which has supplanted it has been heavily influenced. The names of plants, animals, objects in daily use, places, as well as many common expressions are derived from *lingua geral.* These and many other culture elements and complexes of Indian origin have been blended with Iberian and Negro elements to form the modern culture of rural north Brazil.

Although the formation of this northern folk culture began in the sixteenth century, the process continues in modern times in a few out-of-the-way areas of the interior. It has been a long and steady process of detribalization and incorporation of native groups, such as the Tenetehara, into Brazilian rural society. In early colonial times both the paternalistic missionary activities of the Jesuits and the violent slave-hunting parties of the Portuguese colonists contributed in their different ways to its formation. Many towns of north Brazil, such as Viana on the lower Pindaré River, Breves, Gurupá, Monte Alegre, and Santarem on the Amazon main stream, were originally Indian mission villages that were slowly transformed into Brazilian communities. The colonists made slaves of the Indians and also brought them out of their native villages into colonial society. In modern times, the Brazilian Indian Service has in a sense taken over the battle of the Jesuits in defending the Indian against his would-be exploiters; and the Indian Service is contributing toward the amalgamation of the Indian into rural society by teaching him Portuguese, by attracting the forest Indian to settle near Indian posts, and by teaching him to work in extracting industries. Rural Brazilian commercial men, eager to get the Indian to collect rubber, Brazil nuts, *babassú* nuts, or pelts from the forest, or equally eager to remove the Indian from his lands so that they may be developed into ranches or plantations, have in the same sense supplanted the slave-hunting colonists. The process of transforming autochthonous tribesmen into peasants, or in other words, Indians into rural Brazilians, is still under way in north Brazil.

The Indian tribes which have survived into the twentieth century as distinct ethnic units are not numerous, nor is any tribe very large. Many of them, such as the Tapirapé of central Brazil, the Canella, the Apinayé, and the Krahô of Maranhão, number less than two hundred people. Others such as the Carajá of the Araguaia, the Tucuna of the upper Solimões, and the Tenetehara are relatively numerous, with tribal populations of from one to three thousand or a little more. Among the remaining tribal groups examples may be found at various stages of culture change. The Chavante Indians who live west of the Araguaia are still at war with Brazilians. The Urubú, the western neighbors of the Tenetehara, made peace with Brazilians less than twenty years ago. The Carajá have had casual contacts with Brazilians for almost two hundred years but still retain the bulk of their aboriginal culture. The Mauhé on the other hand, who live along the Amazon mainstream, have become so changed during the last three centuries of contact with Luso-Brazilian culture bearers that their present way of life is hardly distinguishable from that of the Amazon *caboclo*.

Furthermore, these tribal groups offer a great range of culture contact situations. There are Indian groups in contact with missionaries, with mining camps, with soldiers, with government expeditions exploring the possibilities of certain regions for colonization or tracing political borders, and with settlers. Subgroups of some of these tribes are simultaneously in varying conditions of contact with Brazilian or *caboclo* culture bearers; one segment of a tribe may have, for example, only sporadic contact with Brazilians and retain most of its aboriginal culture, while other villages of the same tribe may have continuous contact with Brazilians and their culture may be profoundly modified.[31]

Obviously, these tribal Indians do not form an important segment of the population of north Brazil nor will the assimilation of the few remaining groups seriously modify the rural culture of the region. They do, however, offer a rich "laboratory" for the study of acculturation, especially in view of the unique conditions which Brazil offers. Furthermore, the study of culture change as it is taking place in north Brazil among these variegated Indian groups gives us insight into the process of the formation of the contemporary folk culture of these regions. *Caboclo* culture of north Brazil is a result of a fusion of Iberian (and in many cases Negro) with American Indian elements through the assimilation of numerous Indian tribes. The process continues into the present day. As the Tenetehara lose their identity as tribal Indians and are incorporated into the rural society of the region, both physically and culturally, they will strengthen the Indian heritage of north Brazil. It is only a question of a generation or so until the Tenetehara become peasants and Brazilians.

[31] See Pierson and Viera da Cunha, pp. 66–67, for an excellent summary of culture contact situations among the extant Brazilian Indian groups.

APPENDIX

TENETEHARA KINSHIP TERMS
(m. sp. = man speaking; w. sp. = woman speaking)

EGO'S OWN GENERATION

He-rikiyra (m. sp.): older brother; all male cousins older than ego
He-riwyra (m. sp.): younger brother; all cousins younger than ego
He-reinyra (m. sp.): sister; all female cousins
He-rikéra (w. sp.): older sister; all female cousins older than ego
He-kipiyra (w. sp.): younger sister; all female cousins younger than ego
He-kiwyra (w. sp.): brother
He-mén: husband
He-remirekó: wife
He-menikiyra: husband's older brother
He-meniwyra: husband's younger brother
He-ukeyi (m. sp.): brother's wife
He-ukéi (w. sp.): husband's sister
He-rikewém (w. sp.): older sister's husband
He-kipýwém (w. sp.): younger sister's husband
He-rairuyra (m. sp.): wife's brother; sister's husband
He-remirekó-ikéra: wife's elder sister
He-remirekó-kiyra: wife's younger sister
He-rikiy-raty (m. sp.): older brother's wife
He-riwý-raty (m. sp.): younger brother's wife

FIRST GENERATION ASCENDING

He-rú (m. or w. sp.): father
He-ruwyra (m. or w. sp.): father's brother

He-hy (m. or w. sp.): mother
amaí (m. or w. sp.): mother, vocative
He-iyra (m. or w. sp.): mother's sister
Ke-tutyra (m. or w. sp.): mother's brother
He-zaihé (m. or w. sp.): father's sister
He-ratyú: wife's father
He-raihó: wife's mother
He-men-ú: husband's father
He-me-hý: husband's mother

FIRST GENERATION DESCENDING

He-raýra (m. sp.): son; brother's son
He-memýra (w. sp.): son; daughter
He-memi-raíhé (w. sp.): sister's son
He-memi-kuzã (w. sp.): sister's daughter
He-razyra (m. sp.): daughter; brother's daughter
He-péng (w. sp.): brother's son and brother's daughter
He-riyra (m. sp.): sister's son
He-ratipéra (m. sp.): sister's daughter
He-rai-taty (m. sp.): son's wife
He-memi-taty (w. sp.): son's wife
He-raiwén (m. sp.): daughter's husband
He-peúm (w. sp.): daughter's husband

SECOND GENERATION ASCENDING

He-tamúi (m. or w. sp.): father's father; mother's father; extended
  to brothers of these relatives and to distant relatives of the same
  approximate age
He-zarýi (m. or w. sp.): mother's mother; father's mother; extended
  to sisters of these two and to other distant female relatives of the
  same approximate age

SECOND GENERATION DESCENDING

He-remiminó (m. sp.): grandson and granddaughter; widely extended
He-remiriró (w. sp.): grandson and granddaughter; widely extended

The phonetic recording used above, and in native terms throughout this study, has been simplified and, with a few exceptions, conforms to the system used by scholars of Tupí-Guaraní. *Ch* has the value of *ch* in children; *w* as in water; and *h* is aspirated as in have. The *y* is used by students of Tupí-Guaraní with the approximate value of *y* in the English *yes* or *j* in the German *ja*.

THE PINDARÉ RIVER

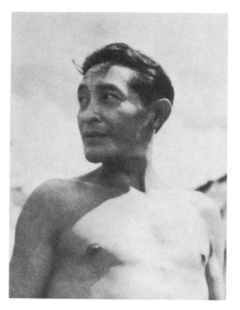

MIGUEL

CAPTAIN ANTONINHO

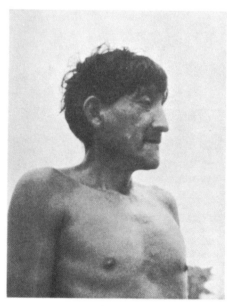

JOSÉ VIANA

CAPTAIN CAMIRANG

INFORMANTS

MANUEL VIANA AND TWO URUBU VISITORS

VAQUEIRO

JOÃO BOCHECHA AND HIS WIFE

JOÃO BOCHECHA AND
CHICO MANCHA WITH A
CATCH OF *surubim*

INFORMANTS

MODERN TENETEHARÁ HOUSES

TENETEHARA GARDEN SITES

TENETEHARA BOYS

PUBERTY RITES

GIRL INITIATES

MAIZE FESTIVAL

AMBROSIO, LEADER OF THE CEREMONY, AND HIS SON

MAIZE FESTIVAL

BOYS DANCING DURING THE PUBERTY RITES

SHAMANS PERFORMING AT THE MAIZE FESTIVAL

INÁCIO FALLS TO HIS KNEES,
POSSESSED BY THE SPIRIT

SHAMAN INÁCIO INDUCES A TRANCE

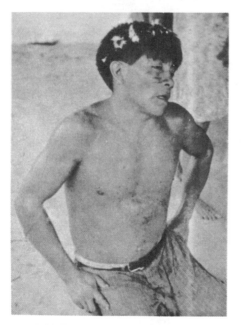

POSSESSED BY A SPIRIT, HE
GROANS AND SINGS

OVERCOME BY THE DANGEROUS
SPIRIT, HE FALLS UNCONSCIOUS

INÁCIO HOLDS IN HIS RIGHT HAND THE "OBJECT" EXTRACTED FROM HIS PATIENT'S BODY

ON THE UPPER PINDARÉ RIVER

BIBLIOGRAPHY

Abbéville, Claude d'. Historia da Missão dos Padres Capuchinhos na Ilha do Maranhão. 1614. New ed., São Paulo, 1945.

Baldus, Herbert. Introduction to "Os Cuduveo," by Guido Boggiani. São Paulo, 1945.

Barbosa Rodrigues, J. "Tribu dos Tembés; Festa da Tucanayra." Revista da Exposição Anthropologica. Rio de Janeiro, 1882.

Bettendorf, João Filippe. "Chronica da Missão dos Padres da Companhia de Jesus no Estado do Maranhão." Revista do Instituto Historico e Geographico Brasileiro, Vol. LXXII (1910), Part I.

Cardim, Fernão. Tratado da Terra e Gente do Brasil. 4th ed. Rio de Janeiro, 1925.

Costa Eduardo, Octavio da. The Negro in North Brazil; a Study in Acculturation. American Ethnological Society, Monograph XV. New York, 1948.

Couto de Magalhães. O Selvagem. 1876. New ed., São Paulo, 1940.

Dodt, Gustavo (Gustave). Descrição dos Rios Parnahyba e Gurupy. 1873. New ed., São Paulo, 1935.

Fróes Abreu, S. Na terra das palmeiras; estudos brasileiros. Rio de Janeiro, 1931.

Hartt, Charles F. Amazonian Tortoise Myths. Rio de Janeiro, 1875.

Leite, Serafim, S. J. Historia da Companhia de Jesus no Brasil. Rio de Janeiro, 1943. Vol. III.

Levi-Strauss, Claude. "The Social Use of Kinship Terms among Brazilian Indians." American Anthropologist, XLV, No. 3 (1943), Part I, 398–409.

Linton, Ralph. The Study of Man, an Introduction. New York, 1936.

Lopes, Raimundo. "Os tupis do Gurupy." Congresso Internacional de Americanistas, XXV (La Plata, 1932), 140–172.

Marques, Cesar Augusto. Diccionario historico-geographico da Provincia do Maranhão. 1870.

Metraux, Alfred. La Civilization matérielle des tribus Tupí-Guaraní. Paris, 1928.

Metraux, Alfred. La Réligion des Tupinambá et ses rapports avec celles des autres tribus Tupí-Guaraní. Paris, 1928.

Moraes, José de. "Historia da Companhia de Jesus no Pará e Maranhão." In *Memorias para a Historia do Extincto Estado do Maranhão, editado por Candido Mendes de Almeida.* Rio de Janeiro, 1860.

Nimuendajú, Curt. "Sagen der Tembe-Indianer." *Zeitschrift für Ethnologie,* XLVII (Berlin, 1915), 281–301.

Pereira do Lago, Antonio. "Itinerario da Provincia do Maranhão." *Revista do Instituto Historico e Geographico Brasileiro,* Vol. XXXV (1872), Part I.

Pierson, Donald, and Mario Wagner Vieira da Cunha. "Research and Research Possibilíties in Brazil, with Particular Reference to Culture and Culture Change." *Acta Americana,* Vol. V, Nos. 1–2 (1947).

"Poranduba Maranhense." *Revista do Instituto Historico e Geographico Brasileiro,* Vol. LIV (Rio de Janeiro, 1891).

Ramos, Arthur. O folk-lore negro do Brasil. Rio de Janeiro, 1935.

Snethlage, H. "Meine Reise durch Nordostbrasilien." *Journal für Ornithologie,* LXXV (Berlin, 1927), 453–484.

——— "Unter nordostbrasilianischen Indianer." *Zeitschrift für Ethnologie,* LXII (Berlin, 1931), 111–205.

Soares de Souza, Gabriel. Noticias do Brasil. 1851. New ed., 2 vols., São Paulo, 1946. Vol. II.

Stewart, Kenneth M. "Spirit Possession in Native America." *Southwestern Journal of Anthropology,* II, No. 3 (1946), 323–339.

Wagley, Charles. Notas sobre aculturação entre os Guajajara. *Boletim do Museu Nacional, Antropologia,* n.s., No. 2 (Rio de Janeiro, 1943).

——— Tapirapé Shamanism. *Ibid.,* No. 3 (Rio de Janeiro, 1943).

Wagley, Charles, and Eduardo Galvão. Tupí-Guaraní Kinship. *Boletim do Museu Nacional, Antropologia,* n.s., No. 6 (Rio de Janeiro, 1946).

INDEX

Abnormalities, infant: causes, 64, 65

Abortion, 67

Acculturation, research as part of program on, vii; still taking place, 14, 183; influence of Brazilian culture upon Indians, 128, 129, 167, 176 f. (*see also* Brazilians); process among Indian groups, 166-83; among northern Brazilians, 179 ff.; alternative elements involved in process, 175*n*; why Indians a rich "laboratory" for study of, 183

Acknowledgments, xv

Adolescence, preparation for, and ceremonial of puberty, 81-88

After-life, *see* Death

Agriculture, 32, 34-50, 167, 180; *roça* system of cultivation, 19, 32, 167, 180; tremendous areas required, 32; war-time neglect in favor of collecting *babassú* nuts, 33; myths concerning, 34, 35, 128 (*text*, 132); commercial farming and resulting changes in organization of production: now a man's occupation, 168; *see also* Gardens

Albuquerque, Jeronimo de, 6

Aldeia de S. Francisco Xavier, 7, 8

Alternative elements and beliefs in process of culture change, 175*n*

Alto Alegria, massacre at, 10, 15

Amazon River basin, racial components of population, 179 f.

Amazon Valley, territory inhabited by Tenetehara a part of, 31

Ambrósio, puberty ceremony under patronage of, 83-87

Amigado, meaning and use of term, 177

Animals, domestic, 56, 167; varieties of wild, in forests: purposes for which hunted and used, 56; (*see also* Hunting); pelts, 56, 57, 168; carriers of evil spirits, 58; prohibited in diets, 64 ff., 69, 79 f.; creation of insects and reptiles, 101; protector of animals, 103; human spirits in the form of, 105 ff.; animal spirits, 107 f., 109; relation of Honey Feast songs to, 122; mixed origins of myths about, 129; *texts* of myths, 134, 136, 140, 145-59

Anteaters, jaguar and, *text*, 159

Anthropology, Department of, Columbia University, vii

Antoninho, village: native name for, 17*n*

Apinayé tribe, 178, 182

Appearance, personal, ix, 170

Arapuha azang (deer ghost spirit), 127*n*

Aruwé, culture hero, 101, 122, 143

Azang, see Spirits

Babassú nuts, war-time demand for, 33; where found: varied uses: husking and opening, 60 f.

Babes in the woods, *text*, 163-65

Barbosa Rodrigues, J., 122*n*; quoted, 123*n*

Beans, origin of maize and, *text*, 144

Beautiful Land in mythology, 100*n*, 131

Beauty and the beast, 128; *text*, 160

Behavior, not influenced by conflicting beliefs, 175

Berniz, Helio Mendes, xv

Bettendorf, João Filippe, quoted, 9

Bird-down, decoration with, 84, 86

Birth of child, 67-70

Black-dyed bodies, 83, 84, 173

Blinds, hunting, 50, 58

Bochecha, João, informant, x, 71, 123